Japanese High School Films

Iconography, Nostalgia and Discipline

Peter C. Pugsley

EDINBURGH
University Press

Edinburgh University Press is one of the leading university presses in the UK. We publish academic books and journals in our selected subject areas across the humanities and social sciences, combining cutting-edge scholarship with high editorial and production values to produce academic works of lasting importance. For more information visit our website: edinburghuniversitypress.com

© Peter C. Pugsley, 2022, 2023

Edinburgh University Press Ltd
The Tun – Holyrood Road
12 (2f) Jackson's Entry
Edinburgh EH8 8PJ

First published in hardback by Edinburgh University Press 2022

Typeset in 11/13 Monotype Ehrhardt by
Manila Typesetting Company

A CIP record for this book is available from the British Library

ISBN 978 1 4744 9461 8 (hardback)
ISBN 978 1 4744 9462 5 (paperback)
ISBN 978 1 4744 9463 2 (webready PDF)
ISBN 978 1 4744 9464 9 (epub)

Contents

Figures

Acknowledgements

This book was made possible by the Special Studies Program study leave awarded to me by the Faculty of Arts and the School of Humanities at the University of Adelaide in the initial stages of researching and writing. I would like to acknowledge the support of my colleagues in the Department of Media at the University of Adelaide, and as my background is not in Japanese Studies, thanks to Dr Akiko Tomita (who helped me arrange my annual *Japanese Media Cultures* study tour to Kyoto), Dr Shoko Yoneyama and Dr Kayoko Enomoto in the Japanese programme here at Adelaide. I also thank my friend and colleague at Ritsumeikan University, Professor Akinori Nakamura, for his fascinating insights and encyclopedic knowledge of Japanese popular culture. And thanks to my hosts at Ritsumeikan University, Takeshi Tanaka and Ayako Suzuki, for their wonderful and informative discussions on Japanese culture during our study tours.

My thanks to Dr Andrew Loo and Mr Anthony Gandolfo Miranti at Universiti Tunku Abdul Rahman (UTAR), Malaysia, for the opportunity to present some of the findings of this study at a well-attended forum of enthusiastic Japanese pop culture students on their campus in July 2019. Thanks for the many helpful comments and suggestions from my friends and colleagues at the Asian Film Studies Conference in Singapore 2019 (again, thanks to the University of Adelaide School of Humanities for funding to attend this conference) and at the Screen Studies Association of Australia and Aotearoa New Zealand (SSAAANZ) conference in November 2019.

Thanks also to Ann Jackson for her invaluable proof-reading and comments on an early draft of this book (I take sole responsibility for any errors that crept into later drafts), and to Guillaume Vetu for his film recommendations (mostly zombie-related!).

Difficulties in accessing Japanese films with English subtitles resulted in a somewhat random selection of films for close analysis. Access to a number of films was assisted by the Japan Foundation (Sydney) and the Japanese Film Festival. The use of subscription streaming services such as Kanopy, Netflix and Stan (in Australia) has been invaluable in this respect, as has the SBS On-demand service provided though the national public broadcaster, SBS Australia. Sites including the Internet Movie DataBase (IMDb and a subscription with IMDb Pro), AsianWiki, Eiren (Motion Picture Producers Association of Japan), Box Office Mojo and the Japanese Film Database (JFDB) have been invaluable for detailed cast, production and box office information. The sheer number of high school *seishun eiga* released in the past few years means that I could not possibly capture them all, and there were many on my list that did not make it into this book. I am happy to take recommendations for any that I have missed.

Japanese names traditionally put the family name first. In this book there are exceptions to this rule, as I have followed the usage within the films themselves, where characters are addressed through a variety of styles and nicknames. Similarly, some film titles appear in Japanese first if they are more commonly known in the West by the Japanese name.

Screenshots have been included under the Fair Use rule, although I have attached production company details in credit lines. Any errors or omissions will be addressed in future editions of this book. My thanks to the editorial staff of Edinburgh University Press, especially Gillian Leslie and Richard Strachan, and to the anonymous reviewers for their valuable feedback.

Finally, I would like to acknowledge the support (and patience) of Mandy, Charlie and Louisa as I toiled away in our upstairs loft (during various COVID-19 lockdowns) at this latest venture into Asian cinema.

Introduction

Since 2014, more than 100 feature-length, live-action Japanese films have been set in high schools. This does not include anime such as box-office hit *Your Name/Kimi no Na wa* (released in August 2016 and the highest grossing Japanese film of all time by 2017, dir. Makoto Shintai) or the similarly popular *A Silent Voice/Koe no Katachi* (2016, dir. Naoko Yamada). The use of the high school as a setting is now an established feature in contemporary Japanese cinema, an iconographic visual and narrative coding that is heavily reliant on existing manga and anime texts for source storylines and characters. Schools provide a ready-made cohort of uniformed teenagers (the students) and authoritarian figures (mostly teachers, but sometimes parents), where select themes can be played out in recognisable cinematic styles. Filmmakers universally create these school-based narratives around heavily stereotyped characters: the bully, the introvert, the jock (athlete), the 'popular' girl or the despotic principal. The school therefore provides not only a social setting, but also a site for metaphors on grander hegemonic themes of cultural and political power structures. Yet it is in Japan that high school films have prospered as an ongoing genre. This book therefore explores the uses of the school setting as a device in Japanese cinema to create a holistic on-screen society contained within the school environment.

This book explores the immediacy of high school films, and why they resonate so successfully with teen and young adult audiences and trigger a recognisable schoolyard nostalgia in older audiences. By initially drawing on the work of Michel Foucault and Emile Durkheim, I propose that the school plays a critical role in Japanese society as a form of social discipline, and that this reflected notion of discipline and order allows these films to become popular with Japanese audiences. Enforced discipline has been a critical element of Japanese films set in high schools, from the violence of the earlier *Battle Royale* films (*Batoru Rowaiaru*, 2000, dir. Kinji Fukusaku, *Battle Royale II: Requiem/Batoru Rowaiaru: Chinkonka*, 2003, dir. Kenta

Fukusaku and Kinji Fukusaku) or, more recently, Sion Sono's *Tag/Riaru Onigokko* (2015) through to absurdist sci-fi in *Assassination Classroom/ Ansatsu Kyōshitsu* (2015, dir. Eiichirō Hasumi) and the sexual innuendo of 'pervert' comedy in *Hentai Kamen*/(lit.) *Pervert Mask* (2013, dir. Yūichi Fukuda) and *Yarukkya Knight/Yarukkya Naito* (2015, dir. Katsutoshi Hirabayashi). While these films have been able to stake their own place in Japanese cinematic history, they are not the central focus of this book. Instead, I explore the world of those high school films that maintain a steady popularity in Japanese culture, the arguably 'mainstream' films notable not for their ability to shock, but for their often gentle nature that resonates with audiences of all ages.

Japan's film industry is in an enviable position for most national cinemas due to its ability to stave off the threat of Hollywood. Mark Schilling (2018) notes that Japanese films made up 55 per cent of the market share in Japan in 2017, up from an already strong 48 per cent a decade earlier. Attendance at cinemas in Japan (pre-COVID-19) has remained high in a nation where a relatively strong sense of cultural and linguistic homogeneity creates a notionally 'singular' audience.

Attendance at high school is mandatory in most cultures, and each institution's organisational structures are part of the 'formal processes that bring students into the same orbit [and] facilitate friendships and the construction of peer groups, especially when they bring together students of similar academic statuses and family backgrounds (i.e. propinquity x homophily)' (Crosnoe et al. 2018: 318). In Japan, policies have been enacted to ensure that schools are also sites for the delivery of curriculum-led 'moral education', seen by some as an overreach of the function of the state (Bamkin 2018). Each of these institutional functions helps in our understanding of how school-based films contribute to a steady flow of box-office success in Japanese cinema.

Definitions

While the term *gakuen-mono* 学園もの (lit. school thing) may seem the most readily appropriate for Japan's school-based films, the more commonly recognised idea is that these films are regarded as part of the cohort of *seishun eiga* 青春映画, or youth films, a slightly more expansive notion than the Western-favoured category of 'teen films'. In one study of Western high school texts, Jennifer Bomford (2016: 16) draws on the phrase 'school stories', and traces these back as a genre that then divides into subgenres emanating from the 'literary school story'; she expands this into the 'televisual school story' for her comparative study into selected

'Teen TV' programmes from the US, the UK and Japan. Throughout this book my aim is to turn our gaze from the West to analyse the themes and motifs found in Japan's school-based *seishun eiga* and work toward a greater understanding of why these films resonate with Japanese filmmakers and audiences. What are the particular aspects of Japanese culture that facilitate demand for the school setting? How do these films frame iconographic images and scenarios to capture an imagined, nostalgic view of the past? I also explore the roles that manga and anime play in the creation of cinematic texts that serve as faithful (or not) live-action adaptations of high school-based films.

Another factor to consider in trying to define these films is whether they constitute a genre or a subgenre. Rick Altman (1984: 7) sees one way of thinking about genre as through a binary of the 'inclusive', citing the example of the 'Western = film that takes place in American west', and the 'exclusive', where a text operates 'in connection with attempts to arrive at the overall meaning or structure of a genre'. However, there are problems with this binary, as Altman recognises, asking, what about Elvis Presley films? Extending this, we could ask the same of Alfred Hitchcock or Quentin Tarantino's work, or even that of Seijun Suzuki or Takeshi Kitano. Specifically, for this book, it is instructive to consider how the definition of the *seishun eiga* as a singular genre fails to recognise the importance of the iconographic location of the school. As noted, the alternative phrase *gakuen-mono* could be used, but this tends to lock into Altman's inclusive terms, in this case: *gakuen-mono* = film that takes place in a school, shifting the emphasis to location rather than the themes presented.

Altman's solution to this definitional impasse on genre is to consider a combined semantic/syntactic approach because he reasons that audiences are:

> conditioned by the choice of semantic elements and atmosphere, because a given semantics . . . in a specific cultural situation will recall to an actual interpretive community the particular syntax with which that semantics has traditionally been associated in other texts. (Altman 1984: 16–17)

In the instance of the high school film, despite its 'semantic' institutional setting, the 'syntax' of schoolwork is assumed. Instead, to the audience the space is presented as a site where 'characters are typically learning about themselves and the world' (Bomford 2016: 21) rather than, say, the basics of algebra or history. Thus, the concept of 'school' as a singular *gakuen-mono* genre is not adequate for the purpose of describing the school-based *seishun eiga* and its fictionally transformative role in the lives of its adolescent protagonists.

One further point of consideration, as Doyle Greene points out in his book on American adolescent culture, is to look at how the 'core contradiction of "teen culture" is that it is *produced by adults and consumed by adolescents*' (2012: 6, original italics). As with Mark Harrison, I hold to the definition that 'the film must evolve around the life of high schoolers' *and* its central storylines must involve 'the setting of the high school' (2017: 5). The figure cited earlier of over 100 high school films also excludes the highly popular *terebi-dorama* (TV drama) series, and films that may feature a high school student as a central character but are not primarily set in a school or classroom. A number of films, therefore, such as *Our Meal for Tomorrow / Bokura no Gohan wa Ashita de Matteru* (lit. *We'll Wait for Tomorrow's Lunch*, 2017, dir. Masahide Ichii) and Sion Sono's *Himizu / Mole* (2011), are excluded from close analysis in this study because much of the action takes place beyond the classroom and the general school environment.

Over-representation?

The globalisation of film industries, hastened by increasingly efficient distribution methods, exposes tensions and mimetic patterns across national film industries. As a way of contextualising Japan's high school films, comparisons can be made with other similarly themed films from prominent national film industries. In the popular films of the US (Hollywood), high school films are perhaps dominated by images of cheerleaders, football teams and school proms, the most popular of these tending to be based on senior high or college, with overt and often graphically explicit themes of sexuality (*American Pie*, 1999, dir. Paul Weitz and Chris Weitz; *Easy A*, 2010, dir. Will Gluck) or homosexuality (e.g. *Love, Simon*, 2018, dir. Greg Berlanti), depression and anxiety (*Eighth Grade*, 2018, dir. Bo Burnham), and cultures based around the (over-)consumption of alcohol and drugs (*HIGH School*, 2010, dir. Adrien Brody). Other films offer quirky characters such as independent productions *Napoleon Dynamite* (2004, dir. Jared Hess), *Sierra Burgess is a Loser* (2018, dir. Ian Samuels) or *Ladybird* (2017, dir. Greta Gerwig), or more mainstream works such as John Hughes's *Ferris Bueller's Day Off* (1986) or *The Breakfast Club* (1985). But school-based texts are only one part of the entertainment available for youth in Western media, in which Greene points to

a multiplicity of discourses [in which] teen culture can overtly present itself as 'speaking for the kids' and offer representations of 'teen empowerment' while it can also impose adult lessons and values as to what constitutes acceptable or unacceptable modes of social behaviour. (2012: 19)

Many of these Western films, however, marginalise the role of the school in teen characters' lives.

So, while US films may view the purpose of the high school film through a different lens, the arrival of Japan's *seishun eiga* did not occur in complete isolation. Catherine Driscoll (2011: 161) notes that:

> [t]he conditions for film as youth culture were established wherever industrial modernity met new theories of adolescence and this was the case in Japan as elsewhere. In the 1950s and 1960s [. . .] Japanese film displayed a new fascination with youth and, as in the US at the same time, particular studios (like Nikkatsu) specialised in producing youth-directed 1950s genres, including the high school sex picture and a subgenre of *yakuza eiga*.

While Driscoll poses the question of whether US Occupation and access to US films might have influenced Japan's focus on youth, she continues:

> but pre-war Japan (and especially Taishō Japan, 1912–26) had already linked adolescence, governance and technology in ways we now associate with teen film and *seishun eiga* is an extension of these ideas, and of a dramatic generalisation produced by the colonial situation rather than being simply an imported genre. (2011: 161)

Thus, Japanese youth cultures, and the films that came to represent them, were as much an internally derived project as they were 'imported'.

In this book, I maintain that the proliferation of school-based *seishun eiga* from the 2000s is specifically a Japanese phenomenon and plays a small but important part in its identity as 'another global cinema that was produced in the middle decades of last century, but continues to evolve in the transnational context of its afterlife' (Russell 2011: 3). Even in the geographically and culturally proximate Korea, while there are said to be many proximities with Japanese cinema forms, the *seishun eiga* is not so prevalent, with only three high school-based feature films among the 200-plus films produced in 2018 (KOFIC, 2019). These films consist of a murder mystery, *After My Death / Joe Man-eun So-nyeo* (2018, dir. Kim Ui-seok), a mentoring teacher narrative in *House of Hummingbird / Beol-sae* (2018, dir. Kim Bora) and a lonely-girl drama in *Second Life / Sunhee-wa Seul-gi* (2018, dir. Park Young-ju).

In Australia, where the number of feature films produced each year is low (around thirty), the school setting is mostly found in iconic TV series such as 'Heartbreak High' (1994–9). Produced by the state-funded ABC (Australian Broadcasting Commission), these programmes are aimed specifically at the teenage audience and are screened in the 4–6pm time slot, thereby missing older audiences who are less likely to be watching at that time. Australian films, similar to their US counterparts (*Ladybird*, for instance) based around school-aged teens, also tend to present the school and its classroom activities as only peripheral to the story (see *Looking for Alibrandi*, 2000, dir. Kate Woods; *Head On*, 1998, dir. Ana Kokkinos; or *Girl Asleep*, 2015, dir. Rosemary Myers).

While these examples of US, Korean and Australian cinema reflect very different cultures and film industries to those of Japan, they serve to highlight the extent to which Japan's cinema audiences have an ongoing appetite for high school films. I further note that Japanese high school films interrupt the commonly viewed notions (mostly from the Western perspective) of Japanese cinema as driven by genres such as horror and anime. This ready identification is also found in the near-deification of particular filmmakers, and as Phillips and Stringer note, 'the brand name of the *auteur* continues to provide the terms of reference through which cultural institutions both inside and outside Japan present and promote Japanese cinema' (2007: 15). This book's focus on high school films, however, deviates from the reductive *auteur*-led views of Japanese cinema to focus on films that serve local audiences first and foremost. They are generally not blockbusters, nor do they, on the whole, necessarily aspire to the artistic 'greatness' of film festivals and awards. Directors such as Takahiro Miki and Shō Tsukikawa may not be internationally recognised, but within their field of high school films they have proven to be relatively prolific and successful at attracting continued funding for their work.

Hierarchies and Heterotopias

Like any formal institution, schools have a teleological function in mapping changes in a society. Arai writes of the ways that Japan's social and economic struggles of the late 1990s resulted in the education reforms (*kyōiku kaikaku*) of 2002, which 'gained much of their legitimacy from this aura of anxiety or moral panic surrounding the youth' (2003: 368). Fear of developing a society that fails to raise its children as faithful subjects has long troubled Japan, especially in the post-World War II era, when much introspection took place. Earlier films of rebellious youth, such as *Crazed Fruit/Kurutta Kajitsu* (1956, dir. Kō Nakahira) or *Season of the Sun/Taiyō no Kisetsu* (1956, dir. Takumi Furukawa), did little to calm those who saw Japan's future as one dependent on a disciplined society that needed to control its wayward adolescents. Similar feelings have been perhaps universally expressed for generations, especially following crisis events, as Durkheim stated in Europe's post-World War I period:

> School discipline [. . .] must appear to children as something good and sacred – the condition of their happiness and moral well-being. In this way, when they are

men [sic], they will accept spontaneously and consciously that social discipline which cannot be weakened without endangering the community. (c. 1916, in Pickering 1979: 161)

The development of the adolescent through institutionalisation is therefore an important step in the creation of an orderly society. For Durkheim, at the beginning of the last century, the shift from childhood becomes a crucial moment where 'it is possible and relatively easy to impart to the child the sentiment of moral authority and discipline, which constitutes the second stage in the formation of character and will' (Pickering 1979: 154). Schools play an instrumental role in this process, where:

[i]n addition to their roles as educational institutions structuring human capital development during a critical period of socioeconomic attainment, high schools organize the peer contexts in which young people come of age during a critical period of development. (Crosnoe et al. 2018: 317)

In the quotation above, Crosnoe et al. go some way toward explaining the 'complex social ecology' (317) that is found in the institutional setting. The importance of the peer networks that develop is found in the non-institutionalised hierarchies that form between students across the many and varied cohorts that must 'survive' their term of state-enforced 'incarceration' during their school years. Drawing on earlier research into high schools, they note how findings corroborate the 'contemporary notion of schools as contexts of human development – organised by class and other stratifying systems – and potentially detrimental to or supportive of the educational missions of schools and the educational prospects of young people' (322). In other words, the school presents as a microcosm of society. In the US, high school, with its lack of uniforms (mostly), is 'a critical turning point in the lives of most youth', where they are required to 'step out of the life conditions they had earlier experienced' (Rubinstein 2001: 281). In this new environment, *sans* the markers of regimented school uniforms, 'they must establish an identity' (282). In Japan's case, it can be seen that the 'transition from childhood to adulthood is more structured than in other highly developed nations' (Tanioka and Glaser 1991: 71), and as described in Chapter 3 of this book, the school uniform is a significant part of this transition.

As with the earlier-mentioned archetypes (the jock, the bully and so on), there are other ways of constructing school-based characters, with Harrison setting the parameters for his study based on a gendered reading that concludes that there are 'only three types of female characters in high school movies in relation to hierarchy': those 'ruled by the Queen Bee';

those that 'actively rebel against this system'; and 'those who lack agency and wilfully try to ignore anything remotely related to such a system' (2017: 6). That such hierarchical structures also exist for young males is unarguable. Each of these examples indicates that, as a setting for a text, the school is able to provide a highly dynamic space for constructing multiple narratives around adolescent behaviour.

Power Metaphors

A useful way to consider the school as a setting arises from the work of Michel Foucault into the institutionalisation of societies. In his *Discipline and Punishment*, for instance, he contends that schools must be able to reflect to students, and society in general, the 'legitimacy of the institute'. He maintains (in one subheading) that 'School [is] Part of [the] Process that Creates Citizens in Formative Adolescent Years' and that it is 'organized around multiple groups with meaningful identities that define the prevailing norms and values to which adolescents entering the school are exposed' (Crosnoe et al. 2018: 317). Finally, Foucault turns his attention to 'The Division of Disciplinary Spaces' (Foucault 1977: 143), interrogating the physical, walled spaces of schools, sites that are witness to generations of adolescents and their growth and development. Each of Foucault's categories captures the purpose of the institute as an arm of state or societal power.

With these categories in mind, films like the *Battle Royale* series emerge as perhaps the ultimate nihilistic metaphor for institutionalised power. The original controversial film created a school setting with its last-person-standing plot (later successfully replicated by Hollywood in the *Hunger Games* films), seizing on the perception that Japan's youth were on the brink of rebellion, with the term *gakkyu hōkai* (classroom chaos) coined in an attempt to understand the social changes taking place. Set in a very near future, where schoolchildren are viewed as a threat to 'adult' society, the government introduces the Battle Royale Act, whereby the children are 'pitted against each other in a lethal game of survival' (Martin 2015: 72).

The links between the high school of *Battle Royale* (albeit a non-organic school environment, given that the students have been sent to a deserted school on an island) and the military are not just coincidence. Foucault's work on the institutionalising of discipline is based on the idea that 'a necessary precondition for the appearance of modern disciplinary institutions was the gradual dissemination of disciplinary techniques from marginal institutions [monasteries, armies and workshops] during the seventeenth and eighteenth centuries' (Jones 1990: 80). In a further example of the link between the ruling bodies of the state and the school, 2017's *Love and Lies/Koi to Uso* (dir. Takeshi Furosawa) sets up a slightly futuristic premise where the (fictionalised) state Ministry of Health, Labour and Welfare is charged with repopulating the nation through an initiative overseen by the 'Super Declining Birthrate Countermeasure Committee', which matches students with their future marriage partners on their sixteenth birthday. The partner is someone of the opposite sex, reiterating the heteronormative standard of Japanese society, and the couples are soon married in a formal Western-style church service where most of the attendees are still in their school uniforms. In Chapter 1, I investigate how these types of disciplinary links in Japanese high school films illustrate the significance of institutional order in Japan.

The narrative structure of Japanese high school films, in many ways, parallels that of other national cinemas. Naturally, differences are found in the cultural aspects of the films. For instance, in Mark Harrison's study of US high school films, he notes that many of those in his focus feature narratives that 'lead towards a prom, subsequently presenting a setting which sees a resolution of conflict and personal growth in characters, potentially redeeming a character after their actions preceding the event' (2017: 3). Therefore, the culturally specific event, 'the prom', serves as a plot point around which tensions and resolutions can be found. In Japan, the concept of the prom is rarely found, so films tend to choose graduation and the passing of college entrance exams, or a music or sporting performance, as the key event around which to structure the narrative.

In a Japanese context, replicated in the role of the teacher in many films, the rigidity of the system is presented through the unwavering teacher who 'exemplifies the cold, impersonal world of the education system' and is 'a creature of rules and regulations, a stranger to kindness and imagination' (McDonald 2006: 145). Throughout this book I show how Japanese school-based *seishun eiga* utilise this authoritative figure in a wide range of styles, from the severity of the 'drill-sergeant' teacher, principal or education official to the kind-hearted empathetic teacher. Firstly, though, I will explore reasons why this particular type of film resonates so strongly with Japanese filmmakers and audiences, and how changes in Japan's approach to education fostered the image of the school as central to adolescent life.

One further distinction in Japan's high school system is found in the power structures that Okano and Tsuchiya define as headed by the 'elite' schools, seen as 'the top prefectural and national academic high schools in urban centres, and a handful of private high schools' (1999: 64). These schools contrast with the 'non-elite' schools, 'which aim to prepare students for less prestigious universities and junior colleges' and make up the majority of Japan's high schools, supported by a mix of government and private vocational schools (1999: 65). These distinctions are an important feature of Japanese society and the nation's educational structures, and many of the films in this book quickly signal what type of school the characters attend in the opening minutes of the film through establishing shots and dialogue.

Why Japan?

Japan's societal shift in the late 1990s edged toward the neoliberal ideology of a 'discharging onto the individual (and individual community) of former responsibilities for education, the child, and the home' (Arai 2003: 372). What this shift failed to take into account was the embedded social structure where the parent(s) was/were so busy trying to hang on to their jobs, and in many instances re-educating themselves to remain relevant in the workforce, that children were tasked with their own responsibilities around education, especially in regard to getting themselves to and from school. This does not mean, however, that children could determine their own fate within the educational structure, as once within the perimeter of the school, students were expected to continue following the instructions of their teachers. After all, the institution (the school) is a site where '[a] relation of surveillance, defined and regulated, is inscribed at the heart of the practice of teaching, not as an additional or adjacent part, but as a mechanism that is inherent to it and which increases its efficiency' (Foucault 1977: 176). For Japan, this 'mechanism' is centred on a balance of the desire for individual responsibility against an equally strong desire for discipline and order.

The school is also part of the 'life-cycle' of almost all global cultures, and as McVeigh proposes in relation to the Japanese experience, it 'is in no small way driven by, ordered and configured by massive political and economic institutionalizing forces' (2000: 48). In other words, it is a heavily embedded and contextualised part of the human experience. This also reinforces the concept that hierarchies of responsibilities under institutional rule are both determined by and reinforced through the selection of participants for different tasks. As Foucault was to point out, disciplinary power was first apparent in the divisions of labour found in educational settings, where, 'selected from among the best pupils a whole series of "officers" – intendants, observers, monitors, tutors, reciters of prayers, writing officers, receivers of ink, almoners [distributors of charitable monies] and visitors' were appointed to attend to their chosen task (in Jones 1990: 95). Each of these responsibilities was part of a holistic

disciplinary approach based on an apparent (or imagined) decline in adolescent behaviour, a decline that has concerned societies for centuries, with
Durkheim noting in 1912, 'I admit, and I am the first to deplore it, that
the notion of authority has become more lax in the family and at school'
(in Pickering 1979: 156). In Japan at around this time, the creation of girls'
high schools, and boarding schools in particular, saw girls from elite families moved beyond the confines of their immediate family to large cities,
where they experienced a modicum of freedom. For many, this meant that
'the emerging schoolgirl culture made it possible for the girls to position
themselves in public spaces that had previously been off limits', such as
the gender-mixed regions of Tokyo's Hibiya Park (Czarnecki 2005: 49).
Thus, while the school itself may have offered military-like surveillance,
once the students had free time, they were able to escape the disciplined
environment.

Foucault notes two developments that were to formalise advancements
in education in France: the first was 'the gradual move toward a national
education system', resulting in standardisations whereby schools were set
up under the watchful eye of universities (Jones 1990: 82). Instrumental
in the creation of this national education system was the second advance-
ment, the setting up of an examination system across the schools where
they acted as a form of surveillance to ensure all students were regularly
and uniformly tested. This also involved a process whereby, 'to ensure
uniformity between these colleges, they were all required to use the same
textbooks and set the same exams' (Jones 1990: 83). This had the further
benefit of imposing a form of surveillance over the teachers, as officials
could monitor, via exam results, each teacher's performance. In Japan,
the strict adherence to forms of institutional education based on a formal
examination system also acts as a type of surveillance, fraught with tensions and anxieties for students, parents and educators. In her study on
the pressures faced by Japanese children, Andrea Arai relates this path to
the challenges faced by the *Battle Royale* students, which mirror a reality
where:

> In the post-bubble economy, despite the rhetoric of the end of competition, in edu-
> cation reform, the new reality of survival is that not all will reach the top, but those
> who do, like the kids in the film, will have to engage desperately (*hisshi ni*) to become
> worthy competitors for Japan in the amorphous battlefield of the global economy.
> (2003: 374)

In other words, the formality of the institution and its examination system replicate the demands of 'real-world' Japan in the global environment.
The nation's 'nose-to-the-grindstone education systems' (McDonald

2006: 138) are seen as providing the perfect, controlled setting to engage young people as they enter the 'battlefield'.

To what extent, then, do school-based *seishun eiga* operate within a cinema industry that can be seen as representative of contemporary Japan? As David Bordwell was to note, Japan's film industry developed across several stages, interrupted by natural disasters and wars, each of which saw filmmakers assess their approaches to their craft and take note of external influences: namely, from European and Hollywood cinema. Bordwell suggests that, once 'distinctively "Japanese" representational strategies showed up in films, they were not spontaneously and unreflectingly transmitted across centuries, but operated more as knowing *citations*, marking the product as distinctly "Japanese" as well as achieving particular formal and cultural ends' (1995: 17, original italics). In other words, the on-screen signs and symbols of Japanese culture were there not simply because the film was created in Japan, but because they were purposely added as a defining characteristic of the film's Japaneseness.

Japan's history was forever marked by the student uprisings in the 1960s, and this era is captured in films as a result of college and university students leading the charge against what it saw as an increasing authoritarian state. Films such as Nagisa Ōshima's 1960 *Night and Fog in Japan/Nihon no Yoru to Kiri*), the series of *pinku* (erotic or soft-porn) films by Kōji Wakamatsu across the 1960s and 1970s that were loosely based on student protests, or the 2010 Haruki Murakami-based *Norwegian Wood/Noruwei no Mori* (dir. Anh Hung Tran) focus heavily on the leadership of these older students and their *Zengakuren* (aka *Zenkyōtō*) anarchist and communist groups. Few of today's popular high school films draw from such pivotal historical events; one film that does draw from past events is *Hyouka: Forbidden Secrets/Hyōka* (lit. a type of frozen dessert) (2017, directed by female director Mari Asato). Based on a 2001 novel by Honobu Yonezawa, *Hyouka* explores the events leading up to the explosive 1968 clashes, through the eyes of present-day high school students who are looking back on what happened. Although worlds apart in many respects, it would seem that some parallels could be made with Ōshima's *Cruel Story of Youth/Seishun Zankoku Monogatari* (1960). The use of newsreel footage in both films harks back to political protests (in Ōshima's film it is footage from South Korea) and looks to set up a strong political narrative that 'simultaneously foregrounds and conceals contemporary socio-political issues' (Yoshimoto 2007: 175). As with *Cruel Story*, though, *Hyouka* (although much lighter in tone) also pulls back from a critical engagement with political struggles. This avoidance of serious political historicisations suggests that today's high school films are positioned primarily as light entertainment rather than as adopting a heuristic approach for young audiences.

Structure

In Chapter 1 of this book, I examine the formal delineation of the school as a site for creating disciplinary spaces within the physical, built structure of the institution. I show how each tangible space serves a deliberate purpose in the school environment and is used by filmmakers to recreate the lived experience of the school ground. This chapter therefore explores the universally recognised iconography of the classroom and school hallways. In Japanese films, these images are supplemented by Japan-centric indicators of place, including the school rooftop, gymnasiums, toilets, and even the window settings in classrooms.

Chapter 2 moves beyond the physical confines of the school itself. Equally important in Japan's school-based films is the passage of student movement to and from school, mostly on foot, sometimes by bicycle and, less frequently, by bus or train. These pre- and post-school moments provide a place for narratives to develop and for the reinforcement of relationships, including moments of quiet contemplation of individual characters (often via voiceovers). Representations of a character's home environment provide a diegetically permanent physical site for domestic issues to play out, and to indicate the socio-economic or class stature of a student's family. Finally, this chapter shows how the student's bedroom provides a place of retreat for teen characters, removed from the pressures of institutional and familial life.

In Chapter 3, I investigate the ways that schools serve to create a regulated society distinct from the familial and political structures that otherwise govern the lives of Japan's citizens. This chapter explores the use of the school uniform both as an iconic disciplinary marker of the institutionalised child/youth and as 'a dictated form of performance of ethnic loyalty' (Tamura 2017: 37). The cinematic use of the school uniform provides the audience with an immediately recognisable character in terms of age and gender, and allows costume designers and colour consultants to expand on the usually drab colours of the uniforms to create a dynamic palette for filmmakers and cinematographers.

In Chapter 4, I delve into the ways that school-based films create a site for student protagonists to signal cohesion as a distinct societal group, or to move outside the assumed traditional collectivist values so often placed upon Japan's institutionalised students. I explore the role of the family in high school-based films and the significance of parental and family decisions that impact on the lives and maturation of the adolescents under their care. Finally, in this chapter I investigate the ways that these films create representations of unorthodox Japanese student behaviours to deliver inventive and entertaining films that indicate the use of artistic imagination in film production.

Chapter 5 looks at the ways that school-based films appeal to audiences by creating a sense of nostalgia and by building on existing audiences through the extensive 'media mix' adaptation processes from manga and anime, and literary or online novels that find their way into production as live-action films. The films are also produced with an eye towards promotion and intertextuality through the use of stars from the fields of pop music, modelling and television. This chapter also investigates the use of seasonal imagery as a way of furthering tropes of nostalgia and representing the temporality of the school experience.

In Chapter 6, my focus moves toward analyses of the taboos and controversial narratives and imagery found in school-based *seishun eiga*, beginning with what may seem to some readers a non-controversial issue: the notion of shame. The importance of this emotional response needs to be seen in the light of Japan's strict formal (and informal) codes within its arguably collectivist society. High school films also create sites for an open discourse on physical violence and the trait of bullying, whether through physical force or psychological means. I also show how the more universalistic notions of adolescent awkwardness appear as a major plot device in these films. This chapter then explores the more overtly taboo nature of images that may be sensationally violent or sexually explicit.

In Chapter 7 the focus moves to the 'tamer' (compared to most US high school films), but no less controversial, issue of sexual relationships in the high school film. I then examine the narratives of forbidden love between a student and their teacher, or between a student and an older man or woman. This chapter then investigates the use of same-sex relationships and the ways that they are employed as either a major plot device or, more frequently, as a subplot that attempts to normalise homosexuality, while maintaining a marginalised approach by using supporting characters to carry out same-sex narratives.

This book's focus on Japanese high school-based films is the first to single out this increasingly popular subgenre of *seishun-eiga*. In an environment where Japan faces an uncertain future centred on its fears around its ageing population, the popularity of narratives based on adolescents in a disciplinary environment puts forth a youthful and mostly optimistic view of contemporary Japanese life. The large corpus of films presented here captures a moment in Japanese history, pre-COVID-19, where concerns were not with human survival from a global pandemic, but with more 'trivial' issues of (mostly) boy–girl romance. At the time, the seemingly straightforward trajectory from school to college to employment is presented as a predetermined destiny, with no sense of the health and economic crises just around the corner. At the time of writing, the pandemic has seen a return to the need for the adherence to strong disciplinary rules, one in which Japanese adolescents are well prepared due to the beliefs and values that have shaped them through their school years. The Japanese high school film therefore plays a significant role in reflecting back those behaviours and highlights the important role of institutional compliance in the formative, adolescent years of the high school student.

CHAPTER 1

The Division of Disciplinary Spaces

The physical, built structure of the school serves as an imposing reminder of its institutional role, whether in a state-run or privately administered education system. In film, the audience's first encounter with the school is most commonly through an establishing shot of the gates or school entrance that clearly locates the institutional setting. These establishing shots reflect the disciplined, organised flow of students into or out of the institution. They represent a funnelling of the youth from freedom to entrapment, a 'pedagogical machine' designed as a 'mechanism for training' (Foucault 1977: 172). Within this machine, in the cinematic experience at least, it often seems as if 'career prospects and plans do not exist, as the students are more focused on "the moment" and current school affairs (or, simply, survival)' (Kiejziewicz 2018: 86). For students, the focus on the self and 'the moment' is a vital factor in their psychological development, and for filmmakers (screenwriters in particular) it provides a site for the development of focused narratives that appear, to a large degree, as 'natural', and necessarily framed within the institutional, disciplined space.

This framing of the imposing institutional structure is not restricted, of course, to Japanese films but found in other cinemas where the school building is easily recognisable, such as in American films like *Ferris Bueller's Day Off*, *Stand By Me* (1986, dir. Rob Reiner), *Fast Times at Ridgemont High* (1982, dir. Amy Heckerling) or *Easy A*. In the UK, *To Sir, with Love* (1967, dir. James Clavell) presents the fortress-like brick structure of the inner-urban school, or the majestic, castle-like boarding school Hogwarts in the *Harry Potter* series of films, images that draw directly from the imposing nature of the military academies on which present-day schools were modelled. Filmmakers utilise low shots to increase the dramatic presence of the institution, much as the set shot of the haunted house is exemplified by the looming view of the Bates House in Hitchcock's *Psycho* (1960). The use of the external establishing shot serves not only to determine the physical location but to code the text for the audience, creating expectations for the film to deliver iconographic images essential to the high school environment.

In films such as *ReLIFE/Riraifu* (2017, dir. Takeshi Furusawa) and *Principal! Am I A Heroine in Love?/Purinshiparu: Koi Suru Watashi wa Hiroin Desu ka?* (2018, dir. Tetsuo Shinohara) (Figure 1.1), establishing shots feature the physical building dominating the upper half of the screen, with the flow of students tapering toward the school entrance. Both films also include the school's name in a lower corner, as if to reinforce the notion that an otherwise nondescript building could be mistaken for any kind of institution. While both of these images indicate forms of contemporary school architecture, the low, multi-storey buildings nonetheless portray a sense of entrapment, their height squeezed into the frame and blocking out the expansive sky to reinforce the sense of an oppressive, restrictive environment.

In *My Little Monster/Tonari no Kaibutsu-kun* (2018, dir. Shō Tsukikawa) (Figure 1.2), the school building is again presented in a low-angle shot, but this time symmetrically framed from straight in front of the building. Again, the building occupies the top half of the screen, and the stairs (which double as open-air stands for the running track and sportsground at the bottom of the screen) expand upwards and outwards, opening up to draw the audiences' attention to the building itself. The turrets of the central building create an imposing castle-like structure, flanked by the austere functionality of the modern classrooms to each side.

Figure 1.1 School frontage in *Principal! Am I a Heroine in Love?* (Aniplex, 2018).

Figure 1.2 Imposing structure in *My Little Monster* (Toho, 2018).

Other films, such as *Ouran High School Host Club/Gekijōban Ōran Kōkō Hosutobu* (2012, dir. Satoshi Kan), use a 'cold open' to establish the premise of the film (in *Ouran*'s case, this lasts for over seven minutes), before the film's titles and introduction to the actors and their characters. Following this, the major establishing shot, similar to the one in *Principal!*, tracks past the school sign, 'Ouran Gakuin Senior High School' (in English and Japanese), toward the main building before a continuity tracking shot inside the building where the students are mingling.

The Classroom

Once inside the formidable structure of the school building, disciplinary actions are performed in the segregation of individual rooms, each designed for a specific function. The classroom is the most recognisable of these spaces, featuring (mostly) a conventional size, layout and furnishings. Within the classroom, a microcosm of individuals, is also a delineated disciplinary area governed by hierarchies (as noted), and a range of what Foucault calls 'judgements', where students are:

> subject to a whole micro-penalty of time (lateness, absences, interruptions of tasks), of activity (inattention, negligence, lack of zeal), of behaviour (impoliteness, disobedience), of speech (idle chatter, insolence), of the body ('incorrect' attitudes, irregular gestures, lack of cleanliness), of sexuality (impurity, indecency). (Foucault 1977, in Jones 1990: 96)

Foucault noted that assigning individual places (seats and desks) made it possible to supervise each individual and the simultaneous work of all of the students (1977: 147). The creation of desks further adds to the disciplinary control, and Foucault muses on the importance of the '*correlation of the body and the gesture*' (original italics, 152) that enables practices such as the confident learning of handwriting. Quoting from a 1783 document, the *Conduite des écoles chrétiennes*, Foucault refers to the detailed instructions relating to how students should sit at their desks:, for example, 'they should hold their bodies erect, somewhat turned and free on the left side', extending this instruction to the physiological warning to maintain distance (of 'two fingers') from the desk because 'nothing is more harmful to the health than to acquire the habit of pressing one's stomach against the table' (152). While, in contemporary societies, this instruction may appear over-regulatory, in Japan, the 'correct' posture is important in relaying to the teacher/authoritative figure one's readiness to learn and be part of the attentive collective of the classroom. The way one sits is a performative act that is taught and modelled to students, even at preschool age, when Japan's children, little more than infants, are required to sit at desks for at least part of their day.

The Western education systems of today tend to offer flexible seating arrangements to encourage less focus on teacher-led classrooms and to foster group learning among students sitting freely around the room or grouped together at tables. Within the more formal classroom of desks lined up in rows, the students' ability to rebel against their institutionalisation is reduced, yet still manifest in behaviours such as the slouching or reclining long exhibited in Western cinematic examples such as *Blackboard Jungle* (1955, dir. Richard Brooks). These anti-authoritarian mannerisms are replicated in *Assassination Classroom*, where Akabane's (Masaki Suda) rebellious nature is shown when he is seen in the back row with his feet up on the edge of his desk. Similarly, in one classroom scene in *ReLIFE*, the teacher is clearly placed at the front of the class as the authoritative figure (the only figure *sans* uniform), while made to stand beside her are two nervous students on whom all attention falls. The students nearest the front of the class are within the immediate field of view of the teacher, so can be seen displaying 'good' posture, yet towards the back of the class other students slouch over their desks, partly shielded from the teacher's gaze.

The physical design of the classroom therefore plays an important role in the organisation of the students. The teacher-focused arrangement of chairs and desks is reiterated when the teacher enters the classroom, as shown in *Missions of Love/Watashi ni XX Shinasai* (lit. *Do XX to me!*) (2018, dir. Tōru Yamamoto), when the teacher arrives and a class monitor instructs the classmates to stand, and then bow, which the students do while calling out 'Good morning'. The task of keeping the classroom orderly both in terms of disciplinarity and as a physical space is often assigned to individual or group monitors in Japan. In *One Week Friends/*

Isshūkan Furenzu (2017, dir. Shōsuke Murakami), a group of students is seen after class (without any teacher supervision), sweeping the floors and then choosing (through a game of rock, paper, scissors) who will take the rubbish bags out, while others restack the chairs on to the floor.

On occasion, the classroom features for reasons other than education. In *Your Lie in April/Shigatsu wa Kimi no Uso* (2016, dir. Takehiko Shinjō), for instance, Kaori Miyazano (Suzu Hirose) uses the excuse of having left her bag at school to lure Kōsei Arima (Kento Yamazaki) back to the classroom at night. In the near-darkness, she admits that her bag is not at school, but rather than use this as a ploy for a romantic or sexual encounter with Kōsei, she takes the chance to confess to him that she is ill and that her illness is more serious than first thought. She stands at her desk, gently touching a musical emblem that she had once scratched into its surface. The moment serves to highlight her wish to continue a 'normal' life at school, but she knows that she must return to hospital. When Kōsei tries to persuade her to leave with him, she runs off, only to collapse in the nearby hallway.

One of the few films to feature a slightly different classroom design is *My Brother Loves Me Too Much/Ani ni Ai Saresugite Komattemasu* (2017, dir. Hayato Kawai), where the classroom is in a new school which has modern floor-to-ceiling glass panels lining both sides of the room. The hallway therefore becomes much more open, and the classroom is filled with light. But while most classrooms present a walled-in, closed environment, students exiting the classroom immediately find themselves confronting another highly enclosed space: the hallway (or corridor).

The Hallway

The school hallway offers a confined (walled) setting that channels and restricts movements of students throughout the institution. It is also subject to the enforced scheduling of time; a common cinematic use of the hallway is at the end of class, when students stream out of one confined space (the classroom) only to exhibit a more casualised (sometimes rowdy) behaviour in the hallway, generally on their way to the freedom of the outside world. As Foucault notes, this is part of the institution's disciplinary function to 'provide fixed positions and permit circulation' (1977: 148). From a technical aspect, the hallway allows the filmmaker to utilise long shots and vary the depth of field to focus the action on the characters in the foreground. This can be used to highlight a romantic link, such as in the coy moment in *Have a Song on Your Lips/Kuchibiru ni Uta o* (2015, dir. Takahiro Miki), when shy boy Satoru Kuwahara (Shōta Shimoda) receives a compliment from a girl in his class, Kotomi Hasegawa (Mayu Yamaguchi) (Figure 1.3). Shot with a low depth of field, this scene places the students in the background and out of focus, as is Satoro (slightly) despite his figure (with box and backpack) filling a third of the screen. The focus falls on Kotomi, head bowed, as she politely passes on the compliment.

The hallway can also operate as a site for intimate moments between friends, or for confrontations, such as in *Principal! Am I a Heroine in Love?*, when Shima Sumitomo (Yuina Kuroshima) confronts her friend, Haruka Kunishige (Rina Kawaei), in a pivotal, confessional moment (Figure 1.4). Again, the low depth of field concentrates attention on the key figures, this time in order to capture the reaction of the person receiving bad news (Haruka).

The hallway is not an exclusive setting for student interactions and movements; it also features as a site for confrontation between teachers and students. For instance, in *Close Range Love / Kinkyori Ren'ai* (aka *A Short Distance Relationship*, 2014, dir. Naoto Kumazawa), Ryū Matoba (Nozomu Kotaki) sees the girl on whom he has a crush, Yuni Kururugi (Nana Komatsu), in tears and realises that she has been romantically hurt by her teacher, Haruka Sakurai (Tomohisa Yamashita). In a jealous rage, Ryū runs down the hallway after Sakurai-sensei and brutally punches him in the face. Sakurai falls to the floor as Ryū stands over him and menacingly warns: 'Don't come near Kururugi-san ever again!' The only other witness is Mirei-sensei, as all the other students are outside on a break

Figure 1.3 Hallway intimacy in *Have a Song on Your Lips* (Asmik Ace, 2015).

Figure 1.4 Confession time in *Principal! Am I a Heroine in Love?* (Aniplex, 2018).

(Ryū himself has just run down from a rooftop break area), and the incident is therefore given heightened prominence due to the otherwise silent hallway.

In *Nisekoi: False Love/Nisekoi* (2018, Hayato Kawai), the hallway is a site for Raku and the blonde-haired Chitoge to figure out if they really like each other. The reluctant Raku finally confronts Chitoge and, once again through the use of shot reverse shot, the focus alternates between the two protagonists in the 'neutral' setting of the hallway. The hallway provides sanctuary for the two characters, where they can be momentarily shielded from the warring *yakuza* who have been dispatched to keep the young 'lovers' under surveillance. In contrast to this potentially romantic scene, Bomford points to the US teen drama *Glee* and its use of the hallway as a centrepiece for bullying behaviours, where students are thrown against lockers or have drinks thrown in their faces (the infamous 'slushy facial') (2016: 14). This type of personalised bullying also occurs in Japanese high school films such as *Sayounara/If That's True* (2018, dir. Yūho Ishibashi), where the hallway provides a site for retaliation when Yuki Kishimoto (Haruka Imō) hears her classmates making disparaging remarks about her friend, Aya Seto (Kirara Inori), who has just died. Yuki walks up to the girl who is speaking and slowly empties a vase of flowers over her head. While the film's title seems to indicate the well-known Japanese word for 'goodbye', it is 'actually a romanized spelling for the Japanese characters which mean "if that's true" and is part of a passage recited by Yuki at the opening and at the close of the movie by a chorus of characters from the movie' (Dimagmaliw 2019). This, in turn, references elements of the narrative regarding the gossip around the cause of Seto's death, and also the relationships (perceived or real) that the various classmates had with Seto.

The hallway, as noted, also serves as an indicator of time: a physical site used for the institutionalised movement of students from one space to another within fixed schedules, or as Foucault writes, through the use of the timetable, whose 'three great methods . . . establish rhythms, impose particular occupations, regulate the cycles of repetition' (1977: 149). As with the institutional prison, students are taught, Pavlovian-style, to react when the bell rings, and either file into the classroom (the cell) or are released from their confinement, as in the image from *Forget Me Not/Wasurenai to Chikatta Boku ga Ita* (2015, dir. Kei Horie) shown in Figure 1.5. This temporal incarceration or emancipation follows set patterns governed by an unseen authority who dictates the flow. Even the teacher must abide by the bell. Again, from a cinematic view, this can be utilised as a marking point within a narrative, signalling interruption or movement of plot. Entry into the hallway can be used as an edit point or for the creation of establishing shots.

Characters can be seen in the hallway having epiphanies or, as in one comical scene from *Nisekoi: False Love*, using it as an avenue of escape for Raku from a would-be assailant. Raku is forced to run along the hallway, but in trying to dodge the *yakuza* henchman, propels himself from side to side by leaping against the walls, using his feet to push away and create momentum.

Figure 1.5 Busy hallway in *Forget Me Not* (Nikkatsu, 2015).

Hallway (corridor) design also has its precedents in the French military *école*, where student 'cells' were created with surveillance in mind through windows 'placed on the corridor wall of each room from chest-level to within one or two feet of the ceiling'; this not only provided a 'pleasant' environment, but was done for 'disciplinary reasons that may determine this arrangement' (as cited in Foucault 1977: 173). Similarly, school classroom design has high-level windows adjacent to the hallway so that, when students are seated, they are not distracted by others passing, or watching, in the hallway. Their view is of the blackboard at the front, the hallway wall to one side, and a wall of windows to capture the light on the other.

For the hallway wanderer, whether miscreant or authoritative figure, the high-level windows and portal-like classroom door allow a better view into the room than the students have as they try to see out. In *Close Range Love* this takes on a voyeuristic tone: newly arrived teacher, and Sakurai-sensei's former lover, Mirei Takizawa (Asami Mizukawa), catches sight of him secretly kissing his student, Yuni, under the lectern while class is in progress, and from a reverse shot, Mirei can be seen looking in as Sakurai pulls away from the kiss (Figure 1.6).

The hallway also provides a space where filmmakers can frame their shots, in the same way that director Yasujirō Ozu is noted for his framing of internal shots using the neat geometry of the traditional Japanese house. In his analysis of *Street Without End/Kagirinaki Hodo* (1934, dir. Mikio Naruse), Bordwell similarly notes how Naruse uses the structure of a hospital corridor to frame a sequence of intriguing shots immediately after the central character's husband has died:

> Abruptly, Naruse presents three shots having the same pattern. There is a blank frame, into which Sugiko steps. She stops. Cut to a new blank frame, into which she steps, moving in a different direction. She stops. Cut to a new blank frame. She steps in, from yet a different direction, and stops. The three shots maintain narrational uncertainty: is she returning to the deathbed in a final gesture of love?; is she

Figure 1.6 Mirei observes Sakurai and Yuni in *Close Range Love* (Hakuhodo, 2014).

moving away in a definitive act of rejection?; is she hesitating? At the same time, the momentary disorientation provided by the empty frames and the sudden, accentual close-ups provide decorative geomatricisation. (1995: 22)

The use of such imagery, from the non-dynamic, 'neat' symmetry of the fixed structure to the dynamic action of the protagonist entering the frame, is often found in shots of the school hallway. In *The Kirishima Thing/Kirishima, Bukatsu Yamerutteyo* (2012, dir. Daihachi Yoshida), for instance, the solitude of the empty hallway is broken several times when the classroom door bursts open and geeky, aspiring filmmaker Maeda runs out.

The Rooftop

While filmmakers can utilise the inside cells and passages of the school to provide an enclosed, structured environment for their characters, the Japanese school often lacks the physical grounds with their large parks and sporting areas found in depictions of Western schools, due to space constraints in the mountainous island nation. This leads to students utilising rooftops (the *okujō*, or literally, top of the building) as a relatively unchecked, unobservable haven for quieter moments. The school rooftop has therefore become a common space in Japanese school-based films where students (and sometimes teachers) can find sanctuary. This differs from American films, where the school roof is generally out of bounds, or used to show especially rebellious or suicidal students. US films instead tend to use sporting fields and open-air stands as the location for more emotional or confessional scenes. In Japanese films, the rooftop is presented as a delineated space, with the straight concrete ledge of the rooftop providing a visual reminder of the ability to confine, while beyond the 'line' there is a sense of freedom – expanses of forest, sky or a city: a binary of inside/outside, or of nature/built environment. Students can find togetherness (drama or singing group practice), friendship, love or isolation. For instance, in *Shino Can't Say Her Own Name/Shino-chan wa Jibun no Namae ga Ienai* (2018, dir. Hiroaki Yuasa), the rooftop is a space where the cripplingly shy Shino (Sara Minami) can speak with her friend Kayo (Aju Makita) (Figure 1.7).

In *Have a Song on Your Lips* (2015), the rooftop is a sanctuary for Nazuna (Yuri Tsunematsu), where she can let her emotions out after confessing quietly to her teacher that her father has left her, again: 'I have been thrown away by my father, twice.' Nazuna runs from the classroom, blurting out that she is looking for the other students, but instead she runs

Figure 1.7 Shino opens up to Kayo in *Shino Can't Say Her Own Name* (Nippan, 2018).

for the rooftop, where she soon bursts into tears at the sound of her teacher playing the piano in the classroom below (Figure 1.8).

The framing of each of these shots utilises the sharp diagonal lines of the rooftop, perhaps as David Morrison notes of Edward Hopper's famous 1927 'Automat' painting, where reflected lights form a diagonal image above the lone girl with her coffee, 'exacerbating the sense of a void behind' (2012: 207). The angular framing in these films directs attention to the actors and their movements. The visual distinction of the roofline, and what lies beyond, mirrors what Bordwell sees as a 'pictorialist approach' in Japanese film that 'emphasises the individual shot as a rich visual design, summoning light, texture, and geogramatic shape to create stable, graceful

Figure 1.8 Nazuna weeps in *Have a Song on Your Lips* (Asmik Ace, 2015).

compositions' (1995: 22). In the image from *Have a Song on Your Lips*, the roofline recedes away from the action (the crying Nazuna), yet in *The Kirishima Thing*, an external shot from down in the school grounds shows the roofline jutting towards the audience, isolating Aya Sawajima (Suzuka Ōgo) as she plays her saxophone. In the foreground, the shot is framed by the silhouettes of the boys she has been secretly observing, with romantic intent.

In *Hentai Kamen*, shy, bullied teenage boy Kyōsuke Shikijō (Ryōhei Suzuki) finally meets the girl of his dreams, Aiko Himeno (Fumika Shimizu), and the rooftop is a place for them to escape. Unable to fit the normalised structures of the school's micro-societies and cliques, Kyōsuke retreats to the roof because, as Foucault notes:

> In a sense the power of normalization imposes homogeneity; but it individualizes it by making it possible to measure gaps, to determine levels, to fix specialities and to render the differences useful [or not] by fitting them one to another. It is easy to understand how the power of the norm functions within a system of formal equality, since within a homogeneity that is the rule, the norm introduces, as a useful imperative and as a result of measurement, all the shading of individual differences. (Foucault 1977 in Jones 1990: 96)

Thus, Kyōsuke's retreat to the rooftop with Aiko to eat their lunch reiterates their outsider status as they shun the 'power of the norm', and their individual difference signifies their inability or unwillingness to belong to the homogeneity of friendship groups that congregate at lunchtime in the schoolyard or cafeteria. Their isolation conjures the 'commonly recurring trope of loneliness' and in a universal manner triggers in audiences the understanding that there are 'historical and cultural associations of eating and drinking as something that has typically been seen as a group activity, whether with family or in a community' (Morrison 2012: 207).

As *Hentai Kamen*'s Kyōsuke and Aiko sit on a towel placed on the concrete rooftop, their actions also show their weariness, which comes from trying to find their place in the social milieu of the school. Yoneyama (1999: 5) points to a small study where students overwhelmingly 'indicated that school is a "tiring" place, and that most tiring of all is relating to friends, i.e. making the necessary efforts to stay on the right side so as not to be considered weird and therefore ostracised and bullied'. Kyōsuke and Aiko's slumped appearance reiterates this tiredness, exacerbated by their lack of self-confidence.

A pivotal rooftop moment in *Forget Me Not* occurs when Azusa (Akari Hayami) records an emotional video for her boyfriend, Takeshi (Nijirō Murakami). The central plot of *Forget Me Not* revolves around those who meet Azusa, but then forget she exists after just a few hours. Takeshi, it seems, is the one exception, but as the story unfolds, his memory also fails to hold on to Azusa. Choosing the rooftop allows Azusa the privacy to record her emotional message for Takeshi to try to keep remembering her. The emotional intimacy of Azusa in extreme close-up, framed by nature (the sky and the trees), is interrupted by the harsh functionality of another wing of the school building, the ridge of the roof line immediately behind Azusa and the nets over the distant baseball field. Even in her grief, Azusa is unable to retreat from the institutional confines of the school.

One Week Friends uses a similar memory-loss premise as *Forget Me Not*, only in this case it is the student, Kaori Fujimiya (Haruna Kawaguchi), who forgets her classmates after one week because of a possible psychological disorder. Her knowledge of this memory lapse sees her deliberately distance herself from her classmates. Again, the rooftop is Kaori's lunchtime sanctuary, interrupted only by her admirer, Yūki Hase (Kento Yamazaki), who follows her up there as he tries to befriend her. In a twist, as Kaori comes to have more contact with Yūki, she invites him up to the rooftop, where she confesses to the difficulties associated with her memory loss. She explains that she does not want to become friends with him and burden him with having to explain himself to her each week.

The rooftop then continues as a site of importance throughout the film in several key dramatic scenes. When all seems lost for Yūki, he begins retreating to a part of the roof that another student notes is restricted for student use. There, Yūki sketches small manga drawings, defacing a library book, a poetry volume that he explains has 'a lot of blank areas' for him to draw his small pictures. In the film's final climactic scenes, Kaori is reunited with the book and sees the real meaning of the drawings. She searches for Yūki, before finding him, again in the restricted area, and *One Week Friends* closes with their touching reunion on the rooftop. The very final image, under the closing credits, is of the two shaking hands and smiling at each other on the rooftop.

In *The Dark Maidens/Ankoku Joshi* (lit. *Girls in the Dark*) (2017, dir. Saiji Yakumo), the rooftop serves as the location for two pivotal scenes. Firstly, from an aerial view, it provides a place of solace for isolated 'new girl', the homely Nitani Mirei (Yūna Taira). She becomes a tiny isolated figure, almost lost against the formidable multi-storied structure (Figure 1.9).

Secondly, it creates a private site, away from the glare of other students or teachers, for a dramatic confrontation between four of the girls from the literature club and their 'leader', Itsumi. The girls line up facing Itsumi, placing her at the front like a teacher in a classroom. The isolation of the

Figure 1.9 Lonely Nitani Mirei in *The Dark Maidens* (Hakuhodo, 2017).

rooftop and Itsumi's slight height advantage highlight the powerlessness the girls feel against the formidable girl. The stark concrete rooftop presented in many films is countered in *Rainbow Days / Nijiiro Deizu* (2018, dir. Ken Iizuka), which shows a rooftop where the male characters eat their lunch (conveniently, also a place for looking down on the girls sitting on benches in the yard below). Their rooftop setting is planted with flowerbeds and shrubs, and contains brightly coloured (thematic 'rainbow'-patterned) benches and tables.

A more colourful setting is also found in *Your Lie in April*, where bespectacled music nerd Kōsei has been smitten by Kaori, who he has just seen in a violin recital. Entranced, Kōsei retires up to the green rubber-lined rooftop in a trance-like state, captured in an off-kilter aerial view (Figure 1.10).

In a later scene, Kōsei is again lying down on the roof, but Kaori finds him and declares that he has been hiding from her to avoid accepting the role of providing the piano accompaniment in her upcoming violin recital concert. He sits up, suddenly.

Kōsei: What are you doing up here?
Kaori: Of course [I'm here], I came to fetch my accompaniment.

Kaori strides toward him to berate him for not joining her to practise for her recital. As she stands above him, he weakens, before admitting:

Kōsei: I'm scared.

Figure 1.10 Kōsei in love in *Your Lie in April* (C&I Entertainment, 2016).

Kaori softens her approach:

Kaori: I'm here. [he looks up at her] I'm here you know.

The camera circles as Kaori delivers a heartfelt monologue and Kōsei remains sitting on the roof, anchored to the place that gives him comfort. The rooftop setting and multiple shots allow this emotional scene to play out against a background of the natural environment with its blue sky, ocean and green hills, yet with the 'grounded' support of the school building, literally beneath their feet. Kaori begins to weep, telling Kōsei that she needs him for her support while playing. She bows low to show the gravity of her requests and he finally stands and agrees that he will help her. The dynamic of the scene has quickly shifted from Kaori having the height advantage (the position of power) and expressing her anger, to her in a lower position (subservient) than Kōsei, now standing, and already taller than Kaori. The scene is mirrored later in the film, this time on a hospital rooftop, and with Kaori uttering the line 'I'm scared,' only this time the stakes are life-threateningly higher.

In the independent, and partially improvised, film *Infinite Foundation/ Mugen Fandēshon* (2018, dir. Akira Ōsaki), the rooftop is used as a site for a flashback to take place, intercut with present-day scenes of a teacher (Gōichi Mine) yearning for a past love, a ukulele-playing girl who had once promised to meet him on the rooftop to sing his songs when he was at high school. The film opens with this girl, Cosame (played by actor/musician Cosame Nishiyama), singing in what looks to be a field littered with rubbish, reminiscent of the aftermath of a tsunami, but later is assumed to be part of the junkyard where she befriends the shy Mirai (Sara Minami). The significance of the school rooftop does not become apparent until late in the film, when connections between Mirai's teacher and Cosame are directly addressed.

One of the points of commonality in all of these rooftop scenes is, as noted, their framing, which mirrors the

> strategies for evoking loneliness [that] range from general qualities, such as blankness, stillness and emptiness, to more specific lonely tropes: the downward gaze, the act of eating and drinking alone, the isolation of characters within the frame or the gaze from the window. (Morrison 2012: 205)

The fact that this takes place in Japanese high school films signals the contrast of the human form against the fortress-like built environment of the institution.

The Window

Back in the classroom itself, the sense of isolation found on the rooftop can also be felt, often more fleetingly, in the framing of shots where a character gazes out of the window, often filmed from behind with finely curtained windows filtering the light from outside. As with painted still images, these captured moments present cinematic characters 'in a contemplative, often melancholic, state', and can be seen as representing 'a pause within the action, whereby an individual becomes lost in thought or feeling' (Morrison 2012: 213). The character can be either teacher or student: in *Have a Song on Your Lips* it is teacher Yuri who stands by the gently billowing curtains, but as she sees Nazuna enter the room she turns away to face the window to reflect on her own behaviour and the crippling emotional state that prevents her from playing the piano for her students. She is also concerned about the impact it has had on Nazuna (Figure 1.11).

A short time later, following a disagreement, Nazuna runs from the room, and this time Yuri turns away from the window to gaze down at the piano, tightly framed by the horizontal lines of the window frame and the vertical lines of the curtains. Yuri hesitantly reaches for the piano keys but then pulls her hand away. In a repeat of the mid-shot, partly silhouetted against the window, Yuri stands silently, barely moving as she contemplates her next move. The shot lasts for almost twenty seconds, reflective of Morrison's reading of a scene in Aki Kaurismäki's 2006 *Lights in the Dusk / Laitakaupungin Valot*, where 'the static sense of timing'

Figure 1.11 Nazuna (right) and Yuri in *Have a Song on Your Lips* (Asmik Ace, 2015).

is used (not for comic effect, as in Kaurismäki's film) to enhance the melancholic effect that will 'allow us to linger on the image, have time to feel something of the loneliness there, as a spectacle of understated emotion is privileged' (2012: 212).

The emotion portrayed here forces the school environment to recede into the background. The partially silhouetted scene could represent anywhere that grieving takes place: a family home, or perhaps more fittingly, a hospital. Yuri's downward gaze at the piano becomes reminiscent of a mourner looking down upon a corpse. The length of the shot 'has little to do with progression but everything to do with feeling and tone' (Morrison 2012: 214), until Yuri's tentative movements toward the piano progress the action.

In *Close Range Love*, a similar window scene is employed when Sakurai-sensei spends time contemplating his illicit will-they/won't-they romance with his student, Yuni; after all, Japan's 'teachers are committed to moral development [. . .] as part of "educating the whole person"' (Bamkin 2018: 78), so he needs to consider his obligations as an educator, rather than an individual or as a man. Yuni's guardian, and Sakurai's fellow-teacher, Kazuma Akechi (Hirofumi Arai), is well aware of the moral dilemma inherent in a teacher–student liaison, and steps in to try to prevent a relationship from developing. Sakurai, however, is torn between his love for Yuni and his devotion to what is morally right. This leads to several contemplative window shots throughout the film as a recurring motif.

The window also creates a site for symmetry in framing, the orderly structure of the institute locking characters into position. In *The Kirishima Thing*, quiet sportsboy Hiroki Kikuchi (Masahiro Higashide) and music nerd Aya Sawajima (Suzuka Ōgo) gaze wistfully out of their respective windows in a neat side-shot that makes them look as if they are travelling on a bus or a train (Figure 1.12). This set-up creates a physical distance, and an awkward silence stretches between them, isolating them perhaps just beyond arm's length of each other, thus heightening the romantic tension. Outside, the town is in the foreground, while the green hills of the natural environment beckon in the distance.

In *Ano Ko No, Toriko/Girl Envy* (lit. *That Girl's (Love) Captive*) (also written as *Anoko no Toriko*, 2018, dir. Ryō Miyawaki), Suzuki (he is referred to by his family name throughout the film) meets Shizuku in the hallway, viewed from inside the classroom, creating a double-framed effect between the classroom, hallway and outside (Figure 1.13). The focus draws toward a pensive Shizuku as she stands framed by the first, open, window. In this scene, Shizuku has just found out that Suzuki's acting career has overtaken her own, yet she is slowly coming to the realisation that she has romantic feelings for him. Again, the natural setting of the hills, visible through the diamond-shaped window, is contrasted with the high-rise, built environment that stands 'between' the couple.

In *Closest Love to Heaven/Kyō no Kira-kun* (lit. *Today's Kira-kun*) (2017, dir. Yasuhiro Kawamura), Yuiji Kira (Taishi Nakagawa) physically drags the girl he likes, Ninon Okamura (Marie Iitoyo), into the curtains in the classroom, wrapping the curtain around them. Taken by surprise, Ninon blurts out an astonished 'What the hell . . .', but Kira just explains 'Behind the curtains . . .' and leans in to kiss her. She pulls away from

Figure 1.12 Hiroki and Aya gaze outward in *The Kirishima Thing* (AX-ON, 2012).

Figure 1.13 Multiple frames in *Ano Ko No, Toriko* (Hakuhodo, 2018).

him, then smiles and they resume their kissing as the camera moves to a medium shot inside the classroom, then tracks back into the hallway as other students walk by, happily chatting but unaware of the lovers in silhouette, wrapped in the cocoon-like twist of the curtains. This imagery would be familiar to many Japanese adolescents and young adults, as it is undoubtedly mimetic of the famous music video clip for girl band Nogizaka46 in their debut hit of 2012, 'Guruguru Curtain' (lit. 'round and round curtain'). In the clip, mostly set in a classroom, girls share secrets and play with each other's hair, as well as exchange intimate looks and touches, all while continually twirling themselves in the classroom curtains. The song's lyrics suggest that the curtains provide a private space, where 'guys aren't allowed'. The scene in *Closest Love to Heaven* reflects the romantic ideal that the song sets out in its opening lines: 'Inside the curtain, the sun, her and me, enveloped in our privacy'. While the music video is apparently innocent in its perception of female friendships, it has also been seen as having erotic *yuri* (girls' love/*gāruzu rabu*, or same-sex relationship) undertones, despite the lyrics pointing toward heterosexual romance.

In *The Senior and the Girl/Senpai to Kanojo* (2015, dir. Chihiro Ikeda), the ground-floor location of the student's clubroom (see Chapter 4), overlooking the sportsfield, sees the characters using the window as a space that can be easily climbed through, and from which they can conduct conversations with those outside, breaking the internal/external mode that is usually created in window shots. The senior, Keigo Minohara

(Jun Shison), also uses the window ledge as a place to sit, sliding back the window to make room for himself, and allowing the 'natural' light of the outside to create a glowing overexposed background, placing him in a dream-like (near-)silhouette that reiterates junior student Rika Tsuzuki's (Kyōko Yoshine) deification of him each time she enters the room.

On occasion the view is shifted to outside the window, a voyeuristic observational shot, looking inward as either a static long shot, or a slow-moving crane shot of a character standing alone, again deep in thought. *After the Rain/Koi wa Ameagari no Yō ni* (lit. *Love is Like After the Rain*) (2018, dir. Akira Nagai) opens with a long aerial shot, a single-take zoom sweeping across the school playing fields, toward a block of classrooms (an obvious establishing shot) as it moves to a single classroom window. Inside the window (as the shot continues moving), a lone student, Akira Tachibana (Nana Komatsu), is sleeping at her desk. Just as the shot reaches the window it cuts to a slightly giddying interior shot, this time pulling away from Akira towards the front of the room. At other times, such as in *Assassination Classroom*, a more rapid, sweeping shot is used to accentuate a noisy classroom or to emphasise students fighting in the room. Again, the framing of the shot is important as it has the power to trap the character; imprisoned in a doll's house-like view (reminiscent of the framing in Hitchcock's *Rear Window* or one of Wes Anderson's films) of the institutionalised body.

The Gymnasium

As with many US-based films, the school gymnasium becomes a site for conflicts to escalate or play out and be resolved. At times this is sport-related, as in *Run! T High School Basketball Club/Hashire! T Ko Basuketto Bu* (2018, dir. Takeshi Furusawa) or dance-related, as in *Let's Go, Jets! From Small Town Girls to U.S. Champions?!/Chiadan: Joshi Kōsei ga Chiadansu de Zenbei Seiha Shichatta Honto no Hanashi* (2017. dir. Hayao Kawai); at other times the large room is used as an auditorium. This is exemplified in US films such as *Election* (1999, dir. Alexander Payne), when students sitting on the gymnasium benches erupt after Tammy Metzler (Jessica Campbell) makes her anti-authoritarian speech while running for student council. In Japan's *The Black Devil and the White Prince/Kurosaki-kun no Iinari ni Nante Naranai* (lit. *I'm Not Just Going to Do What Kurosaki-kun Says*) (2016, dir. Shō Tsukikawa), the gymnasium becomes the showdown site for Kurosaki and Takumi (as he is mostly referred to) as they stage a ferociously exhausting basketball playoff to see who can win Yū's heart (Figure 1.14).

Figure 1.14 Showdown in *The Black Devil and the White Prince* (Hakuhodo, 2016).

The echoing isolation of the disused gym is also used as a site for deception. In *Peach Girl/Pichi Garu* (2017, dir. Koji Shintoku), Kairi uses the pretence of basketball hoops practice to discuss Sae's manipulative behaviour, jealously toying with Toji to destroy his relationship with Momo. Kairi draws a confession from Sae, and as she leaves, Momo and Toji appear from the upper level of the gym, having heard everything. In *ReLIFE*, Chizuro uses the empty gymnasium to let out her frustrations through practising her volleyball serving, the loud sounds of the ball crashing to the floor providing her with some solace.

In *You Are the Apple of My Eye/Ano Koro, Kimi o Oikaketa* (lit. *Those Years, We Went After You*) (2018, dir. Yasuo Hasegawa), the gymnasium features as a site for cheerleading practice, for basketball and, in a refigured mode, for a final assembly, where Kōsuke's love interest, Mana Hayase (Asuka Saitō), gives a valedictory speech. This scene is a visual reminder of the institutional importance of the school as a place of order and discipline. The students sit upright on chairs in their formal uniforms, lined up with an exacting military precision.

The Toilets

In many high school films, the school toilets (bathrooms) are featured as a space away from authoritative figures where students can conduct anti-social behaviour (bullying, smoking), or as a private confessional space. Often, a toilet scene operates as a lynchpin because of a confessional moment, or a place where the central protagonist faces their foe, as in the infamous 'sectumsempra' scene in *Harry Potter and the Half-Blood Prince* (2009, dir. David Yates) where Harry (Daniel Radcliffe) confronts a momentarily off-guard Draco Malfoy (Tom Felton) and seemingly defeats him. In Japanese high school films, confrontation scenes between male students are depicted more openly in the gymnasium, the school grounds or, as in *Kids on the Slope/Sakamichi no Apollon* (2018, dir. Takahiro Miki), on the roof of the school, where the wayward Sentaro Kawabuchi (Taishi Nakagawa) meets other boys to fight. The toilet scenes therefore are almost exclusively the domain of storylines centred around female students.

In *You, I Love/Ui Rabu* (aka *We Love*, 2018, dir. Yūichi Satō), for example, Koyomi (Tina Tamashiro) confronts her shy friend, Yū Haruna (Hinako Sakurai), in the toilets to ask why she accepted the role of 'pretend girlfriend' with the boy she really likes, Rin Izumi (Shō Hirano).

> Koyomi: I don't really understand this pretend girlfriend business. It's way too weird!
> Yū: I wonder why . . . when I'm with Rin-kun, my heart is beating so fast. It keeps on getting worse by the day. I'm going to be his pretend girlfriend, but . . . that's just making my heart beat faster. [smiling] I'm really weird, aren't I?

Just as they are getting to the point where Yū seems as if she is about to confess her love for Rin, they are interrupted by other girls coming in to use the toilet.

The Kirishima Thing presents the school toilets as a site for Risa (Mizuki Yamamoto) and her best friend, Sana (Mayu Matsuoka), to break quickly from their friend group in the hallway. In front of the mirrors, they check their make-up and briefly gossip about Sana's possible meeting with a boy, Fujita, in order to make another boy, Hiroki, jealous. While the scene is brief, it shows the instant isolation that removes the students from the busy hallways of the school for a private conversation.

In *Principle!: Am I a Heroine in Love?*, Shima, the new girl at school, is in the toilets looking in the large mirror when she is joined by three other girls. They surround her as the scene plays out in reflection through the mirror, framing the girls close together in a threatening group around Shima. Shima is in a white pullover, making her stand out from the other girls in pink, grey and navy blue, respectively. They feel that she has been too friendly with two boys in their class and begin to pace around her:

> Blue Girl: You guys sure are close.
> Grey Girl: You, Wao and Gen.

Pink Girl: It seems like you have a lot to learn because you're new, but . . . Wao and Gen belong to everybody.
Grey Girl. True, true! That's why you shouldn't get too close to them, alright?

Blue Girl suddenly pushes Shima backward against the toilet doors.

Blue Girl: Are you even listening to what we are saying? Hey, say something!

The shot then cuts to a front view of Shima cowering, slightly.

Grey Girl: Hey! [say something]
Shima: Someone being a 'possession' is strange. Gen and Wao are their own people after all!

Pink Girl moves in even closer to Shima.

Pink Girl: Speaking of which, what did he tell you?
Shima [now confident, smiling]: Who are you talking about?

The girls exchange glances, not believing that their bullying tactics are not eliciting the response they expected.

Blue Girl: This chick doesn't know anything.
Grey Girl: Let's get out of here!

They exit, leaving Shima leaning against the door of the toilet. She does not show signs of being overly bothered, and as a previous scene where she angrily confronts Gen has shown, she is not easily pushed around.

The privacy of the school toilets is sometimes not as it seems, such as in the Hollywood film *Easy A*, where Olive (Emma Stone) is dragged into the girls' lavatories by her friend Rhiannon (Aly Michalka), and Olive blurts out a false confession that she had sex on a date. Unbeknown to both of them, their arch-enemy, 'good' Christian girl Marianne (Amanda Bynes), was already in the toilets, and after a quick flush, emerges to admit that she heard all of their conversation. A similar scene occurs in *Heroine Disqualified / Hiroin Shikkaka* [aka *No Longer Heroine*] (2015, dir. Hanabusa Tsutomu), a film that took a box-office gross of almost $US20 million. Early in the film, the main 'heroine', Hatori Matsuzaki (Mirei Kiritani), emerges from a toilet cubicle to overhear two girls talking as they adjust their make-up. The girls stand in front of individual mirrors, but Hatori remains just out of their sight, thinking that they may be talking about her:

Girl 1 [short hair]: Just what is up with that former ugly four-eyes?
Girl 2 [long hair]: Even with contacts an ugly girl is still ugly.

Hatori realises they are talking about the formerly homely Adachi (Miwako Wagatsuma), who is now dating the boy who Hatori has had a crush on since childhood.

> Hatori [v/o]: Oh my, oh my, oh my. About Adachi-san, huh?

Hatori begins to walk towards them.

> Girl 1: After all . . . That girl should just realise that she's not good enough for Terasaka. Right?

Hatori arrives at a basin next to the girls, and Girl 1 suddenly turns to her.

> Girl 1 [cont.]: Huh?
> Hatori: Wh, well . . . Not really . . . Isn't she really a good girl though?
> Girl 2 [applying lipstick]: I think you and Terasaka make a better pair, though.
> Hatori: Why do you say so?
> Girl 1: You are both such a great match. Like you are tied by a very deep bond with each other.
> Hatori [emphatic]: No, no, no way! We're just childhood friends, you know?
> Girl 2: Well that fugly pig-faced girl won't look right in the role as Rita's [Terasaka's] girlfriend, right?
> Girl 1: She hasn't realised it yet, you know?
> Hatori: Well, right. She is Adachi-san, after all.
> Girl 1 [turning to Hatori]: See? We do get along well after all. Let's talk again next time.
> Hatori: Uh huh.

They wave goodbye, and as Hatori turns back to the mirror her face momentarily flashes as a vicious, growling demonic face. She is startled, and then jumps again when in the reflection behind her she sees Adachi standing there, having just emerged from a cubicle. In a voiceover, a horrified Hatori begins to question herself:

> Hatori [v/o]: No way! Since when was she there? How much of our talk did she hear?

Hatori remains frozen, clutching the basin as Adachi makes her way to the basin next to Hatori to wash her hands. With her head bowed, Adachi speaks softly:

> Adachi: I'm sorry.
> Hatori: Huh?
> Adachi: I didn't plan to eavesdrop on your conversation . . . But I lost the timing to escape.

Hatori: No. It's not something you should apologise for, right?
Adachi [smiling]: Oh. Right.

Adachi turns and appears to leave, with Hatori puzzling over the consequences.

Hatori [v/o]: It's over. Everything will be exposed to Rita [Terasaka].

There is a noise, and Hatori is again startled.

Adachi [o/s]: Umm.

Hatori looks up to see Adachi facing her.

Hatori: Uh huh?
Adachi: About what happened now . . . you don't have to worry about it, okay?
Hatori: Huh?
Adachi: After all . . . You like Terasaka-kun, right?
Hatori: Oh!

Through the use of CGI she suddenly tenses, then turns into ice before shattering and collapsing on to the ground. She returns to her human form and climbs up to her feet.

Hatori [v/o]: What did this bitch just say?
Adachi: You've always been together since you were very young, right? That's why . . . you don't need to pay heed to me. Just treat me like you usually do, okay?
Hatori [confused]: How I usually do? Huh?
Adachi: And if ever . . . that Terasaka-kun . . . would go over to you . . . [smiling] I won't harbor hard feelings against you.

Adachi gives a little smile, then bows her head to turn and leave.

Hatori [v/o]: What's with that? The 'righteous heroine's' compassion? Like the 'chosen one' thingy? Stop acting high!

She collects her thoughts, then shouts after Adachi:

Hatori: No, wait!

She runs out after Adachi but, as she exits the toilets, finds Adachi walking away, holding hands with Terasaka. They turn to face the now embarrassed Hatori and Terasaka invites her to join them on the walk home. Hatori refuses, then turns and runs, beginning to wail.

The importance of this scene (it runs for around three minutes) is underscored by the fact that it uses the surprise emerging-from-the-cubicle element twice, firstly when Hatori thinks the girls are talking about her, and then when Adachi appears. In a film that constantly breaks the fourth wall and uses CGI for fantasy or comical moments, the toilet scene remains (relatively) in a realist mode to convey its vital role in setting the narrative path.

In the ensemble cast of *Rainbow Days*, Yukiko Asai (Mayu Hotta) and Mari Tsutsui (Yuri Tsunematsu) chat in the toilets in a scene shot from behind as each girl stands in front of an individual wash basin and mirror. The scene begins as a long shot, but as the camera slowly edges forward to become a medium shot the dramatic tone of the scene builds. Their faces and expressions can be clearly seen, and while Yukiko is bright and smiling (in the reflected image), Mari is more serious. When Yukiko leaves first, Mari stays standing there, her sombre face reflected in the mirror.

Conclusion

The physical environment of the high school provides scope for narrative dramas (and comedies) to play out in standardised and often formulaic settings. The various buildings, rooms and fixtures allow for formal schooling to be shown against a backdrop of the informal, social aspects of adolescent growth and development. There are, of course, other sites around the school that feature for particular scenes. Gymnasium changing rooms feature either as a site for bullying or physical embarrasment, or as a focus for students spying on the opposite sex, as happens in *Assassination Classroom*. The library is another location frequently used in high school films, its quiet environment ideal for establishing relationships as students study together, as in *Hyouka: Forbidden Secrets*, or for meet-cutes, such as in *One Week Friends* when Yūki meets Kaori after he sees her drop something in the library. In *Strobe Edge/Sutorobo Ejji* (2015. dir. Ryuichi Hiroki), Ninako Kinoshita (Kasumi Arimura) is confronted amongst the rows of books by classmate Daiki Korenaga (Jingi Irie), who hints at a possible romance between them. Unsure of herself, or of Daiki's motives, Ninako breaks from his clutches and runs from the library.

Ultimately, the wide range of locations that the high school provides all serve in narrative development. Each iconographic space is recognisable and familiar to the audience, providing a type of ontological 'comfort' for older audiences. Given the relative similarity of the physical layout and designs (including fittings and furnishings) of schools amongst Japan's state-run educational system, and the overall expectation that even private schools will reflect the cultures and the disciplinary structures of Japanese society, high school films are able to capture the essence of an institution-alisation process shared by all Japanese people.

CHAPTER 2

Beyond the Classroom

The disciplinary space of the school extends beyond the physical boundaries of the institution and its classrooms. Japan's Ministry of Education recommendations around the enforcement of 'moral education' in 2015, for instance, looked to 'reallocate moral education as a "special subject" of the curriculum rather than "classtime"', in effect pushing the onus on to the student under the watchful eye of the teachers who previously had the difficult task of assessing student morality (Bamkin 2018: 79). The notion of assessing one's morality has been seen as problematic by Japan's teachers because of the type of assessment that might be required: for example, should it be summative or formative, quantitative or qualitative? Bamkin notes one school that 'kept a whiteboard to tally the nice things students of the class had done' over their weekend (2018: 92), which leads to claims that student behaviours are adapting to be *seen* as fulfilling their moral obligations in order to gain a high mark. In school films, the journey to and from school is often depicted as a scene that provides a space for the portrayal of a character's moral actions within their community, and more broadly as a representative of Japanese culture.

Once beyond the gates of the schoolground, opportunities open up for students to enact their lives (and fantasies), potentially free of the strictures of institutionalisation, yet always in their shadow. The students are seen walking, sometimes cycling, or on a bus or train, and these moments of screen time are used to show the development of personal or familial relationships.

Transport

Japan's public transport systems are seen as global exemplars of efficiency and punctuality. The ability to shift millions of the nation's citizens around and between its urban and rural areas is also testament to the strict institutionalised training of transport staff and the bureaucratic web that supports them. The provision of free or subsidised travel for students means that many travel by public trains, buses or, in some cities, trams (as seen in *You, I Love*) to get to and from school. In a sense the official status of transport workers – the drivers and conductors, the station masters and ticket sellers – operates as an extension of the supervisory function of the officials found in the education system. There is an assumed pastoral care role taken by these officials, who carry out their jobs with fastidious care and devotion to their work, aware that any below-par performance reflects on their entire company, whether state-owned or private.

Schoolchildren in Japan are often autonomous at an earlier age than their Western counterparts when it comes to taking themselves to school. It is not uncommon to see a child barely out of infancy toddling their way to school, unaccompanied, beneath the bulk of their large backpack. Despite the frequency of school students relying on public transport for their daily commute, in the cinematic world these journeys fall into a lesser category, with filmmakers instead making use of the slower-paced walk to school to allow dialogue to take place. What, then, of the films that do use images of students on public transport? In *Sayounara*, Yuki (Haruka Imō) is seen on a local train (the type of single- or dual-carriage train that serves outer suburbs and villages), where the driver is immediately visible through the front window, and there is no conductor on board. She sits quietly, following the rules of public propriety on Japanese transport, where the use of electronic equipment such as mobile phones is discouraged and all devices must be switched to silent. This makes for often near-silent travel, as in Figure 2.1 when Yuki and her classmate sit in silence as they mourn the death of their classmate.

The train scene presents a counterpoint where the girls are sitting, static, engrossed in their thoughts as the train is in motion, the world flashing by. In part, the scene can be thought of in relation to Richie's observations of Ozu's films, which show 'a kind of resigned sadness, a calm and knowing serenity which persists despite the uncertainty of life and the things of this world' (1972: 69). The banal activity of movement from one location to another is heightened by its uselessness; Yuki must persist with the mundane, and nothing will bring her deceased friend back to her.

Silence persists, even on Japan's packed trains or buses, which, from a filmmaking perspective, means that any dialogue will need to be low in tone, resulting in a suppression of emotions on the part of the characters. Often the journey to or from school provides a site for the revealing of important information, where reactions from one's friends are a key feature – squeals of delight at hearing of a new crush, or heated arguments about how one should live one's life; in *Say I Love You*, however, when

Figure 2.1 Grieving Yuki on the train in *Sayounara* (Spotted Productions, 2018).

the large group of friends board a bus, they have an exuberant but quietly restrained discussion about pasta sauce.

Given that the protagonists in high school films are young people, often without a source of income (very few young people have the time for part-time jobs, given the intense nature of study for university entrance exams and attendance at cram schools), Japan's *Shinkansen* (high-speed bullet trains) are rarely shown. These trains are almost exclusively for long-distance travel and are symbolic of journeys between larger cities; they may be used for a daily commute by wealthier businesspeople and government officials, but are beyond the reach of most citizens and high school students, certainly on a regular schedule. There is no question of avoiding fares, as the consequences for failing to pay for a ticket can include arrest and fines, and perhaps more importantly, there are social impacts that reverberate beyond the perpetrator to their family and beyond as a symbol of failure in teaching that child the mores of Japanese society.

The bus also provides a site for students to enact their romance, without the close observation of their teachers or parents. In *Ano Ko No, Toriko*, for example, Shizuku affectionately leans her head on Suzuki's shoulder, the physical closeness further affirmation of their burgeoning romance (Figure 2.2).

In *Your Lie in April*, Kaori and her best friend, Tsubaki Sawabe (played by dancer, musician and model Anna Ishii), take the bus home, a picturesque ride along the seaside, and use the time together to discuss their male classmate, Kōsei. They can speak openly, the two of them being the sole

Figure 2.2 Shizuku's affection in *Ano Ko No, Toriko* (Hakuhodo, 2018).

occupants of the back seat of the bus (Figure 2.3). Kaori uses the moment to probe Tsubaki's feelings for Kōsei, as they were childhood friends:

Kaori: Seems like you really like Arima [Kōsei].
Tsubaki: Hmmmm. It's a bit different from liking him. For me, Kōsei is like a good-for-nothing little brother.

Kaori gives a self-satisfied nod, then smiles to herself, indicating that if Tsubaki does not have romantic feelings for Kōsei, then Kaori is free to act on her sentiments for him.

In *My Brother Loves Me Too Much*, the opening scenes show school-girl Setoka Tachibana (Tao Tsuchiya) travelling on the bus to high school on a mountainous rural road. Setoka stands for the commute and is soon approached by a boy, Suzuki (Fūju Kamio), who asks her if she would like to go out with him. As she is about to reply, a loud bang is heard and the bus suddenly lurches, causing them to lose their balance momentarily. From outside, a male student on a bicycle can be seen kicking the bus. The otherwise calm nature of the bus journey is therefore interrupted, and as the story unfolds, the reason for the cyclist's behaviour becomes apparent.

The motif of a train or bus as a rolling vessel, carrying a departing loved one away, has long been used in cinema, and in Japanese high school films this is no different. Often accompanied by images of falling rain, the general image is highly gendered and it is the girl who is on the train or bus, her boyfriend (or former boyfriend) remaining at the bus stop or on the station platform, as occurs (though *sans* rain) in *You Are the Apple*

Figure 2.3 Kaori and Tsubaki on the bus in *Your Lie in April*
(C&I Entertainment, 2016).

of My Eye when Mana Hayase leaves for medical school in Tokyo. This is a frustrated farewell, as their relationship has not yet developed into a physical romance. Mana is apprehensive about getting on the train, leaving Kōsuke standing on the platform mutely watching as the doors close and the train moves from the station. If the parting is one of two lovers, then the boy will walk alongside the vehicle, and perhaps even run to maintain eye contact with his lover as long as possible, yet Kōsuke remains frozen to the spot. In a twist on this theme, Yūki Hase, in the opening minutes of *One Week Friends*, runs from one train to catch a connection. Although he met Kaori only once, and briefly, she happens to be on the same train and notices that in his rush he has left a library book behind. Kaori quickly grabs the book and throws it to him just as the doors begin to close. She beams at him (in essence the film's meet-cute) and he is smitten, running alongside the moving train shouting his thanks.

Rainbow Days also features a quiet moment when Natsuki Hashiba (Reo Sano) walks Anna Kobayakawa (Ai Yoshikawa) to her train in the glow of the late afternoon sun. They are in their casual clothes after spending a day with their friends, studying for an up and coming exam. She boards the train, and as he stands on the platform, she tells him that she has enjoyed their day together. He agrees, just as the doors shut. As the train pulls away from the station, Natsuki wanders along the platform, his hands in his pockets, seemingly happy with Anna's response. An exception to this type of train station departure is later seen when Anna is on her way home from school and is seemingly the only person on the train. Anna is thumbing through a book in a disinterested way, so she puts it down and stands up to stretch, when she sees Natsuki standing by the side of the tracks, deep in thought. Throughout the film the two have had a crush on each other, but both have been too shy to develop a romantic relationship. As a romantic song plays, the scene drops into slow motion and swaps between internal and external points of view. From outside the train, Anna can be seen with her hands pressed against the glass, and her face showing rapt attention focused on Natsuki. As the train passes, he glances up, just in time to see her, but he makes no attempt to wave or acknowledge that he has seen her.

The purchase of transport tickets is rarely visible in high school films, especially because much of Japan's public transport runs on swipe cards. One of the few films to show this is *My Brother Loves Me Too Much*, which begins with a series of close-ups of students entering the bus and tapping their travel cards.

The use of a bus, whether specific school transport or a general route vehicle, does provide the physical space of the bus stop, which may be in an isolated place. Often there is no bus shelter, just a sign on a pole by the kerbside, as in *Say I Love You*, where Mei Tachibana is seen at several points throughout the film, quietly waiting for the bus to arrive. The solitary figure, or small group of friends, as exemplified in the iconic image of Totoro, Mei and Satsuki standing waiting for the catbus (a fantastical cat creature that transforms into a bus) in Hayao Miyazaki's *My Neighbour Totoro / Tonari no Totoro* (1988, dir. Hayao Miyazaki), is a familiar sight for Japanese audiences. The vision of a student missing the bus similarly carries notions of a character struggling to meet the norms of society, unable to keep to the strict timetable that allows Japan to function. In *My Brother Loves Me Too Much* the bus stop is used for comic effect, as the overly protective brother of the title, Haruka Tachibana (Ryōta Katayose), pulls off an unexpected bike stunt, to the stunned amusement of the other students waiting there (Figure 2.4).

Walking

The number of schools within each district (designated as a *chōme* in cities and larger towns) in Japan means that schools are commonly within walking distance of students' homes. Large suburban blocks remain the realm of Western societies, but in Japan's cities high-density living brings the residents of a *chōme* literally closer together. Frequent images of students meeting up on their way to school can be found in high school-based

Figure 2.4 Bus stop witnesses in *My Brother Loves Me Too Much* (Shochiku, 2017).

films, signalling the start of a new day and offering a moment for narrative development as students (characters) pick up from previous days' events.

Walking alone also provides for moments of quiet solitude that are often accompanied by the character's thoughts in voiceover. In *My Little Monster*, for instance, Shizuku contemplates her relationship with the unpredictable Haru as she walks alone toward the school gates (Figure 2.5). The voiceover goes some way toward making up for the lack of dialogue, such as is found in the lively exchanges and playful ribbing between the characters in *You, I Love*.

Figure 2.5 Shizuku on her way to school in *My Little Monster* (Toho, 2018).

Figure 2.6 Hinano walks alone in *Wander Life* (Spotted Productions, 2018).

In *Wander Life/Kakuga, Mama* (2018, dir. Naho Kamimura), the lack of a voiceover gives Hinano's walk a more desolate tone. She is seen in similar settings, making her way to and from school, highlighting her sense of isolation from those around her (Figure 2.6). This creates an atmosphere that reflects the mental anguish she feels as an 'outsider' within the school community.

In *Ano Ko No, Toriko*, walking from school also provides a visual motif for the strain in Suzuki and Shizuku's relationship, as they are seen in this shot-reverse shot, focus-pulled scene (Figure 2.7), walking in different directions, the other person fading into the distance. The look of despondency on both characters' faces parallels the physical nature of their body language as they clutch their bags and walk away from each other.

Cycling

The compact nature of Japan's cities and villages also makes it a nation where bicycles have become a common form of transport. In school-based films, the cycle to or from school provides a convenient meeting moment for students, whether this is a chance meeting or a planned rendezvous. It can insert a regularity into the narrative, based around the temporal patterns of their institutionalised lives. Although not strictly a high school film, the horror suspense, manga-based *Spiral/Uzumaki* (2000, dir. Higuchinsky) features a male protagonist, Shūichi (Fhi Fan), as a schoolboy with an increasingly unhealthy obsession with anything spiral; he gives his girlfriend, Kirie (Eriko Hatsune), a lift to school on his bicycle and she sits in the common side-saddle position. Higuchinsky

Figure 2.7 Reverse shots in *Ano Ko No, Toriko* (Hakuhodo, 2018).

provides several close-ups of the bicycle's wheels spinning, furthering the spiral metaphor. The closeness afforded by the female passenger sitting on the bike also allows physical contact, romanticising the activity in a way that walking to school together does not in a society where holding hands on the way to school is not regularly seen in a heteronormative romantic relationship.

In *The Kirishima Thing*, Ryūta gives the much bigger Hiroki a lift on his step-through bike, concerned about the extra weight of Hiroki's baseball sports bag. As they cycle away, Ryūta can be seen struggling as they ride up past the sports field. The design of the bicycle as a step-through goes unremarked in this and any of the films, as it is a culturally accepted form of transport, with no gender significance attached to the design. In the West, and Australia in particular, these bicycles have been known for generations as 'girls' bikes' because of the low crossbar that enables girls (or women) in skirts or dresses to ride them easily.

In *Honey / Hanii* (2018, dir. Kōji Shintoku), earlier flashback scenes show Nao Kogure (Yūna Taira) as a child, being taught to ride a bicycle by her uncle, Sōsuke (Yū Takahashi), after she becomes orphaned and he is appointed her sole carer. The bicycle motif then becomes symbolic of her freedom, and therefore appears in the film's finale as Kogure rides off to school, meeting her boyfriend, Taiga Onise (Shō Hirano), on the way. As they cycle off together into the distance and along the seashore on their way to school (Figure 2.8), the film's theme song plays, until there is a reference to an earlier daydream of Kogure's in which two bikes appeared to be parked by the shore. This time, the image of the stationary bicycles is followed by an intimately romantic scene on the beach.

The bicycle is used extensively as a motif of Japanese life throughout *You Are the Apple of My Eye*, from the opening scenes as the students travel to school, and then post-school as they ride to get snacks and meet their friends. An old delivery bike is carefully framed in establishing shots as it sits outside Kōsuke's family tofu shop. There are even jokes that push the boundaries of decency (for Japanese high school films), when the boys show their immaturity by fantasising (aloud) about being the girls' bicycle seats. While many of these films show students ambling along the streets and lanes of Japan, Kōsuke is seen in full flight, riding his bicycle quickly as he dashes from one location to another (Figure 2.9). At times he skids or is forced to take evasive action to avoid pedestrians and other obstacles. His haste appears counter to the other events in his life but projects his impatience and his teen desire to take risks.

What unites these films is the utilitarian nature of riding a bike. Rarely is the bicycle featured as being employed for exercise or sport.

Figure 2.8 Onise and Kogure in *Honey* (Toei, 2018).

Figure 2.9 Kōsuke cycles to school in *You Are the Apple of My Eye* (Kino Films, 2018).

Home

Many high school films also provide insights into their characters' home life. In many instances, these are included as a broader comment on the conditions of parental control. This often points to the loss of a parent – mostly the mother – to indicate an adolescent unable to find the nurturing environment expected in the on-screen representations of the mother. In other cases, though, the student may be seen in an environment that is abusive, such as in *Your Lie in April* when (in a flashback), the young Kōsei returns home to his mother, who is violently critical of her son's piano playing.

While the school may be seen as an extension of the hierarchical structure of the (patriarchal) home, the reverse may also be found in high school films where the student/child finds themselves subject to strict disciplinary codes that are seen as preventing their ability to mature or to make individual decisions. In *Flying Colours/Biri Gyaru* (2015, dir. Nobuhiro Doi), this is demonstrated when Sayaka Kudo (Kasumi Arimura) wishes to apply for a top Tokyo university but is explicitly (though unsuccessfully) warned against doing so by her mother. Very few films feature physical torment or corporal punishment of its student characters in their home environment. Sono's *Himizu/Mole* (2011) and *Love Exposure/Ai no Mukidashi* (2008) are perhaps exceptions, although, while both films are centred around adolescent high school students, little of the action takes place at school.

Other films feature characters who have defined responsibilities that they must attend to around the home. In *Have a Song on Your Lips*, this includes Satoru taking care of his autistic brother, Akio (Daichi Watanabe), and in *The Senior and the Girl* there is Tetsuo Yada (Junki Tozuka) looking after the family sushi restaurant with his mother (Makiko Watanabe), so that when his friends come to socialise, he remains behind the counter preparing food for them. This restrictive environment shows a hastening to maturity in terms of meeting familial responsibilities, but also a limiting of social growth, especially in relation to the building of deeper relationships with friends or romantic relationships with members of the (usually) opposite sex.

The socio-economic standing of students is rarely featured as a theme in Japan's high school films, with a seeming flattening-out of characters to the middle-class background of a small but neat house – a typical vision of Japanese living. The small kitchen is rendered as a highly gendered space where either the mother or a daughter (often the central student character) prepares meals. One exception is *You Are the Apple of My Eye*, where it is the bachelor father who is seen cooking in the kitchen but this is presented in a way that suggests this is only a temporary arrangement until his wife returns (even though she has no intention of doing this). Thus, the sense of helplessness fits with stereotypical and heavily conservative images of elder male characters who are only equipped for work beyond the domestic duties of the home.

In *My Brother Loves Me Too Much*, the family appears wealthier than most because they live in a large contemporary house that features a grassy area that runs down to the seaside. To accentuate the house and its open location, the characters are often placed either looking out to the view, or with the view visible to the audience. The father is seen only intermittently and has very few lines of dialogue; he is (conveniently) absent when some major family-related plotlines are divulged. Even though the characters often mention 'Mom and Dad', and the eldest son is seen preparing meals, the mother is absent until almost the final scene, when she is seen unpacking some gifts, to insinuate that she has been away in an undisclosed location, presumably for work.

Bedroom

As a place for personal retreat, a teenager's bedroom is a valuable physical space. This is shown in *Kiss Me at the Stroke of Midnight/ Gozen O ji, Kiss Shi ni Kite yo* (2019, dir. Takehiko Shinjo), where Hinana Hanazawa's (Kanna Hashimoto) bedroom features a number of times in key moments as the place she retreats to, often interrupted by her much younger sister. Early in the film, Hinana has been asked out on a date by the dazzlingly handsome Kaede Ayase (Ryōta Katayose), and is frantically checking through her drawer, trying to choose suitable, fashionable underwear.

In her haste she has strewn garments all over her room, but she stops suddenly and says to herself (aloud):

Hinana: Wait! Why am I choosing? I just want to wear some good panties.

Suddenly the door swings open and her sister casually invites Hinana's male classmate, Aachan, who has an unrequited crush on Hinana and is clutching a bouquet of flowers, into the room. They all freeze for a moment, before Hinana squeals and dives on to her furniture, scooping up all of the underwear.

Aachan [turning away]: I didn't see it! I didn't see anything, okay?

Later in the film, once Hinana knows that both Aachan and Kaede like her, she retreats to her bed, highly confused as to which boy she should choose. At her mother's request, Aachan enters Hinana's bedroom as she pulls the bed covers over her head:

Hinana: I'm not here!
Aachan: What happened? [he closes the door]. Everyone's worried about you. You always look depressed at school, too.

He waits but there is no response, so he grabs the covers and rips them off the bed, exposing Hinana curled up in her pyjamas.

Aachan: Something happened, right? With Ayase-san [Kaede].

Hinana tries to pull the covers back, but Aachan leaps on to the bed, embracing her from behind:

Aachan: Just give up! [pause] On that guy. It looks like you're suffering a lot. If it was me, I would never make you feel that way.
Hinana: Aachan . . . ?

He moves around to face her:

Aachan: I've always liked you. [pause] I know that you don't have any feelings for me, but . . . I don't want to see you suffering. I want you to smile.

Hinana stares at him, stunned. He leaves the bedroom in a high-angled shot that isolates the lonely and still confused Hinana kneeling on her bed. On Adachi Momo's (Mizuki Yamamoto) birthday in *Peach Girl*, her new boyfriend but long-time classmate, Kazuya Tojigamori (Mackenyu), invites her back to his place, informing her that his parents will not be at home, thus setting up a possible scenario for their first sexual encounter. Toji (as he is known throughout the film) has a bedroom that reflects an archetypal Western teenage boy's lair, decorated with various sports items including a dart board, chest-expander, sports trophy and baseball caps hanging on the wall. Of note is the framed #51 jersey (with the name 'I. Suzuki' emblazoned on the top) in homage to iconic Japanese base-baller Ichiro Suzuki, who achieved fame in the US Major League. Toji's single bed dominates the room, furnished in a neutral tone of blue, grey and white. Eventually, Momo joins Toji on the bed and they prepare to kiss, until interrupted by a phone call. In a later scene, Momo's bedroom is shown with its leaf-print wallpaper and subtle pastel furnishings (some peach-coloured), as well as a vase of flowers and numerous potted plants (Momo's room is above her mother's florist shop). Momo's bedroom therefore takes on the expected more feminine tone of soft colours and a 'natural' environment.

The 'feminine' decor and pink-hued colour scheme are also found in Yū's bedroom in *You, I Love*, most notably when her personal space is 'invaded' by Rin, who has a sexual conquest in his sights. Yū's bedroom is a mix of white, cream and pink colours, including a pink birdcage and a pink sweater hanging from a hook. One scene opens with Yū returning from the kitchen with drinks for them both. As she enters, Rin unbuttons his shirt, a reprise of one of the film's opening scenes. He lies down on her bed, telling her to come over and help him to button up his shirt. As she approaches, he pulls her down on to the bed, asking 'It's normal if we do it while dating, isn't it?' Yū manages to stammer out, 'D-d-do it?' before Rin throws her on to her back and straddles her, trying to plant a kiss. She resists, and he abandons his mission. The soft decor and subdued lighting designate the space as her bedroom and carry a sense of childhood inno-cence. In contrast, Rin's bedroom is a mismatch of bold colours, stripes, checks and geometric shapes, suggesting a more 'masculine' mix of func-tionality and a carefree manner.

A different style of girl's bedroom appears in the musical comedy *Kiss Him, Not Me/Watashi ga Motete Dosunda* (lit. *What's the Point of Me Getting Popular?*) (2020, dir. Norihisa Hiranuma), in which *otaku* Kae Serinuma (Miu Tomita and Nonoka Yamaguchi) has a messy room that has splashes of bright yellow decor but is noticeably crammed full of stuffed toys, figurines, cushions, manga and anime DVDs, mostly in homage to her favourite (and recently killed-off) anime character, Shion. Kae initially appears as 'heavy' girl (played by Miu Tomita), the inference being that she has no interest in boys beyond observing 'boys' love', as her self-esteem is low. When she is magically transformed (and now played by Nonoka Yamaguchi), she becomes the centre of attention among the boys at her school and grows (slightly) more self-aware of her appearance as a female. Kae is taken out on a date by four boys from her school but cannot shake off her *otaku* fetish. When the boys later visit her house, Kae's bicycle-obsessed brother, Onī (Shuto Miyazaki), shows them into her crowded, untidy bedroom to try to warn them off pursuing his sister.

Conclusion

The use of locations exterior to the school provides filmmakers with a large palette to extend narratives and create characters that have a diverse range of interests and responsibilities. The inclusion of travel allows for movement of images beyond what can otherwise be relatively static views of the classroom and individual conversations (on the rooftop, for example). Student travel can also add an extra dynamic to the visual elements of a film, with the daily movement of people a universal feature as we move between the different 'platforms' of our existence. The quotidian home–school–home or home–work–home dimensions that regulate our days make them ideal for filmmakers to construct narratives that ebb and flow. The mirroring of our own lives creates a link between the on-screen images that are unfolding and those activities that intrude into our own days. This again reiterates the Japanese high school *seishun eiga* as a text that will resonate with audiences beyond the ages of the characters presented in the films. The presentation of the home as a regular site for familial interactions, meals and bedroom scenes (most often reserved for benign images of homework being completed or phone calls being made) further reinforces the films as part of a recognisable vision of Japanese life.

CHAPTER 3

Iconography of the School Uniform

The conventions found in school-based *seishun eiga* are not limited to the physical architecture and built environments of Japanese schools. The school uniform also plays a significant role in the notion of the disciplinary institution, thereby acting as a form of disciplined 'space'. This significance is applicable to any form of clothing, of course, where it 'can be looked upon in terms of its brute concrete reality or as an element in some greater conceptual scheme transcending its mere materiality' (Corrigan 2008: 1). As in many nations, Japan's school uniform has direct links to historical forebears in the military, but as Kinsella points out, in contemporary Japan, 'in the collective imagination of the nation, the uniformed individual has come to represent the example *par excellence* of the modern subject' (2002: 216). For McVeigh, uniforms in Japan take on a broader role as 'material markers in a general life-cycle', constituting three 'phases' where a citizen is 'uniformised' from ages three to eighteen, then 'de-uniformised' (ages eighteen to twenty-two). They are then 're-uniformised' from the age of twenty-two, when they (following heteronormative traditions) enter the workforce, marry and become parents (2000: 49–50).

In US high school films, unless they are portraying the exclusiveness of the private or boarding school, the uniform is rarely presented, with state schools adopting a more casual approach to uniform wearing. In *Heathers* (1988, dir. Michael Lehmann), for instance, the students, and in particular the group of girls known as 'the Heathers', use different forms of clothing to express their individual personas, and as Harrison notes, their 'choice to dress more akin to adults rather than those their own age gives the aura of a maturity they don't actually possess' (2017: 17). Thus, the non-wearing of uniforms allows older (or older-looking) students to distance themselves from the institutionalised 'branding' of childhood and adolescence.

The uniform indicates, by its very name, conformity and an adherence to a particular set of rules and circumstances; it is part of what Erving

Goffman refers to as one's 'identity kit' (1961: 20). Tamura explains that a 'fabric uniform is one way to singularise and territorialise the [students'] bodies under the name of an institution (whether a nation, corporation, or school) and mark the bodies for a formal belonging to an institution' (2017: 35). In other words, it indicates *inclusiveness* to a group, whether this be a nation – in the case of uniformed soldiers – or a formal or informal institution, as found in the almost limitless collection of groups such as police officers, postal workers, sporting teams, religious officials or high school students. As Tamura continues, 'A uniformed body is a body fabricated into a body of membership, uniformed and unionized under an institutional identity' (35). The uniform may delineate along national lines, but often also along geographic (state or provincial) or even seasonal lines (the 'summer uniform', for instance).

Uniforms and Identity

The importance of any type of clothing as a representational costume in fictional works has a longer precedent than in film, in all realms of arts and theatre, and with Japanese literary authors long recognising 'what certain textile types, patterns, or styles could signify for their imagined community of readers' (Suzuki 2017: 334). In her work on the use of the kimono in Japanese literature of the late eighteenth and early nineteenth centuries, Michiko Suzuki writes that 'informed readers could interpret kimonos through their own real-life experiences' and that scholarly research into clothing styles leads us to 'consider questions of self-fashioning, gendered and national identities, political expressions, concepts of the body, and the changing contexts and meanings of these objects' (334). In the Japanese context, the school uniform exemplifies this in the ways that it presents numerous questions around issues of temporality, class, wealth and gender, each of which takes on its own meaning in each of the films examined in this book. The uniform provides a form of 'ritualised dress' that performs the task of 'expressing one's commitment to the dictates of the group' (Corrigan 2008: 19), with a few exceptions, as noted later in this chapter. This commitment is part of the institutionalised discipline of the school but may also be more readily accepted by the school student because it provides a point of contact with their fellow pupils, and a point of difference from students belonging to 'other' schools, including a visible marker between what Okano and Tsuchiya (1999) designate as 'elite' and 'non-elite schools'.

The school uniform, as the most overt visual sign in a school-based film, carries multiple meanings, and as Suzuki notes, 'clothes are often overlooked or seen only as a tangential aspect of a text' (2017: 333). Indeed, the lack of reference to the uniform in the dialogue in the films tends to render them unimportant to the narrative (again, some exceptions are described later in this chapter), even though their development carries important local, national and international significance. School uniforms first appeared in Japan in 1879 and were based on the nation's military uniform, which borrowed heavily in style from the French and Prussian armies (Kinsella 2002: 217). However, when it came to designing uniforms for schoolgirls in the 1920s, Japan's naval uniforms were chosen as the inspiration, themselves influenced by British naval dress (218), resulting in the universally recognised 'sailor suit' (*sērā-fuku*) design. The shift toward the Western style was part of a widespread move in Japan's 'occupational uniforms' that signalled cultural attitudes toward Western clothing as 'a sign of sophistication and an expression of modernity' (Kawamura 2012: 22). The shift was also said to have been a more practical response to the Great Kanto Earthquake of 1923, which saw 'the loss of people's kimono wardrobes, the cost effectiveness of simple Western wear, the perception that kimonos prevented wearers from moving quickly in emergencies, and the view that Western clothes were more sensible for modern life' (Suzuki 2017: 342–3, n. 15).

While these *sērā-fuku* designs have remained in place, by the 1960s in Japan 'clothes were becoming something to be bought ready-made, and also considered items for enjoyment, not worn just for practical purposes' (Suzuki 2017: 345). This followed on from the ambivalence that has emerged in Japan's post-war culture, whereby the repurposed military-style uniform has been further adopted in multiple ways so that it can operate as a signal of respectability, disciplinarity and conformity, while also signalling disruption, dysfunction and revolution, including as a major visual motif in pornographic and homosexual cultures (Kinsella 2002: 219). In her list of various eroticised 'Lolita' outfits, Kawamura noted the Sailor Lolita (*sērā-roriita*) 'nautical style inspired by Japanese school uniforms' (2012: 72), which blurs the line between a subcultural fashion item and a deliberate cosplay outfit with less (or no) emphasis on the Lolita, under-age sexualisation of the outfit.

By the 1980s, Japanese fashion was impacting global fashion trends, and for designers such as Issey Miyake, the fashion world had become 'an arena of contestation and reinscription of power, where contradictory and complex identities are asserted' (Kondo 1995: 476). Thus, as with the Western-influenced *sērā-fuku* designs for military and school uniforms, clothing that carried the aura of an authentic Japaneseness was equally a product of cross-fertilisation between cultures.

Various music groups and artists in Japan have also made use of military and school-style uniforms as part of image making in mainstream pop, especially all-girl idol groups such as Akiba Nation and Nogizaka46, or the cross-dressing Ladybaby, or those veering toward anti-establishment punk movements including Scandal, Babymetal or Necronomidol (Figure 3.1). Drawing from the rebellious 'girl boss' (*sukeban*) gangs of the late 1960s, these latter groups project a mix of schoolgirl gothic and metal imagery, a deliberate attempt to 'disrupt and reorganise meaning' (Hebdige 2003: 106). Just as punk was to challenge notions of British society in the 1970s, Japanese youth have followed the pattern where 'fragments of school uniform (white bri-nylon shirts, school ties) were symbolically defiled (the shirts covered in graffiti, or fake blood; the ties left undone) and juxtaposed against leather drains [trousers] or shocking pink mohair tops' (Hebdige 2003: 107).

In manga and anime, such as the globally renowned Sailor Moon, the *sērā-fuku* uniform holds an iconically popular place in internationally recognised images of Japanese culture. The performance of wearing the uniform (that is, when it is not worn for the purposes of going to school) can also be linked to other forms of popular culture, often appearing as a major theme in 'maid cafés', with Kawamura recounting his visit to a cosplay restaurant decked out as a school classroom, with the waitresses wearing school uniform, but noting that on other days the cafe would have a different theme, with the waitresses dressed as nurses, for instance (2012: 81).

Uniforms are employed in a variety of ways to send messages about the wearer, and in the Victorian era two different approaches to dress were seen in relation to clothing and the body: using clothes in 'the disciplinary

Figure 3.1 Publicity shots of Nogizaka46 (left) and BabyMetal (right).

job' of shaping the body, or as a way of 'revealing the lines of the body' (Corrigan 2008: 89). In its officious 'disciplinary job', the female uniform often has the task of de-sexualising the female form through the design of straight, shapeless skirts and jackets. In her study of the notoriously violent murder committed by a fourteen-year-old schoolboy in Kobe in 1997, Shoko Yoneyama wrote of how the media portrayed the safe, almost sterile environment of the killer's school, Tomogaoka Junior High. Yoneyama notes that the students were 'extremely neat and uniform in appearance – same clothes, same shoes, same socks folded at the same length, same hair styles, same bags carried in the same way' (1999: 5). In terms of its disciplinary job, Craik (2005: 52) ponders the 'role of school uniforms in shaping the self to create conditions for the habitus of the docile body'. Yet the uniform also offers opportunities for the individualising of the wearer and, in some cases, actively sexualising them beyond the concept of the 'docile' body.

The disciplinary nature of uniforms is also reflected in the fact that students must adhere to a select but finite number of uniforms to be worn for seasonal or utilitarian purposes. In this manner, differences in uniforms worn in summer and those worn in winter are rarely acknowledged in school-based films, although the changes are highly visible, especially from the main uniform to sports uniforms. McVeigh relates an anecdotal viewing of a nearby middle school in Japan where students were seen in training for a sports day, and notes how this took on a military tone, through 'uniformed squads' of identically dressed students that:

> moved here and there as if part of a miniature army on maneuvers. The point of the exercises seemed not to be to compete against each other nor to demonstrate their physical abilities, but rather to learn how to take orders, how to be mobilized and how to move in small units. (McVeigh 2000: 52)

Thus, the uniform is enacted as a disciplinary device to maintain a military-like commitment to the institution, and more broadly to Japanese society. Even for those who might wish to demur from this commitment, 'they may conform to role expectations for dress because of their sensitivity to the reactions of significant others who expect such conformity' (Jasper and Roach–Higgins 1995: 141).

This chapter illustrates how the colour and style of uniforms vary widely in different films, yet each establishes a code that unites all the students from one school but separates them from other schools, and from teachers and society in general. It is this individualising function that means 'an organisation can communicate sartorially only if it is a separate entity' (Joseph 1995: 182). The wearing of the uniform also moves from formal to casual – often students are shown in full uniform (ties and blazers) as they move toward school, but then in the classroom or playground they may revert to more casual wearing. The students know the rules of what to wear, and when to wear it, and this is also the case with variations in the activity – gym wear, for instance, or band uniforms, or even cheerleading clothes. In the following sections, I conduct an analysis of the varied types of uniforms presented in Japan's school-based films.

Colour and Design

Costume design is an important feature of any film and, increasingly, Japan's school-based films exploit the central concept of the uniform to create a colour palette exclusively for each film. The ability of costume designers to come up with an individual look seems to go against the real-life trend, where only a few schools create uniforms that are 'much more conspicuous than most' (Tanioka and Glaser 1991: 62). Recent examples include the bright orange blazers and dresses of the winter uniforms in *My Little Monster*, carefully matched to cream trimmings and shirts, and dark green–grey checked (plaid) trousers (Figure 3.2). The bright orange mirrors the colour from the original 2008 manga, in which the characters wear matching orange trousers or skirts. In the case of the film, the notable change to the bottom half of the uniform from orange check to dark grey first occurred in the thirteen-episode 2012 anime TV series but moved to the more distinctive green–grey in the live-action film. These variations in colour give the live-action film an exaggerated effect that is perhaps more comic-like than the painted styles of both the anime and the manga.

In *Close Range Love*, bookworm Yuni (Nana Komatsu) wears the mustard-coloured blazer of her mixed (co-ed) school, as from the original 2009 '*Kinkyori Ren'ai*' manga on which the film was based (Figure 3.3), teamed with a crimson, striped ribbon bow tie, cream cardigan and short checked skirt. In a streak of individualism, she wears a black cat hairclip, not only as a fashion accessory, but also as a good luck charm. In the live-action TV prequel, NTV's 'Close Range Love: Season Zero' (2014), the blazer does not appear in promotional materials, with the Yuni-like love-interest character, Minei (Anna Ishibashi), dressed (mostly) in a white shirt and a grey-knit vest.

Exaggerated colours are also found in the girls' uniforms of *Nisekoi: False Love*, where the film's colour grading is heightened to accentuate the bright turquoise of the skirts and collars, and the golden ties. These colours are used as a strong visual motif throughout the film; in classroom

Figure 3.2 Uniforms in *My Little Monster* (Toho, 2018).

scenes this includes matching, for instance, the geometric shapes above the blackboard and on posters on the walls.

The students in *You, I Love* wear a vivid dark green winter uniform, also matched to checked trousers and pleated skirts that seem not far removed from the design of the Scottish kilt. In promotional materials for the film,

Figure 3.3 Yuni in *Close Range Love* (Hakuhodo, 2014) and *Kinkyori Renai* Vol. 5 (2009).

the students sport a selection of contrasting pastel colours, an amplification of the more muted shades that they wear in the film (Figure 3.4). Again, a manga, 2015's 'Ui Rabu: Uiuishii Koi no O-hanashi', was the inspiration for the film's colour palette.

The tragedy–romance of *Let Me Eat Your Pancreas/Kimi no Suizō o Tabetai* (2017, dir. Shō Tsukikawa) is mostly told through flashbacks across a twelve-year period from when the narrator, 'I', a high school boy (played by Takumi Kitamura), discovers the private diary of his friend and (female) classmate, Sakura (Minami Hamabe). They wear a uniform of distinctive dark green blazers. When the action cuts to twelve years in the future, 'I' (now played by Shun Oguri) is a high school teacher, but to locate the time period clearly as the film cuts between past and present, he now teaches at a different school where the students wear tan blazers.

My Teacher, My Love/Sensei Kunshu from 2018 (dir. Shō Tsukikawa) also features Minami Hamabe, this time as Ayuha Samaru. This time, she attends a high school where the girls wear the more traditional *sērā-fuku*, a white sailor-type top with blue trimmings, a grey skirt and a crimson neck ribbon. Minami also appears in *Saki Achiga-hen: Episode of Side-A*

Figure 3.4 Screen uniforms versus promotional poster in *You, I Love* (Asmik Ace, 2018).

(2018, dir. Yūichi Onuma), a mahjong tournament-themed film that, at nearly two hours long, provides the live-action cinematic sequel to the anime TV series. As the plot involves inter-school rivalry among teams of female students, *Saki Achiga-hen* features several styles of uniform, from the traditional blue and white *sērā-fuku*, to a range of looks featuring maroon, white, blue and checked skirts, plain ties, striped ribbons and scarves.

While all of these styles reflect a cinematic choice, they also indicate that uniforms are not necessarily static in design; instead, they evolve, whether for stylistic reasons or for wearability, with the advent of new materials that may be more durable or flexible. Craik notes of Western school uniforms that, in some instances, 'schools have increasingly commissioned uniforms from popular designers, thus hoping to create a uniform that is more wearable, more aesthetically pleasing and more acceptable to students' (2005: 69).

The importance of the school uniform as a fashion item seemed to peak in the 1980s, when private high schools in Tokyo began to promote their 'designer uniforms' actively as a strategy to 'maintain the numbers of their pupils in a period of demographic decline in the school-age population' (Kinsella 2002: 227). This signalled a clear shift from the idea that (in general) school uniforms were 'ugly and ill-fitting', designed for function rather than fashion (Craik 2005: 53). As shown above, the trend toward fashionable uniforms continues in contemporary films, where the students wear closely tailored styles or fashion their uniforms to look deliberately casual (such as in Figure 3.4 above (*You, I Love*), where the boys lower their ties and unbutton their shirts in a seemingly nonchalant way). A further distinction in the casual adaptation of the uniform that began to take on a higher significance in the 1990s was when schoolgirls began wearing 'loose socks' (*rūzu sokkusu*) around their ankles, accentuating the amount of exposed flesh on their legs and presenting a particular 'laxness' that contradicted 'the formal expectation that schoolgirls should be impeccably neat and perfectly pure' (Kinsella 2002: 230). Kawamura notes that this was one of the first trends spread by Japan's teenagers that was 'completely independent of the Western fashion system' (2012: 27), although, arguably, it seemed to mirror the early 1980s 'leg-warmer' or 'tube sock' fashion from the US, exemplified by Jennifer Beals in *Flashdance* (1983, dir. Adrian Lyne). In 1990s Japan, this modification of the school uniform was seen as outrageously anti-social behaviour, but now, several decades later, it is considered more acceptable – except, perhaps, at the elite private schools where such behaviour would not be tolerated.

The shift in the ways that students wear their uniforms also draws attention to temporal changes in acceptable behaviours, in which there is a 'possibility that different parts of the very same item [that is, the school uniform] are caught up in different time cycles, and even in different positions with respect to their "own" maxima and minima' (Corrigan 2008: 51). In the school uniform, the most apparent change is found in the length of girl's dresses or skirts (the latter a more common element in Japanese uniforms), often as a way of sexualising the overall image of the teen wearer.

This 'laxness' can also be seen in the wearing of uniforms in a casual manner, and the incorporation (presumably endorsed by individual schools) of less formal-looking garments such as the 'standard-bearer of comfort' (Corrigan 2008: 94), the cardigan, as sported by the male character Keita (Hayato Isomura) in *You, I Love* (on the far right of the promotional image shown in in Figure 3.4 above). The cardigan can be worn in a straight, buttoned-up manner (as in the American-style 'preppie' look), or left undone, with the sleeves pushed up, to suggest a confident, assertive personality. This use of 'untidy' or 'disorderly' fashion (*darashinai fasshon*) can be seen as an obvious attempt to rebel against the institutionalisation of the school (McVeigh 2000: 100), but it also highlights either the schools' powerlessness or their disregard in terms of enforcing uniform regulations. In the manga-based, live-action sequel to the 2015 two-part TV series of the same name, *The Black Devil and The White Prince*, the 'White Prince', aka Takumi Shirakawa (Yūdai Chiba), sports a chunky-knit cardigan that he wears in a relaxed style (Figure 3.5). His tie is loosened and the top and bottom buttons on the cardigan are left undone; he matches this with brown loafers instead of the standard black school shoes.

Despite the important visual motifs that the school uniform provides, it is notable that it is rarely (if ever) spoken about in contemporary films, but rather accepted, adopted and adapted 'off screen', as it were, as part of each character's development. By the time we, the audience, meet the student, their wardrobe is part of the character. Two of the few times when the uniform is focused on, in close-up, occur during tension-filled scenes in *Close Range Love* and *Your Lie in April*. In *Close Range Love* it is the anxious Yuni who grasps at her skirt, bunching a handful of material in scenes of romantic frisson with teacher Sakurai. In a gender switch, it is the boy, musical prodigy Kōsei, in *Your Lie in April* who suffers from a range of anxieties and affects the same nervous manner: in this case, grabbing at his trousers when in stressful situations. The ability to create an even more tense environment is also signalled by a change of clothing style, from the regular school uniform to the Western-style 'performance'

Figure 3.5 Takumi's outfit in *The Black Devil and the White Prince* (Hakuhodo, 2016).

uniform. The standardised appearance of a plain white shirt and black trousers is, in many ways, a less distinct sartorial look, but one that is part of the 'important extension of symbols' that occurs within a particular institutional structure where 'the reading of signs is related to the requirement of the organisation' (Joseph 1995: 183).

Aside from the clothing that is worn, many high school films also feature short scenes or establishing shots of students changing their shoes before entering the main parts of the building, an activity that does not generally occur in Western high schools. Students change from their 'outside shoes' to generic white sandals or slippers known as *uwabaki*. Depending on the school, these slippers may be in a contrasting colour. Yoneyama notes that many institutions delegated decisions about slipper design to the students, but that '[a]lthough it may sound fair to let students take part in the process [of choosing], in reality, everything was decided by teachers in advance and students were just used in an effort to make the operation smooth' (1999: 125). The wearing of these slippers is so commonplace in Japanese culture that it is not remarked upon by the characters; in *Wander Life*, however, they are focused upon when Hinano (Shuri Nakamura) has her shoes stolen by the class bullies; she is embarrassingly forced to wear her scuffed *uwabaki* for the rest of the day (Figure 3.6), even after the other students have been allowed to change into their usual shoes. Even

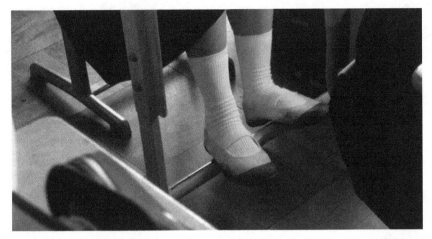

Figure 3.6 Hinano's scuffed *uwabaki* in *Wander Life* (Spotted Productions, 2018).

more belittling, Hinano then has to wear her flat-soled *uwabaki* outside of school on her walk home. During this humiliating trek, she is shown from a distance, in a long shot that isolates her on an empty footpath as the day grows dark.

In one of the rare images of a uniform being altered, a brief close shot in *Flying Colours* shows Sayaka's *uwabaki* with her name (in English) written in marker pen across each strap, along with various coloured flowers, love hearts and smiley faces adorning the front and side white sections. The defaced *uwabaki* reflect Sayaka's anti-authoritarian ways, even to the extent that she wears them with her heels out, pushing down on the back part of the slippers in another small resistance to conformity.

As can be seen in these various modifications to uniforms, including rolled-up sleeves and *rūzu sokkusu*, a degree of individuality is afforded the characters, and as with the kimono, teenage students are often keen to test the limits of what 'defies standard rules of gender and age appropriateness' (Suzuki 2017: 338). As Craik notes (2005: 52), the connotations provided by the school uniform vary, from the accepted disciplinary functions of the institution, to an indication of the levels of 'gender training and performativity', and even an indication of 'sensuality and perversion'.

Gender 'training' in the wearing of uniforms is an important factor in the development of youth during their formative school years. In her discussion of Western, 'Anglo-derived' boys' school uniforms, Craik explains that their attire has 'become a taken-for-granted part of the training in masculinity where certain attributes and characteristics are instilled and internalised' (2005: 62). Furthermore, students themselves are aware of what the uniform represents, with McVeigh citing student anxieties around the clear bond between the wearing of the uniform and their personal sense of self, quoting one Japanese student: 'If we make our appearance disorderly (*darashinaku*), then our interior (the way we feel) becomes disorderly' (2000: 107). A self-disciplinary practice therefore emerges where the student is obligated to uphold the standard around their presentation when in uniform.

For boys, the use of the uniform grants them a partial entry into adulthood via the combination of long trousers, blazer/suit jacket, collared shirt and tie. This is part of the ensemble that emerged in late nineteenth-century Europe and 'helped to create a blocky silhouette, a substantial image proclaiming authority' (Rubinstein 2001: 159), and one that maintained the appearance of the dominating masculinity of military uniforms. The 'Prussian boys suit' (Craik 2005: 225) in films such as *Hentai Kamen* or *Nisekoi: False Love* clearly marks these students as bound to their individual school, whereas those schools with blazers as part of the dress code may allow their male students to be visibly distant from the educational institute, as Western-style blazers (and suits) are found outside this environment. The wearing of the uniform also highlights the 'evaluative aspect' of dress, whereby 'other people decide how well a person meets their expectations for dress as well as the type of behaviour his or her dress helps predict' (Jasper and Roach-Higgins 1995: 141).

The use of clothing to indicate place by accentuating regional difference has its precedents in Japanese culture in all manner of clothing, not the least in kimono. Suzuki points to the designs of author Aya Kōda, who was seen as 'embodying a specific kimono aesthetic, usually associated with the understated, so-called Tokyo style, in contrast to the more feminine Kyoto style' (2017: 336, n.8). In the 2014 film *If You Count to Five, It's Your Dream/Itsutsu Kazoereba Kimi no Yume* (dir. Yūki Yamato), set in an all-girls' school, the student uniforms take on a look that is a cross between a *sērā-fuku* and a *meido* (maid) costume (Figure 3.7).

The styles and colours of school uniforms operate as a visual fashion and colour palette that differentiates between films. As seen in the examples above, recent films have explored colours and designs to create a more enticing on-screen look rather than presenting a realist depiction of Japan's school uniforms.

Delinquency

The central role of the uniform, as noted, is to establish belonging, and for the school uniform this indicates affiliation with a particular school

Figure 3.7 *Sērā-fuku/meidu* style in *If You Count to Five* (Spotted Productions, 2014).

or region, its 'institutional face' (McVeigh 2000: 84), that defines pre-primary, primary, junior or senior high, or adolescent age groups. The overt indicators that the school uniform presents are recognisable throughout the school and its broader community, and also create particular forms of identification, which, for some students, is neither desired nor advisable (Tanioka and Glaser 1991: 62). For students that commit (usually petty) crimes, for instance, their uniform can operate either as a form of disguise because of its commonality, or as something that needs to be removed for the journey to and from school if they anticipate crime-related activities such as shoplifting or visiting a bar (the legal drinking age in Japan is twenty). Yet anomalies exist when 'the strongest predictor of both crime and status-offence incidence and prevalence that is derived from this theory is students' changing from their school uniforms on their way home from school' (Tanioka and Glaser 1991: 68–9). This brings into question the idea that the student may be either mis-recognised as older than they actually are, or involved in an act of deception in order to attract or ensnare an older person into a relationship. For pupils from ethnically or religiously diverse schools, the uniform may draw unwanted attention, and again lead to students discarding their uniform as soon as possible when leaving the school grounds.

The lure of delinquent behaviour can be seen as a form of rebellion for Japanese students governed by a society that sees them, in effect, as children until the age of twenty. Anti-establishment acts of delinquency can be rendered as 'expressions of adultlike autonomy, masculinity or femininity

before society grants adult status; it is a flaunting of adult authority'
(Tanioka and Glaser 1991: 72). Added to this is the idea that, as many studies have shown, 'disaffection with school may contribute to deviation from
the conventional norms that discourage problem behaviors like smoking,
drinking, and sexual behaviors' (Takakura et al. 2010: 549). Furthermore,
Tanioka and Glaser point toward what they call 'status-offense' behaviours
that include: 'smoking inside home or school, drinking at a bar or restaurant, drinking in a friend's house or on a trip, playing Pachinko [. . .],
entering adults-only theatres, and running away from home' (1991: 54).
A number of these activities take on a more overt mode of disruptiveness
when committed publicly and in school uniform. As mentioned, the visible markers of institutional belonging work 'by creating identifiability as a
student and a juvenile'; the school uniform 'seems to inhibit delinquency,
but those most motivated to offend can carry a change of clothing in a bag
or find other ways to be free of their uniforms before reaching home' (62).
While this may have been common in the early 1990s, in the school-based
seishun eiga of recent years there seem to be very few examples of this
anti-authoritarian mood, with a focus on the narrative (usually romance-
based) and a resigned, unstated acceptance of the uniform as a part of the
student's social contract with the school.

In a survey of Japanese high school students (from Osaka), Tanioka and
Glaser note the pattern where 'crimes peaked in the middle year of high
school, regardless of age, then dropped in the final year when Japanese
students are in serious competition to do well on college entrance examinations' (1991: 58). On the other hand, 'status-offense' rates were
seen to increase 'somewhat in the final year, particularly for those aged
18, for whom violations of the norms against youngsters' drinking or
smoking are often overlooked when they are with older persons' (58).
These indiscretions, though, were minor compared to the rebellious
acts found in the films of the 1950s and 1960s, where the youth (high
school or college students) were presented within a frame of moral panic
around delinquency and revolution. The early films of Nagisa Ōshima,
most notably *Cruel Story of Youth* and *Deep-Sea Fishes/Shinkai Gyogun*
(1957), and Kō Nakahira painted a far more destructive image than do
the high school films of recent years, perhaps with the exception of those
of Sion Sono.

In the USA, the push toward individualism from the 1960s on saw a
reduction in school requirements to wear uniforms. By the early 1990s,
moral panic about the rise of teenage gangs and general unruliness amongst
young people meant that there was no ready identification for troublesome
youth. President Clinton publicly called for uniforms to be reintroduced

'with the goal of preventing violence and promoting academic achievement' (Rubinstein 2001: 309). The inference was that this would lead to a more cohesive youth because uniforms provided 'a visible sign of structure, coherence and seriousness; and that uniforms would reduce potentially dangerous situations and minimize violence' (310). Craik cites an example from California, where government reports in the late 1990s stated that 'the introduction of uniforms in all elementary and middle schools was correlated with significant decreases in school crime (fights, sex offences, weapons offences, assault and battery offences and vandalism)' (2005: 71–2). As noted, though, mandatory uniform policies did not emerge across the US, with casual clothes policies still the accepted norm at the majority of schools.

The concept of the delinquent schoolgirl seemed to be amplified with the sudden trend of *rūzu sokkusu*, as mentioned, seen as a rebellious move when they first appeared. While not quite aligned with Hebdige's judgement of punk attire as the 'sartorial equivalent of swear words' (2003: 114), this break from the regulation uniform was deliberately contentious. Kawamura quotes one girl who wore these socks at the time, who later admitted that "'My school had a strict dress code, so I would carry one pair in my school bag, and I would put it [sic] on on the way home'" (2012: 55). Kawamura notes that, by the early 2010s, the long socks fashion was not as strong as it once had been but had settled in to become 'a necessary item for junior high and high school girls' (55).

As a form of discipline, the governance around the wearing of uniforms could be seen in the 1990s as 'meticulous and enforced with military-like "clothing inspections" (*fukusō kensa*) and "school gate guidance" (*kōmon shidō*) at some schools' (McVeigh 2000: 70), but much more lax at others. By the 2000s (as we have seen), a more relaxed approach was taken by authorities. One of the very few high school films to make explicit mention of strict rules around uniforms is *You Are the Apple of My Eye*. In the opening scenes, set as an extended flashback to the early 2000s, the characters are being introduced (via a voiceover narration) as the students make their way to school. An image is presented of a (smiling) male security guard standing at the school gate, and then a female teacher in a business-like blazer, holding a clipboard and explaining to the students that she is carefully monitoring their appearance (Figure 3.8).

In a humorous way, the curly-haired narrator, Kōsuke Mizushima (Yūki Yamada), claims that his school is so strict that students have to provide a certificate of 'naturally curly hair' to prove that he has not had his hair styled in contravention of the school rules. As he arrives at the school gate, the teacher berates him for not providing the certificate.

I'm checking your hair and
the length of your skirts.

Figure 3.8 Uniform check in *You Are the Apple of My Eye* (Kino Films, 2018).

He mockingly plays ignorant and she slaps him, telling him to 'reflect on your stupid behaviour' and dishing out the punishment that he must 'sit facing the wall today'. The teacher is soon distracted by another student, Utako Komatsubara (Honoka Matsumoto), who lifts her skirt slightly to antagonise a nearby male teacher with a tape measure who is trying to determine its length. Utako's behaviour also creates a disruption among the other male students arriving at school, delaying their transit as they stop to watch her display her upper thigh, fulfilling their scopophilic desires. This scene serves to highlight the novel Japanese description of the 'absolute territory' (*zettai ryōiki*), also known as the 'golden ratio' (*ōgonhi*), referring to the distance of visible flesh between the bottom of a miniskirt (or other item of clothing) and the top of a girl's socks (originally overknee socks but casually expanded to include other forms of socks or hosiery). The frustration of the teachers in trying to enforce regulations around the wearing of uniforms is only heightened by the students' carefree manner.

In *Ano Ko No, Toriko*, Shizuku has begun a successful modelling career, seeing it as a path to acting. When she is late due to being nervous about a lingerie photo shoot with former classmate and fellow model Subaru, the latter becomes annoyed and leaves the shoot location, so Suzuki must take Subaru's place. The photo shoot sees Shizuku in pink underwear and the – until now – gormless Suzuki, his glasses removed and in an unbuttoned linen shirt, as they recline together on a bed in an erotic pose. The advertisement is a hit for the advertising company. Despite this, there is no comment on the fact that they are high school students, soon back in their uniforms and taking their place among their student peers.

Cultural Difference and Identity

While differences may exist between Japan's public and private schools, and even between rural and urban establishments, another division is found in the uniforms of students attending *Zainichi* schools: essentially those Japanese youth 'who have lineages that do not originate in Japan but in the colonial migrations' from the Korean peninsula (Tamura 2017: 28). The creation of uniforms that better reflected Korean traditions served not only to celebrate the *Zainichi* Koreans' originating culture, but also to delineate the students from 'regular' Japanese pupils. These uniforms were also highly gendered in that only girls wore the traditional style; boys uniforms remained indistinguishable from the regular Japanese school uniform. This meant that the boys were 'not assigned the same visibility' (30) as the girls, whose uniform was:

> adopted by the first generation *Zainichi* female students themselves in the 1950s to express their ethnic identity (taking from the original uniform design created by patriotic Korean women in the 1920s against the Korean government that promoted Westernization of clothing at that time) and as a feminist statement (against the patriarchal trend of discouraging women's education in the *Zainichi* community in the mid-twentieth century). (Tamura 2017: 29)

Thus, the girls' uniforms are based in tradition: the Korean dress styles that 'take after what Japanese would call *chimachogori* (or *hanbok* in Korean)' (Tamura 2017: 29). The uniforms are therefore coded with political meanings that belie their appearance as a 'neat' link back to a romanticised Korean history.

A series of separate public attacks on over 120 *Zainichi* schoolgirls took place in the early 1990s, in which their uniforms were slashed while the girls were in transit to or from school. These ethnically coded events saw a further reason for these students to change out of their uniform before entering 'the public space that connected their schools and home' (Tamura 2017: 32). The violent acts resulted in the shredding of uniforms, not physical injuries to the girls, yet the incidents drew attention to the fact that 'the female Korean school students in their uniform existing in daily public spheres [. . .] may cause tension for those who believe in the seamless and pure surface of the Japanese national (and homogeneously one-race) body by disrupting the surface appearance' (35). In response to the attacks, Korean schools began to offer their female students the choice of wearing an alternative uniform in the style of Japanese schools, incurring further costs for the girls and their parents. The advantage of this second uniform was to enable the students to 'become invisible', removing their outward signs of ethnicity and allowing 'the Korean girls mass passing, their bodies spilling out of the community, and mixing and coexisting with the majority Japanese bodies in public spaces' (39).

Not all South Korean schools had to alter their use of uniforms so drastically, as at least one establishment already used Western-style gendered uniforms for students while outside school, but 'a unisex *Hanbok*-style dress (not the *Chimachogori*-style uniform [. . .] which was targeted for attacks) inside the school property' (Tamura 2017: 45, n. 13). Thus, the uniform provides a sense of cohesion, and in its communicative practices 'is fundamental to knowing where we are in the world, and what the world seems to be' (Corrigan 2008: 7).

While the *Zainichi* girls were subject to ethnic vilification, physical attacks and a further financial burden in the cost of new uniforms, *Zainichi* boys did not seem to suffer the same consequences, or at least their fate was not broadcast as widely through the media. This could be partly because many Japanese schools, including *Zainichi* ones, used the *Gakuran*-style uniform with 'a raised-collar long jacket that is buttoned up to the neck' and styled in the fashion of European military dress (Tamura 2017: 44, n. 9). This style is still commonly adopted, but newer and private schools began the move in the 1980s toward the more contemporary-style blazer for boys, as seen in *You, I Love*, for instance, where the blazer unifies the characters and creates a consistently striking colour palette for the film.

While the uniform can suggest ethnic, racial or cultural difference for *Zainichi* students, it can also mask these differences, especially in the case of other 'mixed' Japanese, who are often placed in a 'dichotomy of either-or – Japanese or *gaijin* [foreigner] – in the media, and in the national and political discourse' (Osanami Törngren and Sato 2019: 2). When the majority of Japanese high school films are viewed as a whole, it would appear that the nation is made up of a singular homogeneous, mono-ethnic race. Cultural difference is mostly presented as a rural/urban divide, where a new student has moved from a small village to a large city, or from the city to the village. But 'mixed' Japanese people are found throughout Japan (in small but increasing numbers), with Osanami Törngren and Sato pointing out that these people, 'who are visibly distinct from the majority Japanese, not only in phenotype but other aspects such as language skills or surnames, may experience constraints in their claim to be Japanese' (2019: 2). In other words, discriminatory practices may be observed because of the perception of racial or ethnic difference.

Similarly, the notion of the *haafu* (or *hāfu*) student is rarely presented in films (I will discuss some examples shortly), and even less frequently in a central role. Often, he or she appears as a supporting character with an 'interesting' past, such as Diana (Tina Tamashiro, whose father is American) in *The Dark Maidens*; in the case of *Ouran High School Host Club*, Tamaki Suō (Yūsuke Yamamoto) is the son of a wealthy Japanese businessman and a French mother, while 'Princess' Michelle Erika Monaru (Mariko Shinoda) is the daughter of a Japanese mother and a Singaporean father. *Haafu* is an 'assigned term with the connotation of being "half white", but it has since evolved into a self-claimed social identification which embraces all mixed people' (Osanami Törngren and Sato 2019: 4).

One study into the *haafu* phenomenon noted the words of a Japanese interviewee with a Chinese–Thai mother, who said that his school

consisted of only Japanese, 100%. I felt the pressure to conform, and I felt that I needed to follow the others. At times I did experience the gap between feeling the necessity to conform and the realization that I am different after all. (Osanami Törngren and Sato 2019: 9)

This negotiation of his identity resulted in him suppressing knowledge of his mixed background so that he would fit in, a situation that he was able to reverse once he entered university and his mixed identity could be overtly displayed without negative racial consequences. Another interviewee who identifies as *haafu* described how, when she revisited her old high school, she was surprised that students pointed her out as a *gaijin*, claiming 'I was shocked because it was my own high school, I [had] already graduated, so I am an outsider (in that sense), but I was shocked by the fact that I was a person excluded from that space' (12).

One instance where a *haafu* takes a leading role is in *Nisekoi: False Love*, when the cowardly, lovesick son of local *yakuza* boss, Raku Ichijō (Kento Nakajima,) is knocked to the ground by new female student as he makes his way into school. The new girl, Chitoge Kirisaki (Ayami Nakajō from 2017's *Let's Go, Jets! From Small Town Girls to U.S. Champions?!*), gives an insincere apology and then runs on into the school. A short time later, Raku is in class when the teacher announces a new student. The camera focuses on a red hair bow, while an off-screen voice begins:

Chitoge: Greetings! My name is Kirisaki Chitoge.

The shot moves to an extreme close-up of red lips, ultra-white teeth and pale skin, before cutting back to Raku, who suddenly pays attention.

Raku [v/o]: She is Caucasian.

The shot moves back to Chitoge, this time in extreme close-up, showing blue eyes, heavy mascara, long blonde hair and a distinct fringe (bangs).

> Chitoge: I moved here from New York.
> Raku: Her eyes are blue!
> Classmate: She's mixed!
> Chitoge: My father is American, and my mother is Japanese. (Figure 3.9)

Raku suddenly recognises her and stands up, pointing accusingly:

> Raku: Ah! That brutal girl this morning!

Chitoge recognises him, and the class stirs in anticipation of their confrontation, the outsider and the cowardly local. Using a bright, colourful and playful aesthetic, including on-screen text that pops up to introduce characters and dramatic moments, *Nisekoi: False Love* draws heavily on the original Weekly Shonen Jump manga (2011–16). Despite Chitoge wearing the standard uniform of her new school, her vibrant blonde hair makes her overtly different.

While Chitoge's blonde hair is accepted as a result of her *haafu* genealogy, the sense of difference among Japanese high school students can be exacerbated by the common practice of (usually senior high) students dyeing their hair a lighter brown or blonde colour, creating what has been seen as a 'symbolic lightning rod' (McVeigh 2000: 71) for anti-establishment behaviour. While not necessarily adopting a *haafu* persona, students with

Figure 3.9 Chitoge introduces herself in *Nisekoi: False Love* (Aniplex, 2018).

dyed hair are allowed a chance to break from conformity and hint at the foreign, the exotic.

Conclusion

The Japanese school uniform creates an immediate visual reference for the cinema audience that carries with it a symbolic nationalism. While the uniform can be seen as a firm indicator of the institutionalisation process, its representation can take a variety of forms, as McVeigh notes: '[r]ather than pieces of garments associated with being dependent, childlike and asexual, uniforms are transformed into attire laden with messages about being independent, adult and sexual' (2000: 77). Yet the uniform can also reflect conformity with the social expectations of being a student. Girls may use their uniform to detract attention from their body (see the length of Hinano's modest skirt back in Figure 2.6) and signal their deference to expected traditional gender norms. Ultimately, Japanese high school films reflect a broad spectrum of uniform styles and the behaviours associated with wearing them. More frequently, filmmakers have taken liberties with uniform designs and colours to enhance their film's aesthetic, yet still maintain a realistic semblance of life in a Japanese high school.

CHAPTER 4

Marking a Distinct Society

The representation of schools in Japanese films embeds them (almost) exclusively as heteronormative spaces (films such as *Boys Love: The Movie/Bōizu Rabu*, 2007, dir. Kōtarō Terauchi, and the two *Seven Days* films directed by Kenji Yokoi in 2015 are some obvious exceptions). Gender divisions work along traditional lines, where Western studies have shown that:

> [s]chools are popularly held to be sites of cultural feminisation as the diligence, compliance and aspiration they foster are seen to both typify and benefit girls . . ., frequently at the expense of boys for whose failure their success is held responsible. (Paule 2016: xiv)

In many films this cultural feminisation can perhaps be seen in the focus on female characters and their difficulties in navigating romantic relationships, whereas for male-focused storylines the relationship may be secondary to their failure or challenges in their academic or sporting endeavours. Such thematic elements may reflect more traditional roles in Japanese society, and high school films often mirror these roles as a way of creating a more holistic view of Japan, rather than a deliberate or antagonistic binary along gender lines.

As noted earlier, the disciplinary structures found in Japan are aimed at making the nation function efficiently through staged moments of institutionalisation. For students, this means staying not only within the boundaries set by those in charge of their education, but also within the often unspoken social parameters dictated by friends and classmates, each of which prepares them for life within an 'administered society' (*kanri shakai*) (Yoda 2017: 180).

Holistic Society

In *Have a Song on Your Lips*, the gender division between junior high school adolescents is highlighted when a boy decides to join the choir because of the attractiveness of the new teacher, Yuri (Yui Aragaki). Nazuna (Yuri Tsunematsu) leads her friends, Chinatsu (Wakana Aoi) and Eri (Kyōka Shibata), to meet with Yuri to protest:

> Eri: . . . there are only girls in the choir club.
> Yuri: Oh well, he said he wants to join, so that's just fine.
> Nazuna: No, it's not fine! Boys are loud and dirty! And they smell!
> Chinatsu: No, not that. The regional competition is soon.
> Nazuna: Right! If boys join the club, we won't make it to the nationals!

Yuri turns to the girls to justify her decision, bluntly stopping them in their tracks:

> Yuri: Whether boys are around or not, you are not ready to compete at the national level.

The gender discrepancy is soon overcome as the girls unite with the boys (in the way of the collective society) to team up for success in the competitions. They work together to meet Yuri's exacting standards and in honour of their usual teacher, who, in a moment of screenwriting serendipity, is giving birth at the exact time that the choir is singing in the competition final.

In films such as *Let's Go, Jets!*, the theme is one of (female) empowerment and physical prowess against a backdrop of nationalism when Japan triumphs over the USA in the sport of cheerleading, normally designated as a key American activity. The disparate group of schoolgirls (Figure 4.1) – some athletic, some not, some apathetic and anti-authoritarian – show the power of collectivism when they finally gel as a competitive, coordinated team.

The role of sport as a narrative device figures highly in a number of films, either as a bonding group activity (*Let's Go Jets!* or *Run! T High School Basketball Club*) or as a more solitary pursuit (*The Kirishima Thing*). Wada-Marciano (2008: 63) refers to early twentieth-century links between cinematic depictions of sport 'as a national discourse [that] existed in the popular genre called *wakamono supotsu eiga* (youth sports films)'. In the period following the 1928 Tokyo Olympic Games, the focus appeared to shift to the more visibly athleticised Japanese physique as 'already containing Westernness and modernity, erasing, through this absorption, the visible inferiority implicit in the comparison to the Western Other' (63). The role of sport and physical fitness as a national project and a necessary activity within the institutionalised daily and extra-curricular programmes of the school became normalised. That films began to feature sport was

我们一定能办到
We'll do the impossible.

Figure 4.1 Confident girls in *Let's Go, Jets!* (Twins Japan, 2017).

therefore no surprise, and as Wada-Marciano surmises, 'the Japanese genre of the youth sports film should not be taken simply as a transplanted form or an imitation of a Hollywood genre, but rather as a newly created genre under the influence of Hollywood, tailored to suit local needs' (67). From a narrative or screenwriting perspective, this also gave filmmakers the ability to create characters that needed ambition, drive and a sense of a united team spirit to reach their 'quest' of achieving success in their chosen sport.

Other films, such as *ReLIFE*, portray the gendered dynamics of the classroom, represented in the scene shown in Figure 4.2, where stereotypical images are created: the jock (turning, in grey sweater/cardigan), the

Figure 4.2 Gendered classroom dynamics in *ReLIFE* (Shochiku, 2017).

cool guy (blonde hair) and the popular girl (leaning towards him, Crosnoe et al.'s 'princess'), the shy, bookish girl (the 'Brain') and the equally shy boy (the 'basket case', near the window), and the other 'normal' characters (Crosnoe et al. also list the 'criminal', 2018: 327). The casual nature of this image (pre-arrival of the teacher) is reflected in the poses of each student, and in the cool guy wearing his oversized, stretched cardigan with the sleeves pulled over his hands.

Each of these highly gendered archetypes can be found in Western high school films dating back to their popular foundations in rebellion-themed films such as *Blackboard Jungle*, *To Sir, with Love* or the many popular works of the 1980s, such as *The Breakfast Club*, *Ferris Bueller's Day Off*, *Lean on Me* (1989, dir. John G. Avildsen) or *Stand and Deliver* (1988, dir. Ramón Menéndez). Other media forms such as the *Archie* comics of the 1950s (and their reinvention as the *Riverdale* TV series from 2017), and literary works such as J. D. Salinger's 1951 *The Catcher in the Rye*, also feature the high school and the often rebellious transformative moments of adolescence as key themes.

Central to many of these foundational high school films in the West was the authority of the male teachers, 'presented for the greater part as unmarried male middle-aged white people' (Federov et al. 2019: 6). This highly gendered authority reflected the patriarchal notions of broader society, with the teachers' unmarried status marking them as strong disciplinary figures. Their focus was on teaching and shaping the lives of their pupils rather than on family, in the hope of nurturing a new generation of citizens. In Japan, though, Yoneyama writes of the ways in which the 1997 Tomogaoka school murder fractured the vision in which schools represented the ideal model of a local society, 'an epitome of the control society, where school, family and neighbourhood functioned in a coordinated, orderly and watchful manner, just as they were supposed to function' (1999: 6).

The reforms in Japanese education in the early 2000s appeared to recognise the stifling environment that had been created with the overly rigid, highly gendered formal education pathway, including a recognition of overly strict uniform requirements. As a way of countering the breeding ground of teen hostility, the new reforms 'took steps to individualise formal education to better meet the needs of the students', by guiding non-conforming students towards alternatives such as 'mandatory service to the nation' (Pagel 2011: 15). In this way, schools were still able to reflect the holistic ideals of Japanese society while giving students the appearance of a degree of autonomy.

Extra-curricular Diversions

Another part of the institutionalised learning in schools is the provision of institutional support for various sporting and non-sporting (cultural) clubs as extra-curricular activities. These help students not only to develop skills in sports, music and other activities, but also to play a role in forming social bonds between individuals and in developing young adults who 'have more positive self-concepts than students who do not join clubs' (Blackwood and Friedman 2015: 258). In *The Senior and the Girl*, Rika has finally made her way from middle school to high school, and yearns to find a boyfriend. On her first day, she is perusing the displays of her new school's clubs with her best friend, Yūko (Kaho Mizutani), when they are spotted by two senior boys, Minohara and his gregarious friend, Tetsuo Yada (Junki Tozuka). The boys keenly invite them to join their deliberately vague 'modern culture research club'. Rika eagerly follows the boys to their 'club room', while Yūko reluctantly tags along. They arrive at a small storage room, which the boys use to hang out, suggesting they could also call the group the Tama club in honour of the small cat, named Tama, that lives on their windowsill. A strong bond soon forms between Rika and Minohara, with the club providing a reason for them to speak to each other, breaking the hierarchical barrier that often exists between first-year and senior students.

Rika's crush on Minohara sees her daydreaming about him, whispering his name as 'Mino-senpai', a mixture of the brief casualisation of his name and the formality of *senpai* (senior), which she begins to call him when they next meet. A bond between them appears to be forming, but when Rika loses a bet (over a board game) and has to buy a vending machine drink for Minohara, he quickly deposits money into the machine, explaining, 'Stupid! Like I'd allow a *kōhai* [junior] to treat me!' While this can be seen as a chivalrous act, it also signals his understanding that the school hierarchy still exists. Rather than being hurt by the statement, Rika soon re-enacts the scene to Yūko, in a faux deep voice, following up excitedly with 'isn't he just so cool?!'.

The importance of clubs as a social site is also demonstrated in *Hyouka: Forbidden Secrets*, when Hōtarō Oreki (Kento Yamazaki) is pressured into joining the school's classics (history) club by his sister, a former member who is concerned the club will soon fold due to lack of interest. Hōtarō lacks determination and drive, and in a voiceover admits that he lives by the unenthusiastic principle of 'If I don't have to do it, I won't!'. When he is given the key for the classics clubroom, he is not surprised to find that it is the furthest room from anything else in the school. When he enters the cluttered room, he finds one other person there: a mysterious girl, Eru Chitanda (Alice Hirose, elder sister of *Your Lie in April* star, Suzu Hirose), gazing out of the window. They are soon joined by Hōtarō's friend, Satoshi Fukube (Amane Okayama), and the curious library monitor, Mayaka Ibara (Fujiko Kojima), and the classics club grows. Hōtarō's skills as a problem-solver soon see him used as a type of amateur detective. In this way, a small, gender-balanced society is formed, allowing for possible heteronormative relationships to develop.

As the title suggests, there are 'hidden secrets' that emerge from the students' sleuth work as they work toward creating an anthology around the local cultural festival. Thus, the club extends its interests beyond the school out to the town's social structures. They find copies of old anthologies; one in particular links back to a mystery in Chitanda's childhood, and subsequently to mysterious events from thirty-three years ago. As their interest grows, so does Hōtarō's enthusiasm and he becomes acculturated into the newly established friendship group. *Hyouka: Forbidden Secrets* draws its focus from the four main high school characters, with little input from adults, and the film takes on an adventurous air, rather like a Nancy Drew or Famous Five story.

The title of *Ouran High School Host Club* indicates the importance of the 'host club', where the (supposedly) all-male students learn deportment and appropriate behavioural skills for 'hosting' guests or holding formal events. Other clubs in the film reiterate the usual activities, such as sports, including US-style gridiron football, but the school is also host to a black magic club, peopled by comically gothic, black-gowned students who claim to have magical powers that enable them to identify when a student is in love. The wide range of clubs presented may seem unusual, but an estimated 70 per cent of Japanese students take part in school clubs, devoting considerable hours to their chosen one:

> Sports clubs on average practise at least 3.5 hours every day, no fewer than 6 days per week. Cultural clubs are generally not as demanding, but they still meet at least 2.5 hours every day, at least 4 days per week. Moreover, since the clubs do not have 'off-seasons', the students continue to meet at this intense pace all year round so that students in sports clubs put in over 1000 hours a year, and cultural clubs over 500 hours a year. (Blackwood and Friedman 2015: 258)

This commitment therefore creates an often tight-knit community of students within each club, and a sense of a competitive spirit, as shown in the strongly contested battle between the various clubs in *Ouran High School Host Club*.

Fitting in at a new school can also be used as a reason for joining clubs. Sei Saotome (Haruka Fukuhara) arrives at a rural school from Tokyo in *You Are Brilliant Like A Spica / Shigatsu no Kimi, Supika* (lit. *April's You, Spica*) (2019, dir. Kentarō Ōtani), and the loneliness of her first two weeks is broken when she meets Mizuki Ōtaka (Jin Suzuki) from the school's astronomy club. Saotome's family name means 'star', and the 'Spica' in the title refers to a star cluster in the Virgo constellation (Virgo is also Saotome's star sign and she avidly checks her horoscope on her phone). She soon meets the club's other member, Taiyō Udagawa (Taiki Satō), and becomes the third official member of the club. As with *Hyouka*, the club's minimal membership creates a site for social interaction, but simultaneously isolates the enthusiasts from other students who follow more 'popular' pursuits.

Clubs play a peripheral role that creates an intertwined narrative in *The Kirishima Thing*. The mysterious Kirishima is the mainstay of the school's volleyball club but he has gone missing. Meanwhile, the baseball club is desperately trying to persuade Hiroki Kikuchi (Masahiro Higashide) to join them but he is uninterested. The school's film club, led by Ryōya Maeda (Ryūnosuke Kamiki), is trying to make a zombie film, but is in conflict with Aya Sawajima (Suzuka Ōgo) as she invades their space to practise her saxophone for the music club. A number of points of dialogue see other characters denigrating the concept of clubs, including Hiroki's male friends and Kirishima's girlfriend, Risa, and her best friend Sana (Mayu Matsuoka), who distance themselves from their other friends who are active in the badminton club. The complexities and tensions between the various students and their opinions of those in other clubs permeate the film and reflect the way that high schools can create cliques that divide students according to their choice of club.

In *The Dark Maidens*, the literature club frames the entire film. Itsumi narrates how, in girls' schools, the 'dramatic imagination can always beat reality' simply because '[y]ou are becoming increasingly cornered, and life is uncomfortable.' In other films, drama is presented as a compulsory class or school activity rather than as an external club pursuit. In *Ano Ko No, Toriko*, the idea of supporting those around you is reinforced when Suzuki steps out of his quiet comfort zone to volunteer and take on a lead role in his school's stage play of *Romeo and Juliet*. He does this in an unselfish, chivalrous way to further Shizuku's acting career. His devotion to her happiness allows him to overcome his fears and shyness. When Suzuki is suddenly removed from the play to make way for his nemesis, Subaru, he politely accepts as he understands that he has obligations to all of those around him.

At times, extra-curricular pursuits do not depend on a specific club, but may be a class or more open school-based activity. In *Infinite Foundation*, the play chosen for the school production is *Cinderella*, and as with familiar dramatic narrative structures, the production's original lead, Nanoka (Nanoka Hara), is forced to pull out, in this case to attend an acting audition for a film role in Tokyo. In an extended series of scenes, the other members of the drama group react bitterly, their bond broken, and they verbally accuse Nanoka of putting her individual needs before those of their own community. In true teen drama style, Nanoka's withdrawal seems to allow for the film's central protagonist, the costume designer Mirai, to step in and for the drama group to bond once again as a disciplined group. Mirai is reticent, though, and when the play's costumes are vandalised by another disgruntled member of the group, it seems that the play will have to be cancelled. The students vow to continue with the play, hoping to find a new lead at the last minute. When Nanoka suddenly returns from Tokyo, the members tearfully unite again and invite her back into the production.

The Romeo and Juliet motif also appears in the live-action comic romance *Nisekoi: False Love*, reinforcing the Shakesperean motif of a romance between young lovers from warring families. In *Nisekoi*, the class decides to put on a version of *Romeo and Juliet*, with Raku and Chitoge in the lead roles, forcing them together. As with *Ano Ko No, Toriko*, the film opens with flashback scenes of the protagonists together in their early childhood. High school student Raku Ichijō is keen to dispense with his familial destiny to head a *yakuza* clan, instead hoping to make a better fit into everyday Japanese society by becoming a public official. In a deal struck with their parents to keep the warring *yakuza* gangs on friendly terms, Raku must date his new nemesis, Chitoge. Even though they despise each other, they understand the traditionally recognised and highly gendered rules of dating and, through gritted teeth, make sure they act accordingly in public (where they are being closely watched by *yakuza* henchmen from both gangs). While in a cinema watching a romantic film (a parody of Korean romantic drama *Winter Sonata*), Raku is encouraged to kiss Chitoge, but instead, she punches him. They soon realise that they must keep up appearances and make a pledge not to let their classmates know about them being together. They are unable to keep it a secret, though, arriving at school to find that their friends have thrown a celebration for the new 'couple'. Raku, who has a crush on another girl in his class, is forced to pretend that it is really Chitoge that he likes. *Nisekoi* therefore pivots between its characters trying to follow the rules of the loyal *yakuza* gangs and their loyalty to conventional school and post-curricular activities.

Toward the end of *Rainbow Days*, Anna is watching the school production of *Romeo and Juliet*, in which Juliet is played by a boy (in a pink dress)
and Romeo by a girl. Despite the gender reversal, the scene makes Anna
realise that she mistook Natsuki's words to another girl as a confession of
love, when really they were practising lines for the play.

One final aspect is the impact of student involvement in clubs, which
adds to the many hours of commitment on the part of Japanese students
to their regular studies. This results in a situation where, as Mizuno et al.'s
2019 study of over 1,300 high school students found:

> Among the three daytime sleep problems, including subjectively insufficient sleep,
> excessive sleepiness during class, and falling asleep during class, the most severe,
> falling asleep during class ≥ 3 days/week, was answered by approximately one-third
> of the students. The three top associated factors for this daytime sleep problem are
> belonging to cultural clubs, belonging to athletic clubs, and taking evening naps
> ≥ 3 days/week . . . (Mizuno et al. 2019: 380)

In *Please Don't Go Anywhere/Nacchan wa Mada Shinjuku* (lit. *Nacchan
Still in Shinjuku*) (2017, dir. Rin Shutō), Nacchan (Yūko Sugamoto)
falls asleep on her bed while reading with her friend. In *Flying Colours*,
Sayaka falls asleep in class due to her punishing late-night schedule at a
cram school, highlighting the contradictory nature of 'cramming', where,
'Considering the possibility that the academic performance of those students will suffer because of this, appropriate measures should be provided
to ensure sufficient sleep and to keep alert during class' (Mizuno et al.
2019: 380).

The prioritising of club activities over schoolwork features in a number
of films, as noted, including *The Kirishima Thing*, and in sports-related
films such as *Run! T High School Basketball Club*, *Make a Bow and a Kiss/
Ichirei Shite, Kisu* (2017, dir. Takeshi Furusawa) and *Let's Go, Jets!*, where
physical prowess is viewed as superior to academic ability. This is apparent
in the films and also confirmed in an early study by Blackwood, in which
a student responded:

> I didn't like school, but I still wanted to go, because I could play baseball. Classes
> were for rest, so that I could save up as much energy as possible to prepare for base-
> ball practice. (cited in Blackwood and Friedman 2015: 259)

The deep concern about the mysterious Kirishima and his return to school
in *The Kirishima Thing* is completely dominated by a desire to have him
back on the sports team, a club activity, and not for his academic abilities
or even for his friendship.

Family

The notion of the family unit is not consistent in Japanese high school films, reflecting more diversity than many of the other themes. In *Missions of Love*, for instance, while giving the outward appearance of a young man with a stable family life, Shigure Kitami has a step-brother, Hisame (Daichi Kaneko), who is a writer, working under the pen name of Dolce and in competition with Yukina to see whose novel will be made into a film. Shigure is shown as the 'legitimate' child and slated to inherit his father's 'Kitami Hospital' once his father retires. Hisame, on the other hand, is shown as resentful of his brother's status as family heir. When alone with Yukina at home, he explains to her that he has always hated his brother:

> Hisame: I want to see him suffer and in pain.
> Yukina: Your mother is different, but . . . you guys are really siblings. Your hearts are twisted [entwined]. His heart and your heart.
> Hisame: I was born from a mistress. And I have always been compared to my 'excellent' big brother. [pause] Of course my heart is twisted. Every single one of you . . . (shouting) It's always Shigure! Shigure! Shigure!

Hisame suddenly grabs Yukina and throws her back on to the living room sofa. He climbs on top of her.

> Hisame [aggressively]: I want everything he desires!

He pins Yukina's arms back.

> Hisame [cont.]: People were created with the desire to take things! Become mine!

Hisame leans forward to kiss Yukina but she quietly challenges him:

> Yukina: I don't feel excited with you at all.

Before Hisami can reply, Shigure unexpectedly enters the room, startling them. Yukina rushes to explain that it was not a romantic moment, but Shigure is visibly shaken and goes to his room. As Yukina watches Shigure disappear, Hisame breaks into raucous laughter:

> Hisame: That was hella funny [sic]. What's with his face? Holy crap! He was actually serious!

The scene reinforces the fracture in the family, and highlights the way the absent parents (who have gone to America on holiday) have left the late teen boys on their own to deal with the emotional challenges of adolescence.

In *Your Lie in April*, Kōsei Arima (Kento Yamazaki) arrives home to find maternal figure and long-time family friend Hiroko Seto (Yuka Itaya) fixing dinner for him and her young daughter. It is soon established that Kōsei's father has moved away due to work commitments and Kōsei is left alone in their family home. Ms Hiroko reminds Kōsei to 'greet' his mother and he gives a perfunctory nod toward a photo, establishing not only that his mother is deceased, but also that he has little respect for her. In later black-and-white flashbacks, Kōsei's wheelchair-bound mother, Saki (Rei Dan), is shown berating the young boy as he practises a difficult piano piece, and then slapping him across the face after he wins a public performance because she is not happy with how he played. A major plotline of the story (originally a manga series, 'Shigatsu wa Kimi no Uso', then a twenty-two-episode anime screened on Fuji TV) is Kōsei's inability to play the piano any more, despite being a child prodigy. While it seems that the trauma of losing his mother may be to blame, this flashback shows how the immense pressure put on him to succeed (at a young age) caused him to 'stop hearing the music', a triggered response that happens once he begins playing, thus forcing him to stop.

Traumatic family episodes feature with some regularity in Japanese high school films, perhaps as part of Japanese cinema's 'cinematic melodrama [that] is frequently a vehicle for staging a conflict between feudal and democratic social values' (Russell 2011: 13). Yet there is almost no mention of these trauma-heavy episodes as mental health issues afflicting an individual. They are represented as challenges for the young adults to overcome, either by themselves or with friends, and occasionally with other family members. There is little to no mention of school or health counsellors, although, at times, a sympathetic ear can be found in the doctor or nurse at the school medical clinic. Most often, students present there because of a physical injury. In *Real Girl/3D Kanojo Riaru Gāru* (2018, dir. Tsutomu Hanabusa) it is a fainting spell, and in *Close Range Love* it is a sprained ankle, but in films such as *Wander Life* the clinic can be seen as a place of sanctuary when Hinano runs there following a bullying episode. There is little or no interplay with concerned parents; instead, the student is patched up (either literally or figuratively) and sent on their way.

Kōsei's difficulty in playing the piano in *Your Lie in April*, as noted, arises from the trauma of his overbearing mother triggering his anxiety. In other films, a traumatic incident (usually the observation of a death, injury, domestic violence or other event) recurs as part of the ongoing plot with parallels to the post-traumatic stress disorder (PTSD) so often assigned to films about military conflict or sexual abuse. The potential audience for Japan's high school *seishun eiga* perhaps prohibits the use of character development in this way, suggesting instead that, as part of a collective society, the individual must figure out, or solve, their own problems. For Kōsei, his suffering stems from the burden of guilt, as though his perceived flaws as a pianist were the cause of his mother's death. Despite teen mental health being a global issue, the inability to address it (or choice not to) in these films may therefore represent a cultural nuance that favours the concept of the family as a place for comfort and healing, rather than as a site where dysfunction occurs. *After the Rain* is one of the few films to mention divorce, with Akira telling her boss, the dishevelled Masami Kondo (Yō Ōizumi), in a matter-of-fact way that her parents are divorced. When Kondo apologises for being rude by mentioning it, Akira politely responds, 'It's alright, I have a good relationship with my father.' Kondo then admits that he is also divorced and wonders aloud if this will have a detrimental effect on his young son. The avoidance of both mental health issues and the topic of divorce may reflect a reluctance on the part of filmmakers and production companies to avoid disrupting the genre conventions of high school films by making them too 'bleak' for audiences to enjoy.

In *Your Lie in April*, Kōsei's salvation comes in the form of the maternalistic Ms Hiroko. Having known him all his life, Hiroko has observed Kōsei's development and understands the trauma inflicted on him in his early years. She offers sage advice and tries to persuade him to reach back to when he enjoyed playing the piano and playing 'with all your heart'. Together with Kaori's encouragement, this helps Kōsei to acknowledge and accept his trauma, and embrace the memories of his mother when she was healthier and less cruel.

The use of sepia-toned, almost monochromatic flashbacks in *Ouran High School Host Club* also draws on the 'dying mother' trope for the blonde-haired Tamaki Suō, likely heir to a prosperous family finance business. At a meeting with his father, Yuzuru (Takeshi Masu), at an extravagant hotel, they observe a family at a nearby table singing 'Happy Birthday' to the mother of a young boy. Tamaki's mind drifts back to his ill mother lying in her bed as the child Tamaki brings her flowers. The scene cuts back to the father and son watching the hotel guests.

> Tamaki: They look happy, that family.
> Father: Tamaki, I'm sorry for making you suffer because of your mother. Also, not being able to bring her here is all due to my lack of power.
> Tamaki: Ah, that's not what I meant. It's just when I see something like that, I feel happier for some reason.

They both smile, indicating that the relationship between the two is sound.

The parents in *Flying Colours* provide a challenging home environment for Sayaka, the *gyaru* (girl, or fashion-conscious party 'gal') of the Japanese title, as she struggles through her sophomore (second) year at high school. Sayaka's academic level is still that of a primary (elementary) schoolchild, as she has spent years being more concerned about her looks (dyed blonde hair and short skirts) and her popularity than on studying. At home, her father, Toro (Tetsushi Tanaka), shows little interest in his eldest daughter, instead channelling all his efforts into nurturing their son Ryuta (Yuhei Ouchida) in a professional baseball career. When Sayaka's supportive mother, Akari (Yo Yoshida), enrols Sayaka in a private tutoring college, a cram school, the short-tempered Toro protests, claiming that it is a waste of money. As Sayaka begins to engage with her studying, Toro's unabashed praise of his son continues, spurring Sayaka to work even harder in the hope of entering a prestigious university once she completes high school.

The family serves as a basis for comedic moments in *You Are the Apple of My Eye*. When Kōsuke arrives home from school in one scene, he begins to strip off his clothes as he enters the house and is entirely naked (apart from his schoolbag, which hangs on his back) by the time he arrives at a pedestal fan that stands in front of the kitchen. This is startling enough, but then his (fully clothed) mother enters the room; instead of being startled, she just talks to him as normal while he stands cooling himself in front of the fan, which conveniently hides his genital area. In the background his father, also totally naked, enters the room, sits down and pours himself a glass of beer. Kōsuke's father tells him that the teacher rang again about the 'naturally curly hair certificate' (see Chapter 3) and they carry on the conversation in an unassuming way. Later, Kōsuke is seen mostly naked whenever he is at home, but when he walks out in his underwear one time, his father scolds him, telling his son that there is 'no need to hide anything from your family'. The conversation continues, with Kōsuke's mother in the background:

> Kōsuke's father: Your mother should also get naked.
> Kōsuke [nodding]: She should.
> Mother [to herself]: Don't be ridiculous.

The seeming ridiculousness of the father is in contrast with notions of Japanese society as traditionally patriarchal; as Richie observed many decades ago, the father figure is often cast as a 'figure of fun' because Japan's films, 'while apparently supporting things as they are, at the same time attempt to show us what we want to see and, consequently, cannot but completely if inadvertently criticize an existing order' (1972: 101). The comic father in the high school film therefore plays a role that does not threaten the focus of the story: the student.

The comic father is, however, of more use than the absent father. When Rin becomes ill (with a cold) in *You, I Love*, Yū must nurse him because his parents are 'both on a business trip, again'. Yū promises that she will stay with him, keeping watch overnight. The absence of his family means that she takes on the responsibility to cook for him. In an animated stop-motion flashback to when they were children, Yū is seen hiding under Rin's bed when he again has a cold. In another animated flashback after Rin sees a photo of himself and Yū as children, celebrating a birthday with Yū's parents, he is seen on an older-style family telephone listening to his mother explain that his parents will not be home for his birthday.

Mother [o/s]: We wanted to get home, but work just wouldn't end. We'll celebrate your birthday next time, alright?

To hide his disappointment, the pre-teenage Rin answers, 'It's whatever. After all, I'm not a kid [anymore].' Back in the present day, while Rin looks at more of Yū's photographs, he declares that he does not remember anything about the day, salvaged by Yū and her parents who took him on an excursion. Despite Yū's prompting, Rin maintains that he has no recollection, hinting at the deep personal hurt he feels due to his parent's inability to be close to him.

In *Drowning Love/Oboreru Naifu* (lit. *Knife Dropped in Water*) (2016, dir. Yūki Yamato), Natsume Mochizuki (Nana Komatsu) is forced to give up her teen-fashion modelling career in Tokyo to accompany her family back to their seaside hometown, where she has to enrol at a new high school. In the car on the way to their hometown, Natsume looks miserable in the back seat, her young brother sitting next to her, as her father, Naoki (Yōichirō Saitō) chides her:

Naoki: What? You're still sulking?
Natsume: Well, that's because . . .
Naoki [interrupting]: We don't have a choice, right? Your grandpa's old already. He can't live alone [. . .] Natsume, to be honest I had mixed feelings over you joining the entertainment industry. Since you're a girl after all.

Naoki's conservative view of the 'entertainment industry' mirrors traditional, gendered thinking that carries a low opinion of women working in what are viewed as the hedonistic fields of arts and entertainment.

In films such as *Daytime Shooting Star/Hiranaka no Ryūsei* (2017, dir. Takehiko Shinjō) and *Hyouka: Forbidden Secrets*, absent family members frame the overall narrative. In *Hyouka*, for instance, Hōtarō's sister encourages him to join the classics club, and then Chitanda, whose uncle has been missing for ten years. Chitanda notes that Japanese laws allow a funeral to be held to mark the bereavement of any person missing for more than seven years. Neither Hōtarō's nor Chitanda's parents are seen as taking an active role in guiding their children. Similarly, in *Rainbow Days*, when Mari's older brother, Masaomi (Yuki Yamada, from *My Little Monster*), arrives at the school to check on her after an accident, he meets Tomoya and concludes that he is Mari's boyfriend. Tomoya has been trying to attract Mari's attention but only gets a frosty reception from her. He confides to Masaomi:

Tomoya: Ninety percent of our conversations are her condemning me.
Masaomi [laughing]: Her personality used to be so cute, she was so attached to me. Our parents are always working, so she was probably lonely.

This open acknowledgement shows that Mari's absent parents have affected her emotional state to the extent that she is wary of new people entering her life.

Back at *Ouran High School Host Club*, the scene cuts from portraying the trusting relationship between Takami and his father to the Ōtori household, a huge contemporary house, where technical genius Kyoya Ōtori (Shunsuke Daito) sits with his father. This time, the dynamic is different, with Kyoya's father quietly but forcefully suggesting to his son that coming top of the class is not good enough:

Father: You know that something normal will not be tolerated by me?

Kyoya agrees, but there is an apprehension in his answer that suggests his life is about to become difficult.

A similar tone is taken in *Peach Girl*, when 'playboy' Kairi Okayasu (referred to by either name throughout the film, and played by popular TV actor Kei Inoo) returns home from school to his stern father, Takashi Okayasu (Takeshi Masu), who immediately berates him:

Takashi: What happened with your entrance exam results? Were you sleeping during the exam?
Kairi [quietly]: I wasn't.
Takashi: As my son and Ryō's younger brother, aren't you ashamed of yourself?
Kairi: Dad, I . . .
Takashi [interrupting]: Entering a good university will give you better opportunities. The world is a competitive place, and it hasn't changed. Be like Ryō.
Kairi: I . . . I'm different from big brother.
Takashi: Of course. You're inferior to Ryō.

Kairi stares silently at his father. Takashi turns away.

Takashi [cont.]: It makes me feel sad.

The familiar conversation again reiterates the expectations that older Japanese, who came of age during Japan's prosperous period of (seemingly) full employment and life-long devotion to their career, have of their children. As in many of the other films in this book, Kairi is being raised by a single parent after the death of his mother, therefore missing the emotional support he claims his mother would have given him. A similar tone of disappointment is found in *Make a Bow and a Kiss*, when Yota Mikami (Masai Nakao), who has been raised mostly by his uncle, meets his estranged and usually absent father, Kaname Mikami (Hidekazu Mikami). The older man has returned home to see his son, but rather than offer support, simply mocks his son's desire to continue with archery at university.

Beyond the Norm

Not all school-based *seishun eiga* follow the norms of contemporary society, and it appears there is a lot to be gained by exploiting the notions of otherness that set some students apart from the confines of Japanese culture. One film that does this in an intriguing manner is 2017's *The Dark Maidens*, directed by Saiji Yakumo, who also directed the 2016 high school *seishun eiga*, *My Pretend Girlfriend/Momose, Kotchi o Muite* (lit. *Momose, Look Over Here*). Unlike many other school-based films, *The Dark Maidens* opens in a gothic-themed room, reminiscent of a boarding school, where four girls in neat *sērā-fuku*-style school uniforms sit at a dining table, which has a large cooking pot bubbling at its centre. A fifth girl, Sayuri Sumikawa (Fumika Shimizu), approaches and introduces herself as the president of the school's literary club. She informs the girls that they will eat the *yaminabe*, a kind of 'pot luck' stew that literally means a stew eaten in the dark, and while they eat they are to listen to her explanation about the identity of the literary club. Sayuri turns out the lights and begins to explain that, although the girls each put one ingredient in the refrigerator the night before, only she knows what all the dish's ingredients are. In the semi-darkness the girls begin to eat their mysterious meal. By candlelight, Sayuri informs them that this is the sixty-first meeting of the Seibo Maria Girls High School literary club, investing the proceedings with a degree of tradition, as well as linking the Western traditions of the 'strictly Catholic' school to the event.

The setting of *The Dark Maidens* mirrors the Western idea of situating boarding schools in the country, isolating their students from the tempting vices of the city. A socio-economic indicator is also provided when schools that are generally restricted to 'a minority of well-to-do children' (Durkheim in Pickering 1979: 156) are presented on screen. Locating these institutions in such isolated areas also presents them as more punitive detention centres or borstals. These are the institutions housing the recalcitrant, already corrupted youth sent to the countryside for rehabilitation, as seen in François Truffaut's highly acclaimed, semi-autobiographical *The 400 Blows/ Les Quatre Cents Coups* (1959), where the young truant and petty thief Antoine (Jean-Pierre Léaud) is sentenced to spend time in strict institutional care.

Of course, less well-to-do students might also be found in schools through generous scholarship schemes, as in *The Dark Maidens*. Mirei Nitani, played by Yūna Taira, who also appears in *Yell for the Blue Sky/ Aozora Ēru* (2017, dir. Takahiro Miki), *Closest Love to Heaven* and *ReLIFE*, confesses, 'Because my family is very poor, I learned the best I could and finally got a scholarship.' At the first meeting of the literary club, Mirei is chosen to read a handwritten manuscript titled 'Human Like the Sun'. As she reads, it emerges that the story is partly a biography of the group, including Mirei. In a series of vignettes, effectively posing as flashbacks, Mirei's financial hardship is emphasised when she has to ask for part-time work and takes on tutoring at the home of the school's wealthy administrator, whose daughter, Itsumi Shiraishi (Marie Iitoyo), was president of the club when Mirei first arrived at the school. As the story unfolds, it is revealed that Itsumi's father is having an affair with Takaoka (Nana Seino), one of the other girls in the literary salon. Itsumi confides in Mirei before the former appears to take her own life, seemingly leaving the latter as the only person in the group who knows the real reason behind the suicide. Quite shaken, Mirei finishes reading, and Sayuri summarily thanks her for her reading style.

As the next narrative, 'Making Almond Biscuits', read by Akane Kominami (Riria Kojima), begins, it becomes apparent that the story of Itsumi is being told from a different point of view (the multiple narrative technique so famously used in Kurosawa's 1950 *Rashomon/ Rashōmon*). In this version, Itsumi is manipulative, and suggests to Kominami that Mirei is a thief. Every story sets up close friendships between Itsumi and each individual member of the group, while alienating the others. These shifting allegiances and relationships are all underpinned by a possible romantic and sexual frisson.

In the third reading, 'Goddess of Prayer', the story takes an international turn, with Diana declaring that she grew up in Bulgaria with a twin sister, Emma. One summer, they received a visit from a travelling student, Itsumi, part of a group accompanied by their shy, young teacher, Hōjō (Yūdai Chiba). Diana narrates how she fell in love with Itsumi when she saw her emerge, naked, from a lake, 'just like the famous painting of Venus being born'. During this narration, a flashback takes place using a postcard-style two-dimensional 'animation'. Itsumi's contact with the school through her father means that she can offer a place there to one of the twins, and Diana offers to let Emma take the opportunity to study abroad. But fate intervenes when Emma is killed in a freak accident. Diana takes her place, but her experience in the new school is one of isolation, and it seems that only Itsumi is prepared to befriend her. Again, a degree of sexual tension is hinted at, with Diana massaging rose oil into Itsumi's shoulders and briefly across her upper chest, her hand moving slowly under Itsumi's dressing gown before they are disturbed when Akane enters the room. Shortly afterward, Akane serves 'Venus puddings', breast-shaped desserts, that only heighten what appears to be jealousy of Diana's relationship with Itsumi. At the finish of the story, Sayuri concludes that Diana's story was a 'rather erotic script, indeed'.

The penultimate story in *The Dark Maidens* is to be read by Takaoka, singled out to join the literary club because of her acclaimed writing skills. Itsumi wants Takaoka to translate a work of teen fiction but Takaoka is more interested in writing her own novel, one based on vampire mythology. Takaoka also confesses to spending more time with Itsumi's father, although at this stage there is no indication of a romantic tryst, beyond him buying a gift of perfume for her. Takaoka's story sees her witness Diana stabbing a doll, in what looks like a voodoo-style attack aimed at Itsumi. Later, Itsumi appears with visible bite marks on her neck, resting her head against a contented-looking Diana.

Although it seems that the stories are finished, one final tale is proposed by Sayuri: one that she reveals was written by the now deceased Itsumi and aptly titled 'Whisper from the Tomb'. The story opens with an apparently naked Itsumi waking beneath white sheets in the arms of a man, soon revealed as Mr Hōjō, the girls' teacher (see Chapter 7 for more on their relationship). To emphasise the isolation of the school in *The Dark Maidens*, though, Sayuri at one stage quotes her (deceased) friend Itsumi, who said that 'just by being a high school student, everything is perfect, however, that elegance has a time limit, because we will definitely leave this sanctuary as well'.

While only a select few of the school-based films take place in isolated areas (for instance, *The Dark Maidens*, *Assassination Classroom* and *The Werewolf Game* series), in those that do the setting is generally not employed as an indicator of wayward youth, but as a way of promoting the tourist sites of a particular location. The films that do move beyond the urban setting are mostly set in a small seaside village or larger seaside town, such as in *Peach Girl*, which was shot on location in and around Kamakura and its beaches in the Kanagawa Prefecture, south of Tokyo. The beach scenes of *Drowning Love* were shot across various coastal sites in the Wakayama Prefecture, south of Osaka. Following the manga and anime, *Your Lie in April* appears to be set in and around the Nerima Ward in Tokyo, including the (fictional) Totsuhara University Hospital. Yet the location shifts to the bayside, with shooting also taking place in Kanagawa, utilising the city of Fujisawa and presenting views of the coastline and Enoshima Island (as does *Kiss Me at the Stroke of Midnight*). This allows for several tranquil scenes of yachts sailing in the bay, or the characters relaxing in natural settings including riverbanks, replacing the formalised, man-made structures of the school. In one scene in *Your Lie in April*, the spontaneous Kaori leaps from a bridge into the river below, a considerably larger bridge – and fall – than the one depicted in the manga and anime in order to emphasise the danger involved.

The use of recognisable locations therefore helps to locate the films within contemporary culture, so that even if events within the school appear unnatural, the school itself is rendered as a recognisable space. While there is a romanticisation of the larger cities – almost exclusively Tokyo, as in *Real Girl*, or Yokohama, in the case of *My Brother Loves Me Too Much* and *After the Rain* – because these are high school films the locations are often related to a desire for proximity on the part of those hoping to be accepted into one of the nation's top universities, which are found in the major cities.

Conclusion

The conclusion to *The Dark Maidens* offers a unique but telling commentary on the dynamic between a selfless commitment to the group or society, and a wilfully hedonistic individualism that seemingly has no place in the Japanese world. The final act of the film features a monologue, written by Itsumi and read out by her friend (and accomplice) Sayuri, as the four newer literary club members (the Freshmen) react when Sayuri informs them that they have been poisoned. They try to escape but discover that they are locked in the salon. This dramatic finale is heightened by Itsumi's explanation (read by Sayuri amidst a lightning storm and a power blackout in the room):

> Sayuri: This salon will be a beautiful coffin that adorns you. The sentimental ending that only high school girls can accept in puberty with strong feelings and selfishness. [pause] This is the climax of my story.

As the girls struggle to make sense of what is happening to them, Sayuri approaches them as they cower on the floor.

> Sayuri: You guys are drifting in puberty. [laughs] According to the story written by her, Itsumi came back to the salon in the morning . . .

The scene then cuts to a flashback showing Sayuri meeting Itsumi (now in casual clothes, not her school uniform) in the salon, where they discuss their plans. Itsumi, however, paints a future that sees her settle down with her lover (the teacher, Hōjō) and have a child. Sayuri becomes distressed, feeling that she is being cut out of the friendship. She takes drastic, fatal action against Itsumi, and the film returns to the 'present' situation with Sayuri addressing the cowering younger girls.

As discussed, *The Dark Maidens* presents a valuable commentary on school hierarchies and piety for one's elders, highlighting the inequities that arise and that can be exploited by those looking to profit from the misfortune of others. As the story unfolds, it is individualism and blind ambition that corrupt Itsumi, at first, and then Sayuri. As with many of the films in this chapter, it shows how the temptation of being accepted by a group of peers becomes an overriding factor in joining a school club. It also illustrates how adolescent growth and cognition can form beyond the nurturing environment of the family, shaped instead by entry into the sometimes volatile mix of structures and personalities found in and around the school environment.

CHAPTER 5

Playing to the Audience

Central to the success and continued development of school-based *sei-shun eiga* in Japan is the audience. Often these films are not box office sensations, but they do perform well despite their relatively small production budgets for non–blockbuster films (Schilling 2018). For instance, in a country where '[p]roduction budgets for films released by [. . .] leading distributors typically range from $1 million to $5 million' (Schilling 2018), *Let's Go, Jets!* took a gross of US$9.1 million. Many of the other high school films amassed worldwide grosses between $US4 and 10 million, including *Peach Girl* ($4.1m), *One Week Friends* ($5.8m), *You, I Love* ($6.9m) and *Close Range Love* ($9.8m). Other films to have had even stronger success include *Your Lie in April* ($11.4m), *Heroine Disqualified* ($19.1m), *I Give My First Love to You/Boku no Hatsukoi o Kimi ni Sasagu* (2009, dir. Takehiko Shinjō) ($24m) and *Orange/Orenji Mirai* (2016, dir. Kōjirō Hashimoto) ($26.2m). More recently, the 1980s retro-styled high school comedy *From Today It's My Turn!!/Kyo kara Ore wa!!: Gekijoban* (2020, dir. Yūichi Fukuda) became the second highest-grossing film of the COVID-19 restricted market of 2020, taking just over $US50 million (Eiren 2021), suggesting an ongoing popularity for this genre.

So, what is it about these films that makes them a staple part of contemporary Japanese cinema? As shown, there is a distinct ability to reflect Japanese culture in these films, and as found with the US high school films of the mid-twentieth century that 'supported the social values of the American society' (Federov et al. 2019: 6), Japan's films also operate at a strongly nationalistic level. A number of themes can therefore be seen as feeding into the demand for high school films in Japan, ranging from simple nostalgic yearning to the drawing power of specific star actors, some of who have already attracted a fan base through other avenues such as TV-*doramas* or J-pop. Feelings of nostalgia can also be heightened through visual reminders of seasonal imagery and the feelings evoked by recurring cultural (and institutional) events and celebrations at particular times of the year.

Nostalgia

While it is important to consider the fact that high school films create a sense of nostalgia for the audience, equally importantly, they are a form of recreation forged from the school experiences of the writers, producers and filmmakers, all of whom, one would expect, are now adults. Therefore, the perspective is one of an imagined or already lived adolescence, at times coupled with an opportunity 'for many adults to see the bully they always hated get their comeuppance' (Harrison 2017: 4). This means that constructed media texts are, to the adolescent viewer, someone else's view of *their* experience. The nostalgic refrains of teen love and the dramas of the school environment are shaped by past memories and ongoing 'generational schisms' (Greene 2012: 7), in which teens find themselves in a complex situation:

> Adolescents as consumers of teen culture struggle with the *contradictions* of 21st century American [and Japanese] life around issues of adult authority, the computer age, consumerism, education systems, family structures, identity politics, mass culture, neoliberalism, and postindustrial capitalism. (original italics, Greene 2012: 7)

While Greene's focus is the USA, these 'contradictions' can be wholly applicable to contemporary Japan, and this suggests the existence of a universality of problems, conflicts and challenges that face the youth of each nation within 'developed' societies. For the writers, producers, filmmakers, cast and crew who decide to create a cinematic reflection of school and adolescent life, there is perhaps a projection of these contradictions back to their own youth, a vision through a nostalgia-infused lens that distorts the story into a mix of now and then, past and present.

Nostalgia is also woven into the narratives, a nod to the memories and recollections of the filmmakers. In *Have A Song on Your Lips*, for instance, the opening scenes show Nazuna heading to school on her bicycle, picturesque views of the seaside town flashing by, as in voiceover she ponders:

> Nazuna: I wonder if I'll remember all this in fifteen years? The teacher I met, the stories of our lives, and the big changes that happened. I'll make sure to remember it all.

Then, tying into the later narrative where the school choir sings a song titled 'Letter' (written by performer Angela Aki for the 2008 National

School Music Concert and later released as a successful J-pop single titled *Tegami: Haikei Jūgo no Kimi e* (lit. *Letter: Greetings to a Fifteen-Year-Old*), Nazuna muses to herself:

> Nazuna [v/o]: I'll write it all down so that I won't forget it [pause]: 'Dear myself in fifteen years . . .'

Earlier in the film, Nazuna's music teacher, Yuri, sets her students the task of writing a letter to their future selves when they are fifteen years older, in order to understand the meaning of the song that she is teaching them better. At this point the musical score rises and the opening titles appear. The choir's eventual climactic performance of the 'Letter' reinforces Nazuna's sentiments as they sing:

> Dear future me who is reading this letter,
> Where have you ended up, and what are you doing now?
> Right now, I am fifteen and there are things worrying me
> That I cannot speak to anyone about.
> I thought that if I wrote a letter to my future self
> That I could tell you all the things
> That I've kept hidden deep inside me [. . .]
>
> Dear fifteen-year-old me, thank you for writing.
> There are some things I want you to know.
> If you keep asking yourself 'what am I striving for and where am I going?'
> Eventually you'll find the answers inside yourself.
> The stormy oceans of youth are hard to sail through
> But keep sailing your boat of dreams
> Towards the shores of the future! [. . .]

The scene then moves to images of music teacher Yuri at the piano, at times unable to play because of her sorrow, but the choir continues:

> I'm now an adult, but still I get hurt and have sleepless nights
> But I continue to live my bittersweet future!
> Everything in life has its purpose
> So have faith and don't be afraid to follow your dreams
> [in English] Keep on believing!

The lyrics to the song are simple and draw heavily on (arguably) overly sentimental, clichéd images and metaphors, but in doing so reflect the dreamy ideals of youth.

Music continues as a motif in the tragic, manga-based *Second Summer, Never See You Again/Nidome no Natsu, Nidoto Aenai Kimi* (2017, dir.

Kenji Nakanishi), when Satoshi (Nijirō Murakami) forms a pop band with promising love-interest Rin (Madoka Yoshida) to play at a school festival. Despite opposition from the school authorities, who want their students to perform traditional cultural activities at the festival, Satoshi and Rin persevere, and their band is a hit. Rin collapses soon after, and the story reverts to a time travel plot (similar to *ReLIFE*) as Satoshi returns to when he first meets Rin with a view to having a romantic involvement with her. That such a tragic tone is found in a high school film fits with what Richie once referred to as 'the notorious predilection of the ordinary Japanese movie for the unhappy ending' (1972: 75), but it is generally at odds with the highly romanticised high school genre, in which true love is often found.

Nostalgia takes many forms, and while the sentimentality of films such as *Have a Song on Your Lips* is steeped in a romanticising of the school experience, for others school may remind graduates of the various hegemonic structures in place that often extend beyond school into broader society. In his examination of the work undertaken by Bourdieu and Passeron into the French education system (c. 1964), Grenfell indicates how, '[i]n schools, there was a claim to meritocracy: education is available to all. Yet, one function of the education process was social selection: to legitimate and replicate the dominant factions within the social hierarchy' (2007: 87). Grenfell adds that '[s]chools are not simply places where individuals prove their innate worth, but a mechanism by which elites are perpetuated and transformed' (87). This portrayal can be found in films such as *The Dark Maidens*, where the archetypal 'rich' girl, Itsumi, continues the line of assumed wealth or authority, which in turn 'lends itself towards popularity in high school, with many of the most popular and beautiful female students coming from rich families' (Harrison 2017: 19). Itsumi's power itself emanates from her self-determined sense of privilege.

The individual nature of nostalgia also results in what can be seen as the imperfect memory of those adults making *seishun eiga* that contain a temporal shift where, '[a]lmost inevitably, each generation dismisses the teen culture of the subsequent generations while it more nostalgically and more desperately clings to its own teenage cultural canon well into adulthood' (Greene 2012: 22). Thus, in films such as *ReLIFE*, Arata's move back into high school uncovers differences from his recollections of high school, partly because it is now a new experience, even in the relatively short time that he has been away from school.

Notable, too, is the positioning of adults in the films, often more so due to their omission where they are not visible parts of the narrative.

As Kiejziewicz notes, it is significant that 'in the films about bullying the family life is rarely seen and the parents, if they appear on screen, have no contact with the growing youths, thus no influence on what is happening at school' (2018: 86). In relation to issues of bullying, there is perhaps a determined omission of adult and parent characters in school films, lest the blame be put on them for appearing to fail in their role, which could be seen as reflecting broader comments on shortcomings in Japanese society. This, of course, links back to the idea that high school is another step in the institutional pathway toward adulthood, and that once students have entered the gates, the parents can be excused from participating in that disciplined environment. In the Japanese films that are Kiejiewicz's focus, adult characters 'vary from the sacred (and also bullied) teachers, through the passive observers, who pretend not to see the problem' (86). In the broader realm of school films, it is almost always the students that must resolve their problems.

In *My Little Monster*, parents provide a framing role for the central characters. In Shizuku's case, her mother no longer lives with the family due to her devotion to her work as a high-level businesswoman in a distant city. The mother left Shizuku, her young brother and their father after a series of failed business attempts on the part of Shizuku's father. Shizuku therefore exhibits a mature approach by taking on the traditional maternal role of looking after the household and cooking the meals. In Haru's case, the catalyst for his unpredictable and highly emotional behaviour is presented as being the result of a childhood spent with his strict and at times abusive father, an enormously wealthy and ambitious corporate executive. So, while the adolescent boys in each household respond differently to situations where the assumed nurturing dynamic of the nuclear family is missing, it is Shizuku's family, under female 'control', that copes more effectively.

In *Infinite Foundation*, a film notable for its use of improvised scripting and acting, Mirai Minami (Sara Minami) is falling behind at school, more content with dreamily sketching fashion designs in her journal than completing maths equations. When the topic of her grades arises at home with her mother (Reiko Kataoka), Mirai tries to bring levity to the moment. While her mother prepares dinner in the kitchen behind her daughter, Mirai lounges on the couch so they only maintain minimal eye contact. Although the tone of the conversation is light, the mother is deeply concerned:

Mother: I hope you're studying?

Mirai grunts an ambiguous answer.

> Mother [cont.]: I want good test results before my next meeting with your teacher.
> Mirai: Test results, eh?
> Mother: Something to cheer your dad up.

There is a cut to some photo frames on a side table, the father in a frame separate to that of the mother and daughter, who have their arms around each other and are smiling.

> Mirai: Yeah, I'm doing my best.

They both laugh.

> Mother: That's what you said the last time. [pause] Don't you have homework to do?
> MIrai: I did it at school.
> Mother: Okay then, show it to me.
> Mirai: Later.

They both laugh again but this time there is a nervousness that was not there before.

> Mother: That worries me. It really does.
> Mirai: Hmmm.
> Mother: Will you have another supplementary lesson tomorrow?
> Mirai: No, I don't think I have one tomorrow.
> Mother [giggling]: Get your story straight, will you?
> Mirai: No, it's true.
> Mother: Okay, I'll call your teacher.
> Mirai: No! Don't.
> Mother: Why not?
> Mirai: Just don't.
> Mother: It sounds suspicious.

Mirai's mother continues to tease her daughter.

> Mother [cont.]: Did I tell you? He [Mirai's teacher] asked me to contact him secretly.
> Mirai: Really? He said that?
> Mother: Relax. I'll call him later.
> Mirai: No. No need to.

Mirai's mother then explains how important it is for her daughter to continue her education over the summer period, with Mirai grudgingly agreeing that she understands. The father is notably absent through the film, as hinted at with the earlier shot of the photographs, indicating to the audience that he may be no longer alive, and later through a scene where the mother and daughter offer their prayers at a small shrine.

Girls' Encounter/Shōjo Kaikō (2017, dir. Yūka Eda) also features the mother and daughter relationship, and again, an absent father. Miyuri's mother has no confidence in her daughter's academic abilities, and reckons that she will only be good enough to enter a local university upon graduation from high school. As the time for graduation nears, Miyuri and her mother meet with Miyuri's teacher for a discussion about her university entrance exam. He seems to confirm the mother's opinion.

> Teacher: Your grades aren't good enough. You need to study really hard for this last month. Your grades are good enough for a local public university. That's a sure pathway to a good career. [pause] That's what your Mum wants [he nods at Miyuri's mother to confirm] but what about you?
> Miyuri: I want to go to Tokyo.

Her mother glances at her daughter, a wry smile suggesting that she sees this as too ambitious.

> Teacher: I see.

In a scene shortly afterward, Miyuri is seen at the railway station, her friends wishing her farewell as she leaves for Tokyo, an elliptical way of showing that, despite her mother's scepticism, Miyuri did possess the skills to be admitted to the more prestigious university.

Nostalgia draws heavily on notions of tradition, as observed in relation to Japanese school uniforms in Chapter 3, but it can also manifest in adolescent behaviours. In Bamkin's study on moral education, he notes that 'comportment and manners' have been seen as important values in students, and are often traceable back to the students' respect for tradition (2018: 87). But Bamkin goes on to claim that '[p]edagogically, tradition can be a trope of convenience as well as a nationalising myth, which calls into question its relationship to "love of nation"' (88) because it can be constructed through curricula as an unchallenged truth. In school-based films, this can be replicated in subtle ways, such as devotion to traditional activities (festivals, the practice of particular arts) as a form of patriotic duty. In *Drowning Love*, for instance, Kō's devotion to performing in the village Fire Festival briefly outweighs his concern for Natsume. In *Ouran High School Host Club*, the school's annual festival is cause for Haruhii Fujioka (Haruna Kawaguchi) to devote herself to ensuring that the festival is a success, and in *After the Rain*, Akira tells Kondo that she wants to wear a *yukata* (summer kimono) at the summer festival with him, a traditional and symbolically romantic activity.

The theme of nostalgia can therefore work as a subtext within a film, for both adults (post-school) and current students, and each happy ending 'could potentially provide a therapeutic experience for both types of viewers' (Harrison 2017: 4). If, as Miller et al. (2001: 176) suggest, 'Screen studies tell us of men identifying with women in melodramas, [and] women identifying with male action heroes' and 'viewers transcend the dross of their ordinary social and psychological lives' (176), then it is not too much of a stretch to imagine adult audiences identifying with the heartbreaks and first loves of on-screen high school students.

Seasonal Imagery

The prevalence of spring in Japanese films is, as is the case in other cultures, representative of new life and the blossoming (pun intended) of new love. But the use of cherry blossom images also serves to highlight and to embed the iconography of Japan deeply, providing a recognisably nationalistic and nostalgic image of the nation. The most common blossom scenes include ones where the young students walk through an avenue of blossom, either alone and dreaming of their new love, with a friend and being teased about their new love or, more dramatically, together with their new romantic partner. This section of the film is often saved for a particularly poignant moment – it is a shot that filmmakers must plan carefully, as the location shoot is obviously available only for an extremely limited time each year and the complexities of producing a CGI blossom scene (until recent technological efficiencies) would add significantly to a production budget.

The use of blossom in literature and art as a metaphor for Japan's regeneration has a long history, but as Bordwell notes, by the post-World War II era, 'geisha and cherry blossoms already seemed anachronistic in an aggressive industrial economy' (1995: 14). It is this anachronism that makes these scenes so important – a quick reminder of the natural world as a setting in stark contrast to the concretised institutional world of the school.

In *Orange*, Naho Takamiya (Tao Tsuchiya) stands alone beneath the canopy of cherry blossom, deep in thought about the letter she has received from her future self (Figure 5.1).

In *Let Me Eat Your Pancreas*, Sakura (Minami Hamabe) reads in a tranquil setting while classmate and possible romantic interest, the film's unnamed protagonist (Takumi Kitamura), passes by (Figure 5.2). This

Figure 5.1 All-encompassing passage of blossom in *Orange* (Toho, 2016).

scene uses a form of colour saturation as a pink wash across the screen, and utilises depth of field to ensure the focus remains on the characters.

In *ReLIFE*, the blossom scene captures the younger version of Arata Kaizaki (Taishi Nakagawa) when he meets his time-travelling mentor from the ReLife Research Institute, Ryō Yoake (Yūdai Chiba). The latter is impersonating a high school student as he has been assigned to watch over Arata to monitor the company's experiment in age-shifting its clients (Figure 5.3). In this pivotal scene, Arata discusses his decision to opt out

Figure 5.2 Sakura surrounded by blossom in *Let Me Eat Your Pancreas* (Toho, 2017).

Figure 5.3 Arata meets Ryō in *ReLIFE* (Shochiku, 2017).

of the time-travel programme, and they both tearfully accept the questionable morality of the chemically induced activity. The scene is notably different from other blossom scenes because it does not feature the heteronormativity of a boy/girl relationship – although no overt homosexual behaviour is indicated. Instead, the visual imagery of two young men making decisions about their future selves in the otherwise romanticised setting is unusual. The importance of the scene lies in its significance, as Greene notes more generally:

> The struggle between adolescent autonomy and adult authority remains the central aspect of generational politics. Indeed, the drive to canonise the generational signifiers of past decades as an authentic and superior culture to the inauthentic and inferior teen culture is as much evidence of this ongoing struggle as any proof it has diminished in the twenty-first century. (2012: 22).

The fact that this struggle takes place in the natural environment and the temporality of the flowering blossom emphasises the brevity of youth as Arata experiences his 'second' period of adolescence, informed by his adult self.

In *My Little Monster*, blossoming trees line the road leading into the school, framing multiple shots across several spring seasons to indicate the temporal nature of the narrative as Shizuku and Haru enter the school once again. And in *Peach Girl*, the opening scenes feature white blossom indicating the start of spring and the warmer, sunny weather that Momo is keen to avoid because she tans easily. This feeds into larger cultural concerns around whiteness in many Asian cultures that see darker skin as a sign of lower class – related to the concept of farmers and those whose work involves manual labour. In Japan darker skin also has the connotation of the deliberately bronzed 1990s fashion of *ganguro* girls, often seen as a socially defiant anti-traditionalist statement, or suggesting sexual promiscuity. Because Momo is a keen swimmer and tans easily, she cowers beneath a black parasol to ward off the sun (even though it is only the beginning of spring), and expresses the view that, before she can attract a boy, and Toji in particular:

> Momo: I should get my skin white first!

In the classroom before the lesson begins, she plasters her face with cosmetic skin whitener, repeating to herself:

> Momo: More white, more white, more white!

The link to spring through white rather than pink blossom therefore has a more tangible meaning rather than just providing a visual background. Later in the film, when Momo has been rejected by Toji, Kairi presents her with a peach stone to cheer her up. She looks at it, confused:

> Kairi: No matter how cold the winter is, when spring arrives, it will bloom and blossom. It will start here today. Let's plant it together.

They plant the peach stone in a flowerbed at the school before the scene cuts to just one week later, when Kairi drags Momo back to the same location. This time, a branch with blossom reaches up out of the ground. However Momo's background as the daughter of a florist allows her to see though Kairi's ploy:

> Momo: Why did a Japanese quince flower bloom if we sowed a peach seed?
> Kairi: Japanese quince? Well the man next door said it was a peach seed.

He pulls the branch out of the ground.

> Momo: Peach flowers only blossom after three years.

Rather than being annoyed at Kairi's attempt to bring her some cheer, Momo softens towards him and he hugs her as they kneel amidst the flowering garden. In the final postscript to the film (after the end credits), Momo and Kairi return to the school in spring several years later. In a shot reverse shot, the two (now lovers) look at each other through the flowering peach blossom, as Kairi states, '*kawaii*' [cute], then adds, 'I mean you, not the blossom.'

In *The Senior and the Girl*, blossom is used as the first image follow-ing the film's title slide, in which a cold open has established a possible romantic link between first-year student Rika Tsuzuki (Kyōko Yoshine) and senior student Keigo Minohara (Jun Shison). The image of blossom launches the film into spring, the season of love, in contrast to most other films, which lead into spring as a confirmation of the romance that has built earlier on. In the latter parts of the film, as Rika and Minohara's rela-tionship ignites and then seems to come to an end; winter arrives, and all attention turns to the seniors about to graduate in spring, when Minohara will be leaving the school. In the final scenes, though, as the older students celebrate their graduation, several blossom petals can be seen drifting in the breeze, a subtle reminder that sets the tone for the film's denouement: a reconciliation between the two young lovers.

The introductory use of blossom is also a feature of *Honey*, this time after an opening scene featuring Onise, a young man with dyed red hair who is involved in a fist fight with other young men in the pouring rain. Onise is beaten up and retreats to a bridge, where he sits in the pelting rain as people around him go about their everyday business. Suddenly, an umbrella appears over him and someone passes him a small, boxed drink. As he looks up, a uniformed schoolgirl can be seen running away. The scene then cuts to images of a brilliant blue sky and delicate pink blos-som with a (CGI) bee collecting nectar, before it flies away and then twists to spell the film's title, *honey*, in lower-case English, with small *katakana* characters below. There is a marked contrast with the dreary opening scene, the blossom signalling a more comic–romantic tone.

In *Your Lie in April*, Kōsei's first meeting with Kaori (or 'Kao') occurs during spring, when he sees her playing a melodica with a group of young children. He begins to video their performance before a strong gust of wind interrupts, blowing Kaori's skirt up and exposing her legs. She sees him, and rushes over to try to grab his phone and delete the video. Their struggle is seen by mutual friends, who call them over. Kōsei appears to be very attracted to Kaori, and when she rushes over to retrieve her violin for an upcoming recital the image appears from Kosei's perspective, with the blossom in the background framing Kaori and matching her pink violin case, giving the scene a softly feminine feel (Figure 5.4). This image is almost identical (apart from Kaori's clothing) to the scene that is popularly reproduced in online fan depictions of the *Your Lie in April* anime and manga known as 'Shigatsu wa Kimi no Uso', or colloquially as 'Kimiuso'. Kaori runs to meet Kōsei and soon the film's titles (written as musical notation) appear against a background of blue sky and blossom trees.

Figure 5.4 Kaori against the blossom in *Your Lie in April* (C&I Entertainment, 2016).

Blossom again appears the next time they meet, on the pathway lead-ing from the school. The blossom trees form a canopy above them, the confined framing accentuating their physical closeness in their potential developing romance. The reference to the month of April in the film's title itself alludes to Japan's cherry blossom season, and the film takes place over one year, bookended by each spring.

Other films, such as *One Week Friends* and *Rainbow Days*, cycle through the seasons as they track across one, two or three years of their protago-nists' time at high school. Often intertitles are used, as in *Rainbow Days*, in which they state the season and the students' year: 'Winter: Second year', for instance. The seasons mark the highs and lows of their friendships and romances, with spring as the dominant season representing the most opti-mistic and romantic period, coupled with its significance as being the time of graduation from high school or signalling the lead-up to the summer holidays. Importantly, the season is most recognised as a metaphor for life, renewal and love.

Manga and Anime Connections

The majority of high school films over the past decade have been derived from manga and anime (and quite a few from novels too – see Films Cited). This link assists with nostalgic aspects and sets up strong inter-textual connections that aid in the promotion of the live-action films. The commercial advantages of these links are accelerated by the 'convergence' of texts (Wada-Marciano 2012: 80), or as Steinberg (and others) refer(s) to it, the 'media mix' that allows a 'proliferation of visually consistent character images across media forms' (2012: 42), which I detail later in this chapter. While these direct adaptations therefore exist for economic reasons, many of the films also integrate manga and anime into diegetic and non-diegetic images as a constant reminder of the importance of these visual styles in Japanese culture.

In *One Week Friends*, Yūki's small sketches are in the exaggerated manga style, and are presented in a flick-the-page animation that retells the story of his relationship with Kaori (Figure 5.5).

Although not based on a manga, *You Are the Apple of My Eye* demonstrates a heavy reliance on close-ups, constantly framing and accentuating the characters' faces and mimicking the wide-eyed manga and animation styles (Figure 5.6).

Another adapted style features in *You, I Love* when the film occasionally breaks the fourth wall and uses small added animations to reinforce the characters' emotions, such as Koyomi's responses of anger and hurt after being insulted by Keita (Figure 5.7). This non-diegetic style can be found in many other films, often with pounding love hearts bursting from a character's chest or circling their head, as in *My Teacher, My Love* and *Kiss Him, Not Me*.

Figure 5.5 Yūki's manga-style drawing in *One Week Friends* (Shochiku, 2017).

Figure 5.6 Mai's close-up in *You Are the Apple of My Eye* (Kino Films, 2018).

You, I Love also draws on manga styles to accentuate the physique and body movements of characters such as Rin, with his 'bad boy' sexually loaded look (Figure 5.8). *You, I Love* is based on the manga series 'Ui Rabu – Uiuishii Koi no Ohanashi', in which Rin often appears with his head down, hair across his eyes and slouched posture.

Manga stylings are also used in *Drowning Love*, where Natsume's affection for Kō is presented through her point of view, emphasising his manga-influenced looks with his dyed white-blond hair and his posture with his

Figure 5.7 Koyomi after being insulted by Keita in *You, I Love* (Asmik Ace, 2018).

Figure 5.8 Rin slouches in *You, I Love* (Asmik Ace, 2018) and in the 'Ui Rabu' manga.

head lowered and only one eye visible through his fringe (Figure 5.9). Kō's boundless energy sees him leaping and jumping everywhere he goes; like a manga or anime hero, he is unpredictable and enigmatic. When he exchanges bracelets with Natsume, he declares, in a superhero manner,

Figure 5.9 Kō, with one eye visible, in *Drowning Love* (GAGA, 2016).

that it will help protect her. When they attend the summer Fire Festival in their *yukata*, Kō dresses entirely in the traditional white clothes and white rope belt of the male participants, making him look ghost-like.

Manga works both diegetically and non-diegetically in *Hyouka: Forbidden Secrets*, where Ibara puts forward her hypothesis on the events that might have occurred thirty-three years ago that saw Chitanda's uncle, Jun Sekiya (Kanata Hongō), banished from the school. To explain her version of the story, Ibara picks up a black marker and begins sketching out the events. This differs from Chitanda's storytelling, which is punctuated by a live-action recreation of possible events. Instead, as Ibara relates her version of the story, her manga-style diagrams fill the screen. The images begin to move in the form of stop-motion animation, complete with action movement lines and written onomatopoeic sounds (including POKA!, when a punch is thrown). Ibara concludes her brief story and the now live action cuts back to the group as Ibara clips the lid back on her marker with a satisfied grin. In contrast, as Satoshi speaks, a montage of black-and-white archival footage from Japan's 1960s student uprisings and subsequent riots is shown to illustrate his story. This movement across visual styles accentuates the ability of Japanese audiences to consume a convergence of media styles.

Hyouka: Forbidden Secret's own journey from manga to anime to feature film also creates a recognisable continuity in the characters themselves. The deliberate media mix strategy creates an economy around each text, drawing on the power of individual or group characters and the creation of a type of mobility where:

> [t]he character is a particular combination of name and visual design that is in some sense independent from any particular medium. Indeed, the nature of the character image is to travel across media, being embodied in each medium in distinct ways. (Steinberg 2012: 83)

This mobility can be seen in other texts such as *My Little Monster*, where the characters of Haru and Shizuku are not just replicated across the manga to anime to live-action film and associated boxed collections, but distinctly commodified, their images appearing on everything from sweatshirts and t-shirts to pillows, tote bags, posters, stickers, dolls, figurines, sculpted ceramic busts, nail polishes, keyrings and ornaments. Steinberg contends that this mobility also contains a valuable communicative purpose, so that:

> [t]he character is not only materialized in different mediums – celluloid, paper, or plastic – it is also an abstract device that allows for the communication across

media forms and media materialities. It is abstract because it is always in excess of its particular material incarnations. The character cannot be reduced to any one of its incarnations but must be thought of both in its material forms and in the ways that it exceeds them. (2012: 84)

As with many of the films presented in this book, the creation and popularity of the initial fictional characters within the 'My Little Monster' manga (from 2008) saw them become embedded in Japanese popular culture, creating a pulse where 'the effects of synergy are felt both within and across every material incarnation' (Steinberg 2012: 85). Having an established body of texts before the live-action film was made therefore meant that the casting of capable (and recognisable) actors would help to ensure the success of the film. Choosing Masaki Suda for the role of Haru built on his prolific acting career; he appears in both *Assasination Classroom* films, a string of *Kamen Rider* films and other comedies such as *Princess Jellyfish*. Tao Tsuchiya is recognisable from her roles in *Orange*, *Yell for the Blue Sky* and *My Brother Loves Me Too Much*, and earned international recognition through her appearances in Kiyoshi Kurosawa's Cannes Jury prize-winner *Tokyo Sonata* (2008), and as an acclaimed dancer in music videos for Grammy Award nominee Sia. Thus, the characters are commodified across multiple media platforms, further accentuated by the use of star actors (or directors).

Star Power

While nostalgia can drive an older audience (even those newly graduated from high school), the teen audience is more likely to be drawn by the appearance of current and recent pop and television stars. The intertextuality of contemporary stardom can also have a number of crossover points, from the star providing a song or songs for the film's soundtrack – mostly during opening or closing credits – or an association with TV adaptations in the cycle of manga-TV series to film. Others may have voiced the same character in the anime version of the film in the well-trodden media-mix path through manga to anime to film, or occasionally from manga to film to anime. The use of either established or burgeoning pop stars in school-based *seishun eiga* has been a feature of these films for several decades, but increasingly it seems that entire pop groups are cast to maximise the impact and cross-promotional benefits of each film.

In *Forget Me Not* (2015), Akari Hayami plays the lead character, Azusa, the mysterious girl who nobody remembers, except for her new love, Takeshi (Nijirō Murakami). Hayami is perhaps best known in her former role in the idol girl group Momoiro Clover (later known as Momoiro Clover Z). She moved from music into a prolific career in fashion modelling, TV commercials, TV dramas and films, including the cheerleading-based 2011 high school film, *Cheerfully/Chiafurii* (dir. Shō Tsuchikawa). *Cheerfully* also featured members of pop groups such as PASSPO☆ and THE Possible/The Posshibō to make up the eleven cheerleaders signified in the title.

A similarly recognisable star is Rina Kawaei, a former member of AKB48, possibly Japan's most successful all-girl idol band. Kawaei has appeared in films such as *Principal: Am I a Heroine In Love?*, where she plays Haruka Kunishige, and *My Teacher, My Love* as Aoi Nakamura. Kawaei's fame grew even further following a public 'handshake' (meet and greet) event in northern Honshu in 2014, when she and a bandmate were attacked by a man with a handsaw, breaking her thumb and resulting in deep cuts to her hand. Following her recovery, Kawaei left the group ('graduated' from the band, another school-based word that is commonly used in a different context with reference to Japan's pop stars) in mid-2015 and has since concentrated on her acting career.

Tomohisa Yamashita, the handsome teacher and object of schoolgirl desire in *Close Range Love*, is a former child actor, TV star and host. His work includes the popular 2003 TV *dorama*, *Stand Up!!/Sutando Uppu!!*, in which he co-starred with Anne Suzuki and Shun Oguri, and this was quickly followed by the 2005 high school drama, *Producing Nobuta/Nobuta o Purodyūsu*. Perhaps more importantly, Yamashita is easily recognised as a former member of successful pop group NEWS, and is an accomplished solo musician who goes by the name of Yamapi, stylised as 'YamaP'. His inclusion as the forbidden love interest in *Close Range Love* builds on his intertextual worth as a star.

Masaki Okada is a TV star and model, now best known as Takuma Kakinouchi in the manga-based film, *I Give My First Love To You*. This explores the developing relationship between Takuma (Okada), a boy with a terminal illness, and Mayu (former child actor Mao Inoue). As the two grow into their high school years, their relationship deepens, underpinned by the knowledge that time is running out for Takuma. As found in Western 'terminal romance' films such as *The Fault in Our Stars* (2014, dir. Josh Boone), *Five Feet Apart* (2019, dir. Justin Baldoni), *Me and Earl and the Dying Girl* (2015, dir. Alfonso Gomez-Rejon) or *Now is Good* (2012, dir. Ol Parker), starring Dakota Fanning, *I Give My First Love To You* taps into the fears and insecurities heightened by the physical and cognitive changes occurring during adolescence and the fragility of life at any age.

Starring in *Have a Song on Your Lips*, Yui Aragaki began her career as
a model, before turning to acting in TV commercials and then branching
out into TV dramas, film and music, with her three albums all achieving top ten status in the Japanese charts. In the role of Yuri Kashiwagi,
a reserved replacement choir teacher, Yui gets to accentuate her musical
talent and play a mature and maturing character that is eventually sympathetic to the struggles and challenges faced by the girls and boys in the
choir. Yuri has returned from Tokyo and her role as a professional pianist
at the prestigious (partly fictionalised) 'Tokyo University of Music', to her
hometown (and school) on the Gotō Islands in Western Nagasaki, to cover
a maternity leave position. The return to her hometown is poignant, as
not only has Yuri's mother passed away while Yuri was in Tokyo studying,
adding a sense of guilt to her melancholy air, but a flashback scene explains
that the true cause of her malaise is a crippling grief that prevents her from
being able to play the piano. Like her character, Yui is also from a coastal
region of Japan: the Okinawa Prefecture, far from Tokyo.

In the 2014 film *If You Count to Five, It's Your Dream*, five members of
J-pop group Tokyo Girls' Style star in a drama set in an all-girls' school.
The five (Hitomi Arai, Ayano Konishi, Yuri Nakae, Mei Shōji and Miyu
Yamabe) also star together in another high school-based film, based on a
novel: the teen-horror *Kotodama: Spiritual Curse / Gakkō no Kaidan Noroi
no Kotodama* (2014, dir. Masayuki Ochiai). This latter film challenges their
'clean' pop personas by avoiding the usual path of romantic dramas as an
entry point into feature film acting. Furthering the link to their off-camera
personas, the characters in *Kotodama* adopt each actor's given name, so
that, for example, Hitomi Arai plays a schoolgirl named Hitomi. Since
these earlier cinematic roles, none of the girls appears to have acted in any
further films, concentrating on their music careers as a 'post-idol' group,
with the exception of Konishi, who 'graduated' (retired) from the group
in 2015, citing health problems.

Shō Hirano's appearance in 2018's *Honey* is notable within a film
stacked with a number of established and emerging actors and musicians.
As the troubled Onise, Shō was able to capitalise on his ascending acting career and, more importantly, his fame as a musical member of the
idol boy-band group King & Prince and as a former member of Kin Kan.
King & Prince was formed by the talent agency Kansai Johnny's Jr,
a hugely successful music production company founded by the controversial promoter, American-born Johnny Kitagawa. With King & Prince,
Shō's fame was reiterated when the group's popular music videos and
their songs were used as themes on successful TV dramas, as well as
when their singles achieved platinum status in the Japanese music charts.

Shō's co-star in *Honey*, Yūna Taira (as Kogure), is a well-established actor, first appearing as a child in Hirokazu Koreeda's *I Wish/Kiseki* (2011), before moving on to star in multiple TV dramas and high school films (including *Yell for the Blue Sky*, *The Dark Maidens* and *ReLIFE*). Supporting actor Kaho Mizutani (playing Kayo Yashiro) had established herself in the successful 2015 hit, *The Senior and the Girl*, and a string of TV dramas, and released her first music video in 2017. Even the 'oldest' role in *Honey*, Onise's mother, was played by Shinobu Nakayama, a former J-pop singer and veteran TV and film actor.

Another supporting role in *Honey* is taken by Nana Asakawa (playing shy exchange girl, Miyabi Nishigaki); she was a former member of the Super Girls pop group and a model and TV drama actress (she also appears in *The Werewolf Game*). As with many actors in high school films, Asakawa is older than many of the characters she plays. She is also recognisable as a 'gravure' swimsuit model, part of a publishing and video network that posts short, sexualised videos on platforms such as YouTube, which are shared widely on Pinterest and other platforms. Therefore, while Asakawa's feature film persona creates the illusion of an innocent schoolgirl, her modelling persona takes on a more adult tone. The star power of all of the actors mentioned above could be said to have played a role in this manga-based film attaining the ninth highest box-office takings on its release weekend in late March 2018.

Rainbow Days stars Reo Sano (as Natsuki Hashiba), since 2012 a member of the hugely successful GENERATIONS from EXILE TRIBE boy band, a spin-off from the early 2000s group known simply as EXILE, and part of the generation of Japanese bands that have multiple members (up to nineteen in Exile's earlier iterations). Sano earned his acting credentials in the 2014 season of the popular TV *dorama GTO: Great Teacher Onizuka*, before moving on to the big screen as a gang member in four films in the *High & Low* (sic) series of action dramas in 2016–17.

In a somewhat self-reflexive moment, the Cinderella-themed *Kiss Me at the Stroke of Midnight* features a storyline in which a (fictionally) famous heartthrob actor, tall and thin Kaede Ayase (Ryōta Katayose, also of GENERATIONS from EXILE TRIBE fame and an established film and TV actor), visits the school of the bookish, diminutive Hinana Hanazawa (Kanna Hashimoto, former member of J-pop group Rev. from DVL and an actor since childhood) to shoot a new film. Kaede's fame mirrors that of Ryota, both former members of popular boy bands (Kaede's fame arising from the fictitious Funny Bone band) who moved into acting. To further the intertextual nature, the film uses a GENERATIONS from EXILE TRIBE song as its theme over the final credits.

Actors also make their mark in particular genres of film, such as Ryō Yoshizawa, who plays timid, geeky Yori Suzuki in *Ano Ko No, Toriko*, and has starred in at least four other high school-based films including Ryūichi Hiroki's 2018 *Marmalade Boy/Mamarēdo Bōi* (with orange/blonde hair), *Wolf Girl and Black Prince/Ōkami Shōjo to Kuro Ōji* (2016, dir. Ryūichi Hiroki), *Blue Spring Ride/Aoharaido* (2014, dir. Takahiro Miki) and *Daily Lives of High School Boys/Danshi Kōkōsei no Nichijō* (2013, dir. Daigo Matsui). Of course, as actors grow older, their ability to play high school students becomes challenged. In 2020, the then twenty-six-year-old Yoshizawa played a university student in *Blue, Painful and Brittle/Aokute Itakute Mori* (dir. Shunsuke Kariyama), while in *Sakura* (2020, dir. Hiroshi Yazaki), he played an older university graduate.

Singer, dancer and former child-model Anna Ishii is part of the eleven-member girl group E-Girls (Exile Girls, a 'sister act' to Exile), and is able to capitalise on her considerable dance skills in the lead role in the high school film *Girls Step/Gāruzu Suteppu* (2015, dir. Yasuhiro Kawamura), where she is advertised as an E-Girl in promotional trailers. Ishii also appears in *Your Lie in April*, but this time in a non-musical or dance role. As with other actors, Ishii's youthful looks are an advantage for playing a high school student, although she also seems mature enough to star in 'older' roles, such as a young woman starting college, in *Spring Has Come/Supuringu Hazu Kamu* (2015, but released in 2017, dir. Ryūhei Yoshino), not to be confused with the 2018 TV mini-series *Haru ga Kita* (also known as *Spring Has Come*). In 2017 she reverted back to another high school film, the anime-based *The Anthem of the Heart/Kokoro ga Sakebitagatterunda* (lit. *The Heart Wants to Shout*) (dir. Naoto Kumazawa), in a supporting role as Natsuki Nitō. In a 2020 release, Ishii plays a lead role opposite *ReLIFE*'s Taishi Nakagawa in another high school-based film with the lengthy title of *The Ashes of My Flesh and Blood is the Vast Flowing Galaxy/Kudakechiru Tokoro o Misete Ageru* (aka *My Blood and Bones in a Flowing Galaxy*) (dir. SABU, aka Hiroyuki Tanaka).

As noted in the case of Tomohisa Yamashita, there appears to be a clearer pathway for Japanese actors to move seamlessly from child actor to youth and then adult actor. In the US, high school roles can be fortuitous for actors like Reese Witherspoon (*Election*), Sean Penn (*Fast Times at Ridgemont High*) or Emma Stone (*Easy A*), whose high school parts would open the door for long-standing 'A-list' Hollywood status. For others, the high school film may see them locked into typecast roles until age renders them unable to play a school-aged character effectively or, in some cases, spells the end of their acting career. For instance, Mia Sara from *Ferris Bueller's Day Off* continued to act in films and TV programmes but was perhaps unable to replicate the success of the 1986 hit film. *Easy A*'s Amanda Bynes announced a hiatus from acting following the success of that film. In Japan, though, apart from Yamashita, others such as *One Week Friends'* Haruna Kawaguchi (who found fame in her early teens) and *Yell for the Blue Sky*'s Mirai Shida (who began acting on TV aged seven before moving to feature films at age ten), the path to acting success has been consistent.

One advantage with established (young) stars is not only that they have a name that can be used for promotional purposes; using a post-adolescent star avoids the unpredictability of the physical changes that take place during puberty and may occur with a younger actor. This is a common theme in Western high school films, including *To Sir, with Love*, whose 'Babs' was played by pop star Lulu when she was already nineteen years old; her co-star Christian Roberts (Bert Denham) was twenty-three, as was US actor Reese Witherspoon in her standout role as Tracy Flick in *Election*. In *Hyouka: Forbidden Secrets*, all four of the key actors, playing high school students in their first or second year and therefore estimated to be between 16 and 18 years old, were themselves between 21 and 23 years of age at the time of shooting in early 2016 (for a November 2017 release). In *The Ashes of My Flesh and Blood . . .*, twenty-one-year-old Anna Ishii similarly plays a girl in her first year of senior high school, with her twenty-two-year-old co-star, Taishi Nakagawa, in the role of a final-year student.

Conclusion

As with any cinema industry, the ability to attract an audience (with accompanying box office returns) is crucial for its survival. The school setting in Japan's high school films reflects a recognisable contemporary society capitalising on themes of nostalgia. This feeling is amplified by archetypal images of manga and anime, and through the stereotypical framing of characters in settings such as the seasonal bloom of the cherry blossom. Through drawing on the intertextuality of known stars from the fields of music, TV and modelling, the audience is primed to enjoy the films with recognition of a clear genre filled with iconic images and established performers. These factors all combine to create the familiar images of the on-screen high school and its (fictional) student life.

CHAPTER 6

Exploring Taboos

The current flood of school-based *seishun eiga* follows a mostly clear pattern of non-offensive films that would easily pass being rated 'PG' (parental guidance) in the West. Within this cohort, though, a number touch upon issues that are potentially more problematic or controversial. The degree to which they focus on these themes or behaviours dictates each film's suitability for younger or mainstream audiences. *Close Range Love*, for instance, with its look at a teacher/student relationship, suggests impropriety, but there is no indication that the age difference might suggest anything approaching paedophilia, with Yuni clearly established as being eighteen years old in one of the opening scenes. *Assassination Classroom* features violence but no blood, apart from one student's cut lip. In this chapter, I investigate the thematic elements presented in recent high school films, and the ways in which they use varying degrees of subtlety to draw attention to topics that may be seen as taboo within the school environment, or more broadly in Japanese society.

One concern in Japanese society is the possibility, as with the 1997 Kobe school murder, that parents are so caught up with their own responsibilities to their employer and the nation that they have very limited knowledge about what their child is up to during each day (Yoneyama 1999: 6). As already described, children are often responsible for getting themselves to and from school from a very early age, without the assistance of an adult. Their lives, therefore, may not be as sheltered as their parents imagine, resulting in behaviours that break existing taboos and cultural codes. As many of these films illustrate, elements of shame and embarrassment are heightened during adolescence and the forming of an individual's identity.

Shame, Ridicule and Embarrassment

In Japanese society, behaviour can be seen as emanating from a prevailing sense of *Nihonjinron* (Japaneseness) and the collectivist nature of a society in which shame and the loss of 'face' are viewed as letting the nation down. The competitive nature of Japan's examination-led education system provides filmmakers with plenty of opportunities to emphasise the need for conformity within the school system as students strive to avoid disappointing themselves and their family, school, community or nation. In writing on *The Family Game/Kazoku Gēmu* (1983, dir. Yoshimitsu Morita), McDonald refers to a scene where:

> [a] teacher returns exams to students, beginning with the lowest score. It is a girl, who covers her head with a paper bag. Several more bottom-ranking names are called out as exams are tossed out the window. (2006: 144)

While these highly exaggerated notions of shame at poor academic performance may strike a universal chord, they nevertheless stand out against the backdrop of Japan's reputation as a polite society.

Following the Kobe school murder, interviews with other fourteen-year-old students seemed to support claims of offensive behaviour on the part of teachers, with comments such as 'There is a teacher who calls us "you stupid pig"' and 'My homeroom teacher said "you are all stupid"' (Yoneyama 1999: 4). While these sorts of comments may or may not have been widespread amongst Japanese students at that time, they nevertheless indicate that not all teacher/student relationships were on a positive footing. Films such as *Kamen Teacher: The Movie/Gekijōban Kamen Tīchā* (2014, dir. Kentarō Moriya) or 2019's *Prince of Legend* (dirs Hayato Kawai and Kentarō Moriya) deal with the need for a disciplined classroom, and the use of shame as a weapon in bringing students into line. In *Rainbow Days*, the sunglasses-toting, unshaven and quick-tempered Tabuchi-*sensei* (Ken'ichi Takitō) berates a group of (academically) poorly performing male students by shouting at them:

> Tabuchi: It would be better if idiots like you could spend your summer vacation without supplementary lessons, you know.

In *Kamen Teacher: The Movie*, dark images of rioting students preface a move by the state to crack down on lawlessness. The overarching message is the shame of the nation in allowing its youth to rebel. An ominous voiceover drones that, in the year '20xx', 'corporal punishment by teachers was banned', resulting in the latter becoming powerless to stop delinquent behaviour. The voiceover continues, '[t]o control everything with the fear of power, special teachers were despatched throughout the whole nation', before images of motor bike-riding, masked teachers are shown in a variety of hyper-masculine poses, mirroring the decades-old tradition of *Kamen* [masked] *Rider* TV heroes.

The unpredictable power implicit in the teacher/student relationship also flares briefly in *Chihayafuru Part 3/Chihayafuru Musubi* (2018, dir. Norihiro Koizumi), when Arata Wataya (US-born Mackenyu Arata, son of Japanese acting and martial arts superstar Sonny Chiba) asks his teacher about the possibility of forming a new club for *karuta* (a competitive Japanese card game). Wataya gently agrees with his teacher that it might not be the right time, before the teacher aggressively snaps back at him, 'Who are you calling stupid?!' Confused, Wataya quietly responds, 'I didn't say anything.' The teacher does not look up, so Wataya rolls his eyes then politely excuses himself. While the scene is brief, and seemingly not important to the overall narrative, the teacher's unexpected response nevertheless signals a discrepancy in the power structure between the two characters and the teacher's underlying hostile but defensive nature.

In *Have a Song on Your Lips*, students are gathered for an assembly and quietly chatting before proceedings begin, when an older male teacher yells abruptly and aggressively through the microphone, 'You lot are so noisy! Pipe down!' The students immediately fall silent and sit to attention, disciplined and shamed into action. In *ReLIFE*, group shame is replaced by Arata's individual shame when he is transported back to his seventeen-year-old self and finds he is unable to pass a series of elementary school tests. As an adult, his sense of shame is heightened by the underlying thought that he did not try his hardest when younger.

Individual shame is also demonstrated when the formerly anti-establishment Sayaka returns from summer cram school in *Flying Colours*. Sayaka has returned her hair to its natural black but is falling asleep in class due to her constant studying while trying to maintain her active social life. This sleeping behaviour is not unexpected amongst Japanese youth, with a number of research studies drawing attention to the habit of over-tired students, and one recent study by Mizuno et al. (2019) showing the impact of extra-curricular studies and (sporting and social) club involvement on teenagers' sleep patterns, including sleeping in class. In this instance, though, in front of the other students (in an all-girls school), Sayaka's teacher, Takashi Nishimura (Ken Yasuda), wakes her at her desk, sarcastically suggesting that the school could provide her with her own room. She responds that there is no need as she is heading to enrol at the prestigious Keio University in Tokyo. The other students laugh and the constantly sarcastic Nishimura-*sensei* responds loudly:

Nishimura: Are you kidding? How could someone as worthless as you be admitted to Keio?

Nishimura throws down a challenge to the effect that, if Sayaka makes it to Keio, he will perform a naked handstand in the school grounds. One of the girls asks Sayaka to make it a bet, so that if she is not accepted at Keio, then she must perform a handstand (in her underwear). While the strong-willed, confident Sayaka is not bowed by the challenge, such behaviour from a teacher not only shows disregard for the unfair power dynamic of the classroom, but also adds a sexualised element to the bet through the threat of nudity (or near-nudity).

In a reversal of her regular high school teacher's behaviour, Sayaka's cram school tutor, Yoshitaka Tsubota (Atsushi Ito), never resorts to sarcasm or cruelty, no matter how inane Sayaka's comments may be. In the scene following the 'nude bet', Tsubota-*sensei* sits across from Sayaka to review her latest test. He questions her response to the English-language question, 'Is there a Santa Claus?'

> Sayaka: (Of course) Santa Claus exists.
> Tsubota [joking]: Obviously!
> Sayaka: So I do not understand the question being asked.
> Tsubota [serious]: Could it be that you think Santa Claus exists, Sayaka?
> Sayaka: Yes, because he appears on TV.
> Tsubota: Huh?
> Sayaka: Huh?

At this moment, Tsubota could have laughed at Sayaka, but instead he gives her another example:

> Tsubota: Ultraman [the costumed superhero] also appears on television, right?

The truth dawns on Sayaka.

> Sayaka: So it's all a lie? Really! [she hangs her head] What a shock!

Tsubota realises that Sayaka's general knowledge is lacking and is immediately supportive of her trying to gain further understanding of the world around her. His kind and nurturing nature prevents Sayaka from any major embarrassment (even though the students listening behind her are quietly chuckling) by diverting her attention to the new book she needs to read. Tsubota's devotion to teaching is reiterated later when Sayaka's tormenting teacher, the older Nishimura, meets with Tsubota to deter him from trying to make Sayaka take the entrance exam for Keio University. Near tears, Tsubota emphatically protests to the senior teacher:

> Tsubota: She is the existence of the infinite possibilities of a very good girl!

Tsubota then spells out his philosophy to Nishimura: if the teacher thinks poorly of the students, then the teacher him- or herself is not fit for the profession.

Discriminatory behaviour of a different kind is found in *Have a Song on Your Lips*, which tackles the issue of disability and the repercussions this may have for the family of the disabled person. This is personified by Satoru's father and his perceived embarrassment at being seen in public with his eldest son. The young boy, Satoru, has an older brother, Akio (played by rock musician Daichi Watanabe), with autism, and must take him home each day from the waterfront, where he waits while his father works. Satoru does not tell his classmates about Akio but Yuri soon finds out, and realises that Satoru is missing choir practice because of his touching commitment to his brother. As Yuri reads through Satoru's homework task of writing a letter to his future self, we hear his voice saying:

> Satoru: Dear myself in fifteen years, Are you still with your brother? Nah, you must be. His being around is what I'm most thankful for, since if he wasn't born autistic, I never would have been born. I know this much: in the future when my parents are gone, he won't be able to get by alone. So my parents made a decision, they decided to give Akio a little sibling to watch over him after they die. And that's why I'm here now. If he was born a normal kid, I probably wouldn't be here. I have no doubts about my future, I know exactly why I'm here. But sometimes, only sometimes, I wish he wasn't here. There are times I don't feel for him. But I will most likely stay by his side my whole life. That's the reason I'm here, after all.

The scene cuts between images of a visibly moved Yuri reading the letter, and of the two boys walking home in the sunset by the bay. Satoru stops and watches his brother walk ahead, but Akio also stops when he becomes distracted by a bus-stop bench that is jutting out from a wall, creating what Akio sees as a distressing interruption to the order of things. Satoru runs up and pushes the bench back, releasing Akio from his compulsive behaviour, and he begins walking again. The non-diegetic voiceover switches to the diegetic, as Satoru runs toward his brother, calling out, 'I'm glad you're around.'

While Satoru (mostly) keeps quiet about his brother, their father, Kōichi (Shigemitsu Ogi), appears to be shamed by Akio's disability. When the family goes to support Satoru in the national choir competition in the city, Kōichi shepherds Akio to a seat in the foyer, not wishing to bring him into the auditorium and telling Satoru that they can listen from the foyer. After the performance, Satoru discovers that Akio could not hear the song:

> Satoru: So you couldn't hear it then?
> Akio: Not yet.

Kōichi intervenes, roughly grabbing his eldest son and ordering: 'Akio, we're going home.' As Kōichi tries to drag a now agitated Akio from the building, Satoru stands helplessly by until Yuri steps forward and assembles the choir to sing an uplifting song just for Akio.

Japanese high school films also tend to take a guarded approach to the subject of class, considering the divides that exist between the various strata of society. By the close of the Meiji period in the early twentieth century, 'the schoolgirl was unilaterally represented by the daughters of Japan's most affluent families' (Czarnecki 2005: 50). This meant that 'lower-class girls who possessed neither the leisure nor funds to attend higher schools were eliminated from this schoolgirl coterie' (50). In the live action feature of *Ouran High School Host Club*, adapted from a manga and an anime TV series, Haruhii attends the prestigious Ouran Academy on a scholarship for students in need of financial assistance. At one point, she is referred to by a fellow student as 'our school's only "common" person', and the wealthy Michelle condescendingly offers her lunch 'leftovers' to Haruhii. Because the concept of shame runs so deep in Japanese society, Sandrisser notes the feeling that 'the Japanese notion of what is public and what is private transcends class and education in Japan' (2018: 15); therefore, Haruhii's private economic circumstances become public knowledge.

In terms of a benchmarking standard for adolescent behaviour, earlier Japanese high school films were assumed to borrow from US Cold War-era films, in which 'images of teachers [. . .] were the embodiment of high moral principles and traditions' (Fedorov et al. 2019: 7). As seen in the examples above, though, in contemporary films the teachers may be portrayed as lacking such high moral standards. Similarly, female students are not always presented as upholding the expected moral values of Japanese youth society.

The ribald *Yarukkya Knight*, for instance, is an *ecchi* film (in essence, playfully erotic rather than explicit pornographic) that features a number of incidents where male students, overcome with sexual desire, find themselves being punished by the female students who were the object of their crude behaviour. In one such episode, several boys are tied to chairs, their hands handcuffed behind their heads. In front of them, a small group of girls have set up microphone stands with wire devices just above the boys' laps for the purposes of electrocution, should the boys become sexually aroused. The girls then project a picture of a naked girl, with blacked-out sections over her breasts. The boys moan, and as they do so, the girls remove one of the boxes, almost revealing her breasts. The boys are unable to control themselves, and soon all are given electric shocks through their genitals. As the girls begin showing another picture, one of the boys becomes aroused again, and just as his (clothed) erection is about to hit the wire, a hand reaches into his lap. The camera pulls back, and surprisingly the hand belongs to another boy, a new arrival at the school, Gōsuke Makoto (Tomoya Nakamura), who wants to stop the shaming of his male classmates.

While *Yarukkya Knight* maintains a comic tone, the boys' sexually charged actions, such as when Gōsuke assaults a group of girls by lifting their skirts to expose their underwear to onlooking boys – an overt *panchira* (upskirting), the girls soon extract retribution, their 'leader', Shizuka Misaki (Niina Endō), kicking him with great force in the groin. The other girls then pile on top of him, violently punching and kicking him, before removing all of his clothes and tying him to a pillar. Thus, the shame is again turned on to the male character, this time with direct physical violence. In a series of flashback scenes, Shizuka's position is confirmed after leading an attack against their original male teacher, Tetsumi Arashi (professional wrestler Alexander Ōtsuka), an older man with *hentai* (pervert) desires for his female students. Arashi is then humiliatingly banished from the school. Shizuka beats him savagely and (again) leaves him bloodied and bruised, lying naked in the school hallway. She then announces that she will end male control of their lives and will establish the school under what one of the boys refers to as a form of martial law.

Shizuka's rule looks like being established over the school but soon Arashi-*sensei* announces his return. The girls decide that their safest option is to join forces with the boys against Arashi and begin to train the cowardly Gōsuke in martial arts, to be able to overcome Arashi. Their teacher (now possibly part-robot) arrives back at school and they meet him en masse at the school gates. Dressed in black like a *yakuza* boss and with his hair cut in an aggressive mohawk, he summarily dispatches Gōsuke beyond the school roof with one punch. Shizuka steps forward and he throws a dog collar and chain at her feet, ordering her, in a humiliating tone, to put it on herself. Shizuka is about to refuse when the petite, bespectacled Chikako Hoshi (Elisa Yanagi) cuts in front to defend her friend. Arashi kneels down and begins to lift her skirt, peeking underneath, when Takashi Yamada (Reiha Masaki) hits him over the head with a steel pipe. Arashi feels nothing and throws Takashi aside. Shizuka kneels and, to the horror of the remaining students, begins to fasten the dog collar around her neck. He picks up the chain and Shizuka, completely humiliated, kneels beside him like a subservient dog.

There is a shout and the crowd of students parts to reveal Gōsuke, in a classic anime pose, legs wide apart and slightly turned to one side. He warns the much stronger Arashi to stay out of their high school. They begin to wrestle, and in a comical fantasy moment (it is a comedy, after all), Gōsuke manages to draw Arashi into a 'magic circle' drawn on the ground, upon which other boys place erotic magazines. A magical pink glow surrounds them as Gōsuke, according to their plans, 'powers up' to absorb superhuman strength (a common Japanese trope found in texts from manga and anime such as the Sailor Moon franchise, and live-action *tokusatsu* TV series such as Ultraman) from the erotic images. Unperturbed, Arashi insults Gōsuke's masculinity and again flings him away. Gōsuke returns once more, and in their final effort his female classmates form a corridor for him to run toward Arashi. The boys kneel next to the girls, and as Gōsuke runs, the boys lift the girl's skirts, empowering Gōsuke once again in the pink glow. By the time he passes Chikako, she is twirling her underwear on her finger, and Gōsuke's assumed glimpse of her naked midriff gives him an energy burst that allows him to knock Arashi (momentarily) unconscious. Arashi recovers and again throws Gōsuke aside. In a final attempt, Shizuka kneels beside Gōsuke and lifts her skirt. Empowered through a brightly glowing, orange 'erection', he again attacks the larger man, knocking his clothes from his body, so that he ends up wearing only a *fundoshi* (cloth underwear) or *mawashi* (loincloth underwear of a sumo wrestler), and he falls backward into the chalked 'magic circle' like a defeated wrestler. It is difficult to overlook the unabashed and sexist gender bias of *Yarukkya Knight*, despite its overarching theme being that the unity of boys and girls can overcome bullying. As an *ecchi* film, it plays with the same tropes as many Western films that present youthful eroticism in a comic way.

Other films blur the line between *ecchi*, *hentai* and *pinku* films, notably *What's Going on with My Sister?/Saikin, Imōto no Yōsu ga Chotto Okashiinda ga?* (lit. *Recently, My Sister Has Been Acting Strange*) (dirs Yūki Aoyama and Iggy Coen). In this film, which has *pinku* features of overt nudity and sex scenes, the typical gender role of the over-sexed teenage boy is reversed when Mitsuki Kanzaki (Tenka Hashimoto) feels shame at her inability to control her sexual urges. The concept of a *pinku* film is difficult to define, and as Zahlten (2019: 26) notes: '[i]n forming a generic identity, pink film crucially relied as heavily on a set of stylistic conventions and paratexts as it did on various production, distribution, exhibition and reception practices'.

Adolescent Awkwardness

The onset of puberty and the physical, mental and cognitive developments experienced by teenagers forms another readily identifiable trope in high school films. In the West, such films take on the form of the 'teen' film, a genre also popular with TV series such as NBC's 'Freaks and Geeks' (1999–2000) and Fox's 'Glee' (2009–15), both having a heavy focus on the mental and physical dramas that accompany adolescent development. As with these Western texts, the awkwardness of adolescence is a key feature of Japanese films, as it is a theme capable of evoking laughter, pathos and empathy. *Ano Ko No, Toriko*, for example, presents shy, bespectacled Yori, who has just arrived at a new school in Tokyo when he is mesmerised by the beauty of a girl running past. He gapes as she passes, smiling at him, which unsettles him, and he drops the bundle of papers he is holding. Scrambling to retrieve the papers from the ground, he fails to notice that she has returned, until she passes him one of the dropped papers. Yori keeps his head bowed (Figure 6.1), unable to look her in the eye. When he finally raises his head and their eyes meet, the girl, Shizuku (Yūko Araki), realises that they know each other, and were former primary school class-mates back in rural Japan. As Shizuku steps toward Yori, he cowers away from the possibility of physical contact, not because of who she is, but because she is a girl.

In reference to Shunji Iwai's 2001 drama, *All About Lily Chou-Chou/ Ririi Shushu no Subete*, Kiejziewicz notes how the bullied and humiliated schoolboy, Yūichi (Hayato Ichihara), tries to escape reality by obsessing over the music of (fictional) pop star Lily Chou-Chou, but this offers him 'no escape from coming-of-age suffering' (2018: 83), or as the character of Veronica Sawyer (Winona Ryder) in the 1988 US film *Heathers* refers to it,

Figure 6.1 Yori cowers before Shizuku in *Ano Ko No, Toriko* (Hakuhodo, 2018).

'teen angst bullshit' (Harrison 2017: 15). Yūichi's continued torment results in him continually staring at the ground, so that he is unable 'to articulate with even that elementary and intuitive form of communication, the look' (Montano 2018, cited in Kiejziewicz 2018: 83). This lack of articulation or perception is also found in *The Kirishima Thing*, where awkwardness with the opposite sex is clearly apparent when film club geek Maeda notices his female classmate, Kasumi (Ai Hashimoto), in a screening of Shin'ya Tsukamoto's cult classic, *Tetsuo: The Iron Man/Tetsuo* (1989). Afterwards, Maeda buys Kasumi a drink from a vending machine. She sits on a bench as he returns from collecting a drink for himself. When he returns, she slides across the seat to make room for him, but he misses the social cue and remains standing awkwardly beside the bench, facing forward rather than turning to face Kasumi.

While public displays of affection by young people are found in Japan, Sandrisser notes a feeling that 'young people would stop kissing publicly as they got older, since, eventually, embarrassment would overpower rebellious behaviour' (2018: 15). In high school films, though, characters tend to be more circumspect when it comes to kissing. In this way, teen awkwardness plays a role in *Make a Bow and Kiss* when Mikami demands that his new girlfriend, An Kishimoto (Elaiza Ikeda), kisses him while they are on a public thoroughfare, slightly sheltered by darkness. Terrified, she asks:

> Kishimoto: Right here? Now?
> Mikami: I want you to prove that you like me. [pause] Please?

She pushes him and runs a short distance away, before turning to face him:

> Kishimoto: It's impossible! I can't do it yet.

They face each other for a moment, before she mutters an informal, friendly:

> Kishimoto: See ya later. Goodnight!

The tense situation is diffused by her light-hearted dismissal, yet the tension and anxiety she felt just moments earlier have left their mark.

As with high school films from across many cultures, it is 'the notion of popularity, introduced by cliques and hierarchies', which forms a point of similarity in representations of the adolescent high school experience (Harrison 2017: 3). While Japanese society is said to operate at a collective level, rather than the individualism of the West, the period of adolescence is fraught with self-identity issues, often based on perceptions of popularity and fitting in with one's peers. In *The Senior and the Girl*, it is Rika, the 'girl', who experiences the awkwardness in her crush on Minohara. When Minohara admits that he has feelings for another (senior) girl, Rika nevertheless blurts out, 'I like you!' Minohara responds:

> Minohara: What are you talking about? You're being carried away too much by the atmosphere. This is a weird topic. How stupid.
> Rika [sadly]): I'm sorry.
> Minohara [smiling]: But [pause] you do have courage.

The scene finishes with a close-up of Rika's face, confused and uncertain as to whether Minohara likes her or not. Later, after they spend some time together rowing on a lake and attending a festival, all seems to be going well for Rika until the senior girl, now a university student, Aoi Okita (Riria Kojima), runs past them and Minohara turns to go with her. Minohara later apologises to Rika in their club room, but when she asks about Aoi, Minohara admits that Aoi has a boyfriend. Rika struggles to make sense of the situation:

> Rika: That person, Okita-san, had a boyfriend?
> Minohara: She has.
> Rika: Then why do you still like her? Well, after all [pause], the other party has someone she likes, why do you still stay in love with her? After all, she has a boyfriend already!

Rika is getting increasingly agitated but Minohara turns away from her:

> Rika [cont.]: Umm. She doesn't look at you that way, and . . . isn't it kind of pointless?
> Minohara [turns sharply]: SHUT UP!

There is a long silence as the two stare at each other. Minohara apologises:

> Minohara: My bad. (pause) Sorry.

He leaves the shattered Rika standing alone, unsure of what to do, before musing aloud and trying to put a positive spin on the encounter:

> Rika. I see, Senpai [pause] is the same as me.

Dejected, she leaves the room as a voiceover begins:

> Rika [v/o]: The person I like likes another person too.

These scenes develop the realisations that are part of a broader maturation of the adolescents as they attempt to figure out the world around them.

Familiar tropes also occur in *Real Girl* when anime-obsessed, glasses-wearing teen Hikari Tsutsui (Hayato Sano, from *Have a Song on Your Lips* and acclaimed boy band, M!LK) is forced to work with noted 'bad girl', Iroha Igarashi (Ayami Nakajō from *Let's Go, Jets!* and *Nisekoi: False Love*), whom he finds breathtakingly attractive. Known simply as Tsutsui, he is chronically shy around girls, spending his time at home speaking to an imagined anime magical girl, a Sailor Moon-type animated figure, Ezomichi (voiced by Sayaka Kanda). Iroha tries to break the ice with him while they are walking one day, and even suggests they go out together. However, Tsutsui is ill-equipped to speak in a civil tone to a 'real girl' (a '3D girl', as the Japanese title suggests), and unleashes an uncalled-for tirade back at her:

Tsutsui: Don't screw with me! Don't just smile and try to break into a person's heart! All you're going to do is trample all over me! Then I'll slowly start to get feelings for you. Then I won't be able to think straight! Did you think I was going to say 'yahoo!' and jump for joy? Don't think that you can do everything with that face of yours.

Iroha eyes him cautiously before speaking.

Iroha: That's true. [pause] I just meant it as a joke. Sorry.

She walks by him and he turns to face the fence, trying to figure out what had happened.

Tsutsui [aloud, to himself]: Was I in the wrong? Was it my fault?

Once Tsutsui is convinced by his best friend and fellow geek Yūto Itō (played by the actor simply known as Yūtarō) that he really should go out with Iroha, Tsutsui accepts and the two become a couple. Tsutsui is not convinced, and speaking with the (imagined) Ezomichi, explains that Iroha is 'taking me away from my anime community . . . what do I do to get out of this?' Ezomichi is no help, though, acting as a negative force by prompting him to end the relationship, stating, 'There's no way you can love a 3D girl!' Meanwhile, Tsutsui's family can hear him talking aloud while he is alone in his bedroom and fear for his sanity.

In *You Are the Apple of My Eye*, awkwardness is played out through a running joke about Junon's (Keisuke Nakata) quick physical reaction 'down there', as he clutches embarrassingly at his groin each time a girl flirts with him, seemingly unable to control his erection. Such characters are readily found in Japan's popular media, such as Kohta in the manga and anime of 'Highschool of the Dead', an *otaku* who is seen as

'a tongue-in-cheek parody of both the target audience and the creators':
that is, young Japanese males (Greene 2018: 7). Thus, in *You Are the Apple
of My Eye*, the boys playfully chat with the girls and make constant sexual
references, but seemingly with no intention of acting on them. Kōsuke
explains:

> Kōsuke [v/o]: The elements of youth are ambition, uncertainty, delusion, sexual
> desire. Regret, humiliation. And first love.

While apparently addressing the problems all teenagers face, Kōsuke's
explanation is also deeply introspective as he tries to reassure himself and
build his confidence around girls, unlike Junon, whose behaviour is completely controlled by his physical responses.

Embarrassment takes a different form in *Drowning Love* when Natsume's
male schoolfriend, Ōtomo (Daiki Shigeoka), drops by her house and
begins to question her about her latest photo shoot and whether she posed
nude. In a light-hearted, perhaps improvised scene, they pace around each
other as he questions her:

> Ōtomo: Is it true? That you photographed nude?
> Natsume [smiling]: What are you talking about?
> Ōtomo: So it's just a false rumour?
> Natsume: No way would I do that. I just got photographed for a photobook. Ha!
> Ōtomo: Ha, ha!

Natsume's mother interrupts briefly, then they continue.

> Ōtomo: When I finally take a look at it, do you understand what would be the case
> the next time I see you at school?
> Natsume: That's ridiculous. Pervert. [laughs]
> Ōtomo: I'm a pervert! [laughs] Your mother's pretty too!
> Natsume: You like older women?
> Ōtomo: Um . . . I like the face.
> Natsume [pretending not to hear]: What?
> Ōtomo: I like the face!

Their continual pacing and giggling show that this is not a regular conversation, but by keeping the tone non-serious, they are able to avoid the
embarrassment of speaking about nudity and desire.

In *Rainbow Days*, awkwardness appears as a delayed response after
Natsuki Hashiba (Reo Sano), sick with fever, collapses into Anna
Kobayakawa's (Ai Yoshikawa) arms. As he falls, he presses his lips against
Anna's and for a moment they remain frozen, he with his eyes shut and she
gazing at him, but not pulling away. In a later scene, Natsuki confesses to

Anna that he thinks he has behaved badly, bowing deeply at the waist, his arms firmly by his side, in a traditional and emphatic apology. Although he confesses to not remembering exactly what he did (because of the fever), he feels that somehow Anna deserves an apology. Instead, she remains detached, telling him that nothing happened, and then walks away, leaving Natsuki standing, stunned.

Awkwardness appears as a visual response in *Love and Lies* when Aoi subconsciously plays with her fringe if she is lying or speaking about something she does not believe in. Much like the earlier-cited clutching of uniforms in moments of anxiety, these non-verbal movements are a way of dealing with internal suffering through forms of habitual behaviour. Each of the above examples builds on perceptions of adolescence and the multiple embarrassments that seem to accompany the changes occurring during and beyond puberty.

'Real' High School Violence

The rise of violence in Japanese films takes many forms, from the samurai films of the 1960s (to which Quentin Tarantino paid homage in *Kill Bill Volumes 1 and 2*, 2003/4), to the heightened sexual violence in Ōshima's *In the Realm of the Senses/Ai no Koriida* (1976), the ultra-violence of Takashi Miike's *Ichi the Killer/Koroshiya Ichi* (2001), and more recent zombie films such as *I Am A Hero/Ai Amu A Hiirō* (2015, dir. Shinsuke Satō) and *One Cut of the Dead/Kamera o Tomeru na!* (lit. *Don't Stop the Camera!*) (2017, dir. Shin'ichirō Ueda). In school-based films, *Battle Royale* seemed to set the benchmark for violence, and only a select number of films since then have utilised the theme of overt violence, such as the series of eight *The Werewolf Games* films produced between 2013 and 2020. One stand-alone film (not part of a series) is Sion Sono's hyper-violent *Tag*, which features a culmination of recognisably iconic school images, from the built environment of the institutional buildings to the uniformed schoolgirls. *Tag* built on Sono's earlier *Suicide Club/Jisatsu Sākuru* (2001, lit. *Suicide Circle* – as in a 'circle of friends'), a film made and released in the shadow of the *Battle Royale* controversy.

For international audiences, posters and promotional materials for *Battle Royale* consisted mostly of 'a stark grey photograph of the "class" of schoolchildren featured in the film, . . . [which,] while understated, makes the film's children-killing-children content pretty clear' (Martin 2015: 76). Much of the controversy around the film in foreign countries was not just because of its violence (as noted, not necessarily unusual for Japanese audiences), but because its makers were keen for school-aged children to see it. In Japan, however, it seemed that state opposition was mostly concerned with the film's veiled criticism of the nation's education system, and local marketing centred on its 'teenage melodrama and emotional resonance' (78–9). Foreign responses were mixed, with the film soon cementing its place in the pantheon of great Japanese cinema, Patrick Galloway, for instance, referring to it as 'a teenage bloodbath epic with a heart' (2006: 116). Tom Vick was later to write that the 'sight of Japanese schoolgirls mowing one another down with machine guns in between gossiping about who likes which boy is so ludicrously grotesque that it makes you feel guilty for laughing' (2007: 61).

The *Battle Royale* films mirror strict ideals of institutional disciplinarity, with the formal modes of authority, practised under the iron rule of Takeshi 'Beat' Kitano's Kitano-*sensei* (referencing the actor's real name and cinematic reputation for playing violent characters – although he was equally well known as a TV comedian), appearing to reflect Durkheim's views of discipline. For instance, in 1916, Durkheim wrote that '[r]espect for legitimate authority, which is to say moral authority, will have to be reawakened and the religion of the rule will have to be inculcated in the child' (in Pickering 1979: 161), a code seemingly reflected in Japan's educational system but reconsidered in the major reforms of the early 2000s. Yet, in the same paragraph, Durkheim points to the need for the individual to play their part in ensuring that the formal system is effective in controlling and shaping the child: 'He [sic] will have to be taught the joys of acting in conjunction with others, according to the dictates of an impersonal law, common to everyone' (161).

As mentioned earlier, the school environment, and requirements such as those around wearing uniforms, act as a disciplinary space in which 'students are agents, and uniforms are the agency through which the official ideo-institutional forces construct subjectivities' (McVeigh 2000: 48). This plays out to an extent in the *Battle Royale* films as classmates try to work in unison, despite being pitted against each other. Unity also occurs in the *Assassination Classroom* series, where an alien life form appears as a teacher who threatens to destroy the world unless his students can kill him first. Contrary to this, the necessity for survival in the earlier *Battle Royale* films means that this unity must eventually be abandoned for each individual's survival within the disciplinary rules of the 'game'. Durkheim also warns of the danger of a rigid system of discipline where:

[a]ssuredly the mechanical, punctilious discipline that was practised formerly cannot be too strongly condemned, for it worked contrary to its aim that, through its unreasonable demands, it kindled the spirit of resistance and rebellion. School discipline,

on the contrary, must appear to children as something good and sacred – the condition of their happiness and moral well-being. (161)

Thus, for Durkheim, the end-point of discipline is positive, unlike in the
Battle Royale episodes where the conclusion can only be tragic (except,
perhaps, for any student who manages to escape harm). Durkheim's pedagogical aim is not designed for immediate gratification, but ultimately
for the graduated student: 'In this way, when they are men [sic], they will
accept spontaneously and consciously that social discipline which cannot
be weakened without endangering the community' (161).

In the *Battle Royale*, *Assassination Classroom* and *Werewolf Game* films,
students are faced with moral and ethical challenges. Has their prior institutionalised education prepared them for this moment? Once any initial
shock at their predicament has passed, it seems that the students accept
their fate and employ strategies to ensure their survival. In early scenes in
Battle Royale, 'disrespect for authority (of the teacher and the State) is met
with swift and violent retribution' (Arai 2003: 374), setting the parameters for the students' own disturbing, desperate behaviour. One precedent
for the *Battle Royale* films was *Sailor Suit and Machine Gun*/*Sērāfuku to
Kikanjū* (1981, dir. Shinji Sōmai), where a delinquent schoolgirl inherits
control of her father's *yakuza* gang and, toward the end of the film, grabs
a machinegun (as suggested by the title) to mow down a competing *yakuza*
boss. This was one of the earlier films, as Kinsella suggests, that shifted
the focus to 'deviant schoolgirls' concurrent with trends across Japanese
pop culture, manga and anime, which were moving away from 'young boys
(*shōnen*) and towards young women (*shōjo*)' (Kinsella 2002: 224). The violence in this film is, however, tame compared to the visceral, unrelenting
nature of *Battle Royale*.

By 2001, Sono's *Suicide Club* had emerged as a small-budget, independent release that gained worldwide notoriety for its violent images. From
its horrific opening scenes, in which a railway station full of uniformed
high school girls commit mass suicide by coordinating their leap in front
of a speeding train, with predictably bloody results, the film sets off on
a path of destruction and mutilation commensurate with the 'splatter
films' of Western cinema. Pushing violent images to the limits of deprav-
ity is not unique to Japanese cinema, of course. Writing on the cinema of
Luis Buñuel, Bazin refers to the

taste for the horrible, the sense of cruelty, the seeking out of the extreme aspects
of life, . . . [which] are also the heritage of Goya, Zurbaran, and Ribera, of a whole
tragic sense of humanity which these painters have displayed precisely in expressing

the most extreme human degradation – that of war, sickness, poverty, and its rotten accessories. (1982: 58)

It is such degradations that seem to punctuate some, but not all, of Sono's films.

Tag carries forward many of the violent thematic features of *Suicide Club*. Sono has used high school protagonists in a number of his films, including Sumida (Shōta Sometani) and Keiko (Fumi Nikaidō) in 'the never-ending collapse of normality' found in *Himizu*, the manga-based film hurriedly rewritten to act as a tribute to the March 2011 tsunami victims (Furukawa and Denison 2015: 236), and the previously mentioned *Love Exposure*; however, none of these films includes such violent events on a mass scale (although *Love Exposure* does have a gruesome ending, particularly for one high school student, this involves individual characters). *Tag*'s violence begins when a lone schoolgirl narrowly escapes an escalating series of violent events that kill all of the other students around her. From brutal decapitations to unsparing machinegun violence, *Tag* is relentless in its portrayal of mutilation amidst institutional structures that are unable to stop the carnage.

Studies into violence in Japanese schools emerged through the 1990s, possibly a result of the increasingly prevalent nihilism that had crept into Japanese society via not just schoolyard violence, but the rise of religious and quasi-religious cults such as the Aum Shinrikyo group, which carried out the poison sarin gas attack that killed thirteen people and injured many hundreds more in the Tokyo subway in 1995. In terms of schoolchildren, violence or the suggestion of violence was assumed to indicate a reflection of individuals (or groups) finding some means of escape from their increasing detachment from everyday society. Yoneyama (1999: 9) points to a number of studies concerned with the 'emptiness' and 'invisible existence' voiced by students, resulting in a generation of automatons or '"*shijimachi ningen*" (human beings waiting for their instructions)'. These were children who had become 'apathetic, passive, bored, low in energy, unwilling to think or make decisions or initiate any action' (9). This also led to the rise in *hikikomori* (shut-ins), who became wholly introverted and reclusive. Not all automatons, however, were wedded to the end-point of violence, as these students were 'also capable of appropriate action when the recognised stimuli are applied' (9), whether in an institution or a family environment. And while it is all too easy to fall back upon a reductive, generalist approach to Japanese society, and the image of a military-grade disciplinarity that governs all schooling, it is necessary to avoid 'Orientalist notions of a Japanese school system that supposedly encourages students to sacrifice their own interests and devote all their time and energy to fierce academic competition and "cram schools"' (Pagel 2011: 7).

Earlier, I noted the move away from the over-disciplined school environment, but by 2006, Japan's ruling LDP (Liberal Democratic Party) revised existing education policies so that they 'established patriotism as a stated aim of the education system' (Bamkin 2018: 78). In this shift, moral education was to become 'enshrined as one of the three dimensions of education: heart, body and intellect [. . .] aiming to cultivate a "zest for living"' (80). Such an approach perhaps reiterates the themes of Sono's *Love Exposure*, thematically driven by questions of morality and the failure of society in general to give youth a sense of moral worth. In Sono's film it is the Western-based church that is seen as tasked with providing the young with a moral education, but it soon becomes clear that even those following the doctrines of the church – namely, Yu Honda and his father – are corruptible. The idea that society is failing to discipline its children tends to be cyclical, subject to the attitudes of the time, as shown in Durkheim's earlier-quoted insistence in the early 1900s on the role of boarding schools, where 'the notion of authority has become more lax'. Durkheim then counters this claim by adding that 'it should not be forgotten that in the older generation discipline was excessively harsh' (in Pickering 1979: 156).

While the *Battle Royale* films were released some two decades ago, the recent revisions around moral education appear to maintain their relevance in the contemporary environment. Bamkin notes that '[t]eachers tended to believe that reforms were motivated by the nationalist agenda of the current [LDP] government which did not accord with institutional beliefs on the purpose of moral education' (2018: 86). According to Bamkin's research, the conservative LDP government appeared to view education as 'a potential key to normalising a belief or ideology instrumental to the state in debates recognisable as militarisable' (86). In other words, education is available as a tool of propaganda, but educators have resisted this approach because they see the formalising of 'moral education' as having 'the potential for an ideology of Japanese supremacy and aggression' (86). For some, Bamkin notes, this suggests a return to the authoritarian, intensely patriotic fervour of the times preceding World War II, and thus the intensely violent militaristic underpinnings found in the *Battle Royale* films.

Violence manifests in ways other than physical. In Kenji Nakanishi's *The Blue Bird / Aoi Tori* (2008), students are traumatised at first by the suicide death of one of their classmates, and then by constant pressuring from their teacher, Murauchi (Hiroshi Abe), who 'not only openly addresses the students as "cowards", but also forces them to remember that the death of their colleague was their fault' (Kiejziewicz 2018: 84). Himself the subject of bullying because of a long-standing stutter, Murauchi-*sensei*'s behaviour perpetuates the psychology of violence affecting his students, with his underlying belief that this approach will teach them valuable life skills.

Not all violence in high school films can be linked back to the failings of a teacher. In *Honey*, Onise (known simply as Oni, the Japanese word for 'devil') has built his tough-guy reputation on using unprovoked physical violence as a means of expressing himself, but as he confesses to Nao Kogure (Yūna Taira), the girl he barely knows but has sworn to marry, he has changed and now fights only with other boys who are themselves picking on younger students. Although Kogure is nervous about having to meet up with Onise, the latter sits with her at lunchtime and offers her a carefully prepared *bento* meal that he has made for her. Kogure hesitantly tastes it and is surprised at how good it is. She tells him that she is enjoying it, before adding:

> Kogure: I was really worried that you might hit me if I said it tasted bad though . . .
> Onise [surprised]: What the heck! I would never hit you.
> Kogure: But yesterday, you were hitting people, weren't you?
> Onise: Ahh. Those guys were picking on new students. If I complain, they'd just hit me. That's why it couldn't be helped. [pause] I've decided that I won't hit people without a reason anymore.

Kogure turns to look at him.

> Onise [cont.]: You hate it when people get into meaningless fights, don't you?
> Kogure: Yes.
> Onise: I won't do anything that you don't like. I won't do anything to make you sad. I'll protect you, I promise.

This scene appears early in the film while the relationship between the two is still uncertain, but serves as a turning point for Kogure as she realises there is more to Onise than senseless violence.

One of the few high school films films to confront the topic of sexual violence is *Drowning Love*, in which Natsume is drawn away from watching Kō at the Fire Festival by an older family friend, Takumi Hasume (Gōichi Mine), who tells her that her grandfather has collapsed and is in hospital. He bundles her into his car and they take off, but Natsume questions whether he has taken the right road to the hospital. The man drives through an isolated forest setting and tells Natsume that when he saw her in her latest modelling shots, he was instantly attracted to her:

> Takumi: Are you thinking that I'm a weirdo? I think I can be together with you. But you kissed a cheeky boy a while ago, didn't you? [pause] You practised for today.

Takumi pulls the car up.

> Takumi [cont.]: Now, this is the real deal.

He aggressively pulls Natsume toward him in a tight embrace and threateningly tells her to 'be obedient'. Natsume remains silent so he pulls back to look at her:

> Takumi: Smile, like the one in the pictures.

Natsume screams and pushes him away. He tries to restrain her, but she throws her head back, hurting his face as she scrambles out of the car. Kō soon arrives to try to rescue Natsume but is set upon by Takumi, who violently beats him. As Kō lies injured, Takumi catches up with Natsume and pins her to the ground, the weight of his body on top of her. He begins to run his hand under her *yukata*:

> Takumi. We're the same. Let's be adults together.

Just as it appears that Takumi's sexual assault is to advance to rape, help arrives from those who had followed Kō, and Takumi is pulled from Natsume and taken away.

Following the traumatic experience, Natsume becomes withdrawn. She breaks up with Kō and he begins to stay away from school to hang around with a street gang. It is up to Natsume's childhood friend, Ōtomo, to try to help her regain trust in those around her. As it seems Natsume is recovering and puts her modelling career on hold, she is sent a script for a possible movie role. When the famous photographer and filmmaker Shōgo Hirono (Ryōhei Shima) arrives in her village, he confronts Natsume as she is leaving school, to see if she wants to do the film. She turns on him:

> Natsume: Why did you suddenly come here? That scenario [script] was terrible. Why should I have to take the role of being raped? Should I really be in that kind of role? It was all terrible scenes. [shouting] Why do I have to be the one who is humiliated?
> Shōgo: But it's good being the one that is humiliated. You're that kind of weirdo, right?

Shōgo leaves, and a visibly upset Natsume runs away to weep near an isolated canal. The trauma of Natsume's sexual assault and Kō's descent into the violent world of street gangs see them meet again and it seems their unhappiness is affecting them both deeply. Natsume cradles Kō's head as he recovers from yet another beating, and she confesses:

> Natsume: I want you to live while you're glittering. [pause] Say something.
> Kō: The one you're saying, the shining Kō, is already dead.
> Natsume [screams]: Then the two of us are just fine suffering from his curse!

Kō leaps up and throws Natsume to the ground. They stop.

> Natsume [quietly]: Do you want to do a lover's suicide? We've both become hopeless. [she begins to cry] The sea and the mountains. They are all yours. It's not that you become someone you cannot play with.

She hugs him and then offers herself to him. They kiss passionately, and while it seems any thoughts of suicide have passed, the scene cuts to underwater footage of them listlessly (or lifelessly) floating deep in the sea. As with the title of the film, water plays an iconic role in their seaside village, and both characters end up at various times in creeks, canals and the ocean. In a voiceover, while they are in deep water, Kō asks if she is afraid, and Natsume replies that she is not and that she is happy. Their ongoing narrative teases the audience with possibilities: they may commit suicide, they may leave town, they may separate or they may stay together. Kō pulls a switchblade from his pocket and tosses it toward Natsume, again creating possibilities for how the story will play out.

The theme of suicide in *Peach Girl* is presented as a more spontaneous act by Momo when she wants to prove her love to Toji in front of the manipulative Sae Kashigawa (Mei Nagano), a successful part-time model and Momo's (pretend) best friend. While visiting Toji in hospital as he recovers from a minor operation, Sae tries to twist the story of why Momo kissed Kairi in an earlier incident that Sae filmed and uploaded to social media. To prove her loyalty, Momo runs to the open window, climbs up on to the ledge (already established as being several floors high) and, clutching the windowsill, cries out:

> Momo: You're the one I love, Toji! It doesn't matter to me if everyone misunderstands me. But . . . I only need you to believe me. If you won't, I'm better off dead!

A sudden gust of wind blows her skirt up; instinctively, Momo tries to maintain her dignity and puts her hands down to hold her skirt. She tumbles backwards (in slow motion) with a frightened look on her face. In an outside shot her arm is suddenly grabbed from above, soon revealed to belong to Toji, willing to risk further injury from his operation to declare his love for Momo. The scene reflects the depth of teenage emotion and the ability for this to result in spontaneous and often violent actions, sometimes with tragic consequences.

Bullying

Within institutional environments, the hierarchical structures create a series of intended and unintended power dynamics that affect students' attitudes toward schooling, where 'satisfaction with school is [. . .] found to be strongly associated with their perceptions of the general school climate, including fairness and safety at school, and the quality of relationships with classmates and teachers' (Takakura et al. 2010: 545). This satisfaction is challenged in *Girls' Encounter*, whose bullying theme is immediately obvious from the film's opening aerial view of a schoolgirl lying on the ground in a forest and three other girls running from her. A close-up of the girl, Miyuri Obara (Moeka Hoshi), shows her with her eyes closed before she stirs, and then holds a knife to her wrist. Too distraught to carry out the act of cutting herself, Miyuri looks again at her wrist to see a caterpillar has crawled on to it, and she stares, fascinated. A short time later, the action cuts to Miyuri walking home from school, watching the caterpillar, which she now keeps in a box, before her schoolbag is snatched by her bullying classmates who are riding past on their bicycles. When Miyuri catches up with them in the nearby woodlands, they tip the contents out of her bag and then push her to the ground, showing that their bullying behaviour is ongoing.

The independent drama *Wander Life* opens with several scenes of fourteen-year-old schoolgirl Hinano (Shuri Nakamura) being physically (and mentally) tormented by her classmates, who steal her shoes and then her journal, which they later read aloud to the class while the teacher is out of the room. Hinano is able to snatch the journal back and runs to the school's sickbay to hide. The school nurse, Yuki Shindō (Yō Hasegawa), allows her to stay, aware that Hinano needs solitude. After several instances of Hinano running away, Yuki heads to the school rooftop and finds Hinano sitting there, alone. Yuki narrates a story her mother once told her, because Yuki had also been bullied at middle school and had stopped going to school altogether. Hinano listens attentively, silently indicating that she understands Yuki's tale. In a voiceover, with slow motion images of

Yuki walking and Hinano eagerly following, Hinano's respect for Yuki becomes apparent.

> Hinano [v/o]: Nurse [*Sensei*] Shindō, it's nothing, but . . . Nurse, you see me. Though I'm nothing, though I've nothing. Nurse, you see me. [pause] And you find me like this.

At a meeting of senior school staff, Hinano's case is discussed, and the issue of her class absences is passed on to a male teacher, Kōichi Yamano (Yoshiki Ōneda), to deal with; he reluctantly agrees. After the meeting, Yuki walks with him:

> Yuki: Hinano needs our help. The school's reputation is not the issue.

Yamano is more pragmatic, though, and while Hinano's welfare is of concern, he is well aware of the school's position, which demands that the young woman's behaviour be dealt with in an authoritative manner.

Again, the 'broken' family unit is featured as a possible underlying reason for Hinano's passive nature. When her older, adult sister tells Hinano that their mother is bringing her male friend, Shūji, over for dinner, the sister explains: 'After our shitty Dad ran off, Shūji is the one who saved Mum. [pause] He's a saviour! At least you can pretend.' The 'absent father' trope is therefore presented again as an unacknowledged disciplinary void in the lives of the teen protagonist. In such narratives (as noted earlier), the mother figure is often too preoccupied with working to support the family, and the teenage child is left to navigate their own way through adolescence.

Unlike many recent high school films, *Wander Life* approaches the topic of bullying directly, with Yamano-*sensei* telling Hinano, in their deserted classroom, that he is aware that she is being bullied. His straightforward approach is not successful, though.

> Yamano: I'm sure it's hard to talk about it, but you must try. [pause] Otherwise your teachers can't help you.

Hinano does not answer and sits silently at her desk, making no eye contact with him. He is obviously ill equipped for a counselling role and soon gives up, walking away muttering 'You can't stay like this forever.' Ultimately, the film does track Hinano's growth, and while there is no retribution for the bullies in her class, the final shot shows her newfound strength as she enters the classroom and gazes straight at the camera (Figure 6.2), in a freeze frame mimetic of the final shot of François Truffaut's *The 400 Blows*.

Figure 6.2 Hinano's new confidence in *Wander Life* (Spotted Productions, 2018).

In many high school films, bullying is carried out by those of the same gender, such as the girls in the literary salon in *The Dark Maidens* or the team of bullies in *Girls' Encounter*. In *Closest Love to Heaven*, though, the film begins with a bullying episode featuring a boy harassing a female classmate. Entering the classroom, Ninon Okamura (Marie Iitoyo, who also stars in *The Dark Maidens*) is harassed by the class bully, who bumps into her, sending her sprawling to the floor. As she stands up, her long hair now all tangled from the fall, he chides her:

Bully: You're a messy girl, huh?

He then dramatically mimics her, clutching his stomach and bending over, shouting, 'The pain!' Ninon watches on, upset, but he continues:

Bully: What are you looking at? Aren't you supposed to apologise?

Ninon stumbles to say something and then bows, apologetically. The bully's classmates (male and female) all laugh but he sneers at her and snarls, 'Drop dead!' At the back of the classroom, a lone male student, Yuiji Kira (Taishi Nakagawa, also the star of that year's *ReLIFE*), sits, watching quietly. He rises from his seat and walks over to the bully, who acknowledges him with a cynical, 'Huh?' Kira stares at the bully and then, with a quick punch, knocks him to the floor. Kira confidently remains standing there, as Ninon watches in awe at his chivalrous act.

The highly stylised 2019 manga-based *Hot Gimmick: Boy Meets Girl/ Hotto Gimikku: Gāru Miitsu Bōi* (dir. Yūki Yamato) features bullying as its key theme. Wealthy Ryōki Tachibana (Hiroya Shimizu) blackmails Hatsumi Narita (Miona Hori, of Nogizaka46 fame) into becoming his personal slave, and she must carry his schoolbag and acquiesce to any request he makes. Via jump cuts, rapid edits, letterboxing and masked screens, as well as composite (split screen) shots, Ryōki is presented as rough, abusive and manipulative. While these stylistic devices could suggest a light-hearted comedy, they serve here to create an unsettling mood that matches Ryōki's erratic behaviour and quick temper. He is also intensely jealous when Hatsumi speaks to other boys, and of her friendship with orange-haired photographic model (and former childhood classmate) Azusa Odagiri (*Blue Spring Ride*'s Mizuki Itagaki). Ryōki's character is complex, yet it seems that his behaviour is simply a way of covering up the romantic feelings he has for Hatsumi. A similar theme is found in *Wolf Girl and Black Prince* when Erika Shinohara (Fumi Nikaido) becomes 'enslaved' to Kyouya Sata (*Your Lie in April*'s Kento Yamazaki) after fabricating a story for her friends that he is her boyfriend. He agrees to pretend but is sadistic in his treatment of her.

The personal slave theme is also found earlier in *The Black Devil and the White Prince* (feature film), which begins with the dark-haired, dominating, brooding 'Black Prince', Haruto Kurosaki (Kentō Nakajima), telling Yū Akabane (Nana Komatsu) that she is his slave. He kisses her firmly on the lips before she retaliates, pushing him away. As the 'vice head' of Yū's school dorm, the conceited Kurosaki exacts his revenge after Yū snips off a large lock of his hair when he accidentally becomes tangled in one of her cardigan buttons. The punishment is that she has to do whatever he says, so he sets her the gruelling task of cleaning the dormitory building. His behaviour includes kissing Yū without her consent, something that would be viewed as a form of sexual assault in many societies. In class, he pulls her hair (Figure 6.3) and bites her ear so loudly that she yelps.

Some of Yū's female classmates misinterpret all the attention she is getting from Kurosaki as the result of her flirting with him, and they begin their own regime of bullying her, including telling her that she has to use the male-only dormitory bath, setting up a potentially embarrassing situation where her male classmates might see her naked. Yū's gullibility paints her as a passive character throughout much of the film. When they visit an amusement park, the blonde-haired White Prince holds her and tells her that he has strong feelings for her, but she hesitates, signalling to the audience that she may have a romantic attachment for the Black Prince after all. Shortly after, Kurosaki finds her alone and forcibly drags her into a ferris wheel capsule, where he forces himself on her once again, kissing her within the confines of the ride. Back at the dormitory, Yū again gets down

Figure 6.3 Haruto hurts Yū in *The Black Devil and the White Prince* (Hakuhodo, 2016).

on her hands and knees to scrub the dining-hall floor, a chore assigned to her by Kurosaki. She begins to reflect on their romantic actions in the ferris wheel, disregarding his abusive, controlling behaviour:

> Yū [v/o]: Why couldn't I reject him that time? It's happening again . . . I feel like . . . poison is spreading through my body.

She is interrupted by her male friend, Yūsuke Kaji (Yūta Kishi), who tells her she is blushing. She dreamily admits to him:

> Yū: I might be lustful.
> Kaji: Lustful? What does that mean?

But Yū has no answer and can only stare off into space.

Although *The Black Devil and the White Prince* features what can be considered a one-sided, abusive relationship almost up to its conclusion, the final scenes see Yū take on a more forceful role in her relationship with Kurosaki. Kurosaki's hesitation to change could, of course, be seen in line with what Donald Richie once noted as Japan's 'bias', which 'insists that unattractive traits be accepted along with those more pleasing' (1972: 77). Richie argues that, in Japanese cinema (mostly in relation to mid-twentieth-century films), 'bad is accepted with good because it is there; it is part of things as they are' (77). Despite the slight concession where Yū shows signs of empowerment, audiences can still approach the overall tone of domination (after all, the bully still ends up with the girl) as highly gendered and problematic.

This gendered theme also appears early in *You, I Love*, when Rin treats Yū in a demeaning manner, even though he is highly attracted to her. Yū's lapse into subservience whenever he is around is remarked upon by her friends, Koyomi Sakashita (Tina Tamashiro) and Keita Fuji (Hayato Isomura), who are both disappointed in her weakness to stand up to Rin. Although this is treated as a comic storyline, Koyomi challenges Rin:

> Koyomi: This is Rin's fault! Yū's become such a spineless girl because of you!
> Rin: I'm doing a good job.

He moves over to a cowering Yū, who is clutching at her hair in a nervous manner and repeating to herself that she is not good enough.

> Rin: I'm sorry. Don't worry. Nobody's looking at you or paying attention.

She looks up and smiles, despite Rin's comments being delivered in an insulting tone.

> Yū: Thanks, Rin-*kun*.
> Rin: Let's go!

As Rin and Yū walk by, Koyomi and Keita exchange looks and both sigh deeply with frustration. But Rin's dominating behaviour comes at a cost. A short time later, he is seen on the school roof and is joined by Keita for lunch. Rin is near to tears and contemplating why it is that he continues to treat Yū harshly. Keita agrees, adding, 'it seems like you're getting worse and worse'. Rin stares off into the distance:

> Rin: I like her so much; I'm scared of myself!
> Keita: It looks like you're just bullying her. [pause] Why can't you just be honest? You know that you just hurt her when you say those things, right?
> Rin: That's why I'm scared. [sniffing back tears] What if she begins to hate me? At this rate . . . [he begins sobbing].

The scene shifts (through an aerial zoom) to Yū and Koyomi, who are sitting on a bench eating their lunch. Koyomi is concerned for her friend, who looks upset, and asks:

> Koyomi: Do you feel pain anywhere? Did you bite your tongue? Say ahhh! Ahhh!
> Yū: I . . . want to change! So I don't become hated by Rin-*kun*. I want to become a human instead of being trash.
> Koyomi: You are a human! Rin just doesn't treat you like one!

Yū shakes her head desperately in disagreement:

> Yū: Rin-*kun* is the only one who is helping me become a proper human.

Koyomi sighs deeply, again frustrated at her friend's lack of confidence, and asks what she sees in Rin.

> Yū: My Dad always said, the men who treat me nicely are bad people . . . but Rin-*kun* is the only one who has been strict toward me. He is helping me overcome my scaredy cat self.

Koyomi cannot believe Yū's logic and rolls her eyes in frustration. Meanwhile, back on the roof, Rin declares that he does not bully Yū; he is only teasing her, just as her father expects from a man. Keita does not believe him and warns Rin that he is likely to destroy the relationship if he keeps being mean to Yū. Rin tries to change and be more considerate, but Yū's lack of self-esteem is deeply ingrained, and she continues to berate herself for being 'pathetic'.

This form of harsh self-criticism also arises in *One Week Friends*. The memory loss that afflicts Kaori is cited early in the film as being psychological rather than neurological. As more is found out about Kaori, it appears that bullying may be at the heart of an initial trauma that caused her to withdraw socially and begin to suffer episodes of distress. In a flashback, it is revealed that some of Kaori's female classmates at her former junior high school saw her talking with a popular boy, Hajime Kujō (Shūhei Uesugi), and began to spread rumours about her having a relationship. Kaori's classmates all began to ignore her, and when three of the girls saw Kaori on her way to meet Kujō, they confronted her, insisting that she 'stole' Kujō from one of the other girls. Distressed, Kaori abandons her meeting with Kujō and runs away, into the path of an oncoming car.

In *Peach Girl*, Momo is confronted by a group of girls who are keen on local heartthrob, Kairi. The girls repeatedly call Momo (also the Japanese word for peach) 'a bitch', claiming that she stole a kiss from Kairi, denying them the chance. They forcefully slap her phone out of her hands. The phone falls from its case as it hits the floor and one of the girls sticks her foot out and grinds it into the ground.

> Bully [menacing]: The next time you come close to him. Well . . . we'll break your jaw!

Momo is strong, however, and tells the bully to take her foot off the case. When the girl refuses, Momo charges, knocking her out of the way.

Ultimately, Momo is able to gain the grudging acceptance of the bullies when her relationship with Kairi becomes public.

Conclusion

Japanese high school films mostly take a more subtle aim at the taboos and challenges of adolescent life than their Western counterparts. Unlike Western films, which deal with these issues in often explicit, confrontational ways, many of the Japanese ones couch any critique of individual behaviours in nuanced depictions that place any actions within a broader societal context. While the apportioning of blame centres on the individual, ultimately their behaviour can be indicative of broader problems in Japan, and therefore need to be resolved by each film's end. Bullies get their come-uppance and victims prove their worth, shifting from passive to active protagonists.

The various problems faced by school-aged characters in Japanese high school films are often heightened or amplified from real-life scenarios. The use of violence is portrayed as instigated by the institution, its teachers or the students themselves, with some filmmakers choosing to depict extreme violence for its shock value. The increased risk-taking and taboo behaviours exhibited by on-screen characters in high school films may be related to each student's home or school life, with studies showing that 'important predictors of [. . .] students' satisfaction with school are that the students feel that they are treated fairly, that they feel safe, and that they experience that teachers are supportive' (Takakura et al. 2010: 550). In the popular high school genre of contemporary films, the school is mostly presented as a safe and supportive environment within which students can navigate their adolescence. As a number of films show, however, disruptions often occur at an individual level, creating a multitude of complex narratives for the audience to enjoy.

CHAPTER 7

Romance and Sexuality

Japanese cinema is often cited for its *laissez-faire* approach to censorship, yet most contemporary school-based *seishun eiga* take a modest stance on sexuality and violence. The strict formula of the romance-inspired films invariably has a doe-eyed boy or girl aspiring to enter a relationship with their desired partner. The school is an important backdrop to such events because high school students are at an age where they self-reflect on their own development through adolescence by having to 'start negotiating their sense of themselves as sexually reproductive beings and as workers in the economy – the core identities of adulthood' (Fisherkeller 1999, in Paule 2016: xvi). Within the 'tame' parameters of today's teen-targeted Japanese high school films, it is instructive to investigate how romantic and sexualised relationships are presented to audiences. These films explore their characters' ability to recognise their identity and their position within an institutionalised setting that is itself part of a larger series of institutions.

Heteronormative Sexuality

In a reflection of Japan's often-cited conservative values, it is no surprise that most high school films privilege the heterosexual relationship over any other form. The romantic ambitions of adolescent boys and girls fit easily into well-worn narratives of heteronormative lifestyles, where the true destination is marriage and the arrival of children – the endless reproduction of one's own image (as Freud would say). In US high school films, on the other hand, sex is often presented as one of the 'major problems' that provides a narrative focus for their characters (Harrison 2017: 25). Most school-based *seishun eiga*, however, as we have seen, veer away from direct references to sex or sexuality in favour of their romanticised style – but that is not to say that all are innocent. Just as American teen comedies have edged toward more ribald, overt sexual references, Japanese films may face the same future: after all, as Durkheim once noted, 'the morality of the future will probably not be that of today' (c. 1909, in Pickering 1979: 131). For Japan, the duty of the schoolgirl of Durkheim's time was 'to be filial, frugal, and possess feminine modesty' (Czarnecki 2005: 50).

Films such as *Hentai Kamen* or Sion Sono's *Love Exposure*, for instance, are possible exceptions, as they display a kind of comic eroticism or ribald humour that suggests a teen audience rather than being a provocative foray into nudity or graphic sexuality. In *Hentai Kamen* and its sequel, both based on the manga series 'Kyūkyoku!!', reserved schoolboy Kyōsuke's surreal, magical transformation (or *henshin*) to a fighting (but fallible) superhero when he places women's underwear over his face is an exploration of the *hentai* (pervert) trope within the relative confines of the comic/action genre. While the film may push the boundaries of 'good taste', it does not venture into the explicitness of a pornographic text. It does, however, tease with its homoerotic undertones, which stem from portraying near-naked men wrestling and barely clad scrotums being pushed into the face of adversaries. In *Love Exposure*, it is Yū Honda's (Takahiro Nishijima) obsession with photographic *panchira* ('upskirting') that drives him to appease his father, a religious minister who believes his son must repent for any sins he may have committed.

A similar type of ribald comic humour exists in *Yarukkya Knight*, another manga-based film, where Gōsuke Makoto (Tomoya Nakamura) becomes infatuated with the girls around him in the school and becomes lost in ongoing dreams and sexual fantasies. Anne Allison says that, in many manga and anime, 'once the female has been inactivated to form a spectacle [for example, if their clothing has accidentally been removed], the males also become immobile' (2019, c. 1996, 42–3). This 'stunned' reaction is often accompanied by onlookers (mostly male) who are drawn with their eyes bulging. In her analysis of the original manga of 'Yarukkya Knight', Allison notes that the stories are repeatedly fashioned as narratives of boys who, either inadvertently or purposely, remove the clothing of females (43). In the 2015 film, however, the tables are turned, and the boys' efforts are often thwarted, with the girls then rounding on the boys and physically assaulting them.

Earlier examples of representations of sexually active schoolgirls had appeared in manga for generations, preceding the *pinku* films from the 1960s, and later manga such as *The Illusory* (aka *Elusive*) *Ordinary Girl/ Maboroshi no Futsū Shōjo* (1987, by female artist Shungiku Uchida) toyed with notions of acceptability by having a lead character who is a 'high school girl who drinks, smokes, and sleeps around' (Kinsella 2002: 224). In the late Meiji period, as Czarnecki points out, 'the label "degener-ate schoolgirl" (*daraku jogakusei*) had gained currency through Japanese reportage' (2005: 50). While this met with the expected outrage, it also had the potential to mark out rebellious girls as daring and brave. For Czarnecki, the '"bad" girl was depicted as a moral transgressor with no regard for the sanctity of feminine virtues, namely that of virgin purity' (50). In *The Kirishima Thing*, a group of girls laugh as geeky Maeda leaves the classroom, one student sniggering that he makes films with titles 'like . . . "Wipe My Hot Thingy"', and another student responding "Is that porn?" as they descend into laughter. A short time later, the teacher reiterates to Maeda and his film club friends that the title of the film he wants them to make is 'You Wiped That Hot Tear from My Face'.

Drawing on statistics from a nationwide survey, Hirayama notes that, leading up to 1999, there was a continued rise in levels of dating among students across age groups from junior high through to university age, especially 'as co-education spread' (2019: 98). However, while kissing and sex among students increased up until 2005, the surveys showed that this had 'thereafter declined until 2017', for reasons said to be related to anxieties around young people's economic prospects and future employment opportunities (97–8).

As with other cultures, 'feminine values' and expectations become part of wider public discourses. Kinsella (2002: 227) notes the various schoolgirl-related scandals of the early 1990s, beginning with the sexually fetishised 'bloomer sailor' (*burusērā*) shops that sold used (unwashed) uniforms and undergarments, and moving toward widespread media interest in 'the apparent involvement of schoolgirls in a new form of amateur prostitution referred to as "assisted dating" (*enjo kōsai*)' (227). Providing a continuous stream of material for news and current affairs programmes, schoolgirl-led stories and the topic of uniform fetishes became 'part of the erotic imaginary' (Corrigan 2008: 5). These stories came to dominate the media as more and more exposés of immoral behaviour and outlandish consumption practices were played out on screen to suggest a demographic out of control.

In *The Dark Maidens*, an unexpected twist occurs late in the film when Mirei, a first-year senior high student, is revealed to have a 'secret', according to one of Itami's stories. In a flashback, Mirei, a scholarship student, is shown receiving cash from an elderly, wheelchair-bound male patient in the toilets at the hospital where she volunteers. Mirei kneels and reaches over, undoing the man's belt and trousers. She removes her glasses, then smiles at him, before leaning forward to perform a sex act on him. He gently caresses her hair while she fellates him, before the scene cuts to her wheeling him from the toilets. The scene is one of the more explicit to

appear in a high school film (besides those that veer into the highly sexualised domain of *ecchi* or *pinku* films).

The manga-based *Sundome New* and *Sundome New 2* (both directed
by Kazuhiro Yokoyama) are 2017 remakes of the 2007 *Sundome* and 2008
Sundome 2 and *Sundome 3* films (respectively), directed by Daigo Udagawa,
that rely on familiar tropes of virginal schoolboys being suddenly tempted
by a new female 'transfer' student in their class. In true *ecchi* style, the
short school skirts worn by Kurumi Sahana (Maori Hoshino) provide
multiple moments for upskirting views as Hideo Aiba (Ryô Kawai) tries to
control his sexual urges whenever she is near him. This reversal of sexual
power, with Sahana the 'aggressor', constantly alluring and arousing him
but refusing to allow him to climax, replicates what Gwynne (2013: 336)
refers to in the original manga of 'Sundome', where Hideo's uncontrolla-
ble erections:

> reflect male anxieties within postfeminist Japan vis-a-vis the strength and vitality of
> emergent girlhood sexuality, which in Sundome always functions to disrupt the male
> characters' quest for masculine validation and sexual satisfaction.

Unlike films such as *Yarukkya Knight*, where the focus is on the scopophilic desires of their young male characters, the narrative drives of the
'Sundome' series of manga and feature films can be seen as creating a surprisingly rare postfeminist site for schoolgirl characters to 'initiate and
enjoy sexual union' (Gwynne 2013: 338).

While attitudes toward sex have been famously explored in films ranging from *pinku* through to Ōshima's *In the Realm of the Senses*, a recent
study into a perceived 'sexual depression' among young Japanese relates
a range of social, economic and technical changes in lifestyles that have
impacted on sexual development. Hirayama (2019: 100) notes that in
recent decades, for instance, 'sexual deactivation' occurred because of the
uncertain economic climate that saw students studying 'more intensely'.
Concurrent with this was the rise in internet use, whereby 'young students' shifted from having potentially embarrassing discussions with
friends and classmates about sex to searching individually online for information and guidance. Changes to sex education curricula in schools began
to highlight the risks of sexually transmitted diseases and pregnancy, with
the result that 'young people stopped having uninformed and reckless sex,
but tended to fear sex in general' (100). And finally, Hirayama draws on
studies that contend that women's attitudes to sex as a way of expressing
love had changed, while the 'number of women who do not want lovers
has increased' (100).

The sensitivity of the topic of teen sexual relations is highlighted in the innocence of Ninon in *Closest Love to Heaven*. When she is at a café with her friend Rei and Kira's friend, Kazuhiro Yabe (Shōno Hayama), Rei bluntly asks if Ninon has slept with Kira. Ninon becomes evasive, and a shocked Kazuhiro tries to stop Rei from saying any more. When Ninon hesitantly answers that she has not slept with Kira, Rei brags, 'I already have,' and provides a photo on her phone of a shirtless Kira lying on a bed. Kazuhiro drops to the floor and groans at Rei's heartlessness, while Ninon jumps to her feet, snapping 'I have something to take care of!' She rushes from the café, tripping on the way out, while a smug Rei smiles after her. Kira enters the frame, presumably returning from the toilets, and asks where Ninon has gone. Rei holds up the photo and says to Kira, 'Get rid of people who are not mentally strong.' The scene draws attention to the social codes in Japan, which dictate that one's sexual life is not normally open for public conversation, and to the importance of fidelity in a relationship (even though Kira's hairstyle in the photo suggests it was taken some time ago, when he was at a rebellious stage in junior high).

The on-again/off-again relationship between Yū and Rin in *You, I Love* is also couched in a high degree of innocence, with Rin promising that, if he gets to kiss Yū, he will be gentle. The idea that there will be a sexual encounter is far from even being considered. Later, when they both begin to open up about their feelings for each other, Yū states, 'I want to become a suitable lover for you!' Despite many failed attempts, when the two finally do kiss, it is Yū who takes the lead. The concept of the young female taking an active role is also found in *My Brother Loves Me Too Much*, in which the desire for a heteronormative relationship is established early when Setoka breaks the 'fourth wall', addressing the camera to introduce herself:

Setoka: Setoka Tachibana, seventeen years old. Still looking for a prince.

The scene cuts to a montage of her dancing in her school uniform but sporting a crown of flowers:

Setoka [v/o]: It's embarrassing to say that . . . I wish I was able to find true love. I still don't have a boyfriend.

In another montage, Setoka is then seen as a little girl (growing successively older), asking a series of young boys out but being turned down each time.

In *Missions of Love*, the innocence of junior high student Yukina Himuro (Tina Tamashiro) is highlighted when she responds to advice from her online followers who read her short mobile phone novels that her stories need a romantic angle. She is taken aback and confesses to her friend, Akira Shimotsuki (Kanta Satō), that she knows nothing about love. He offers himself as a 'pretend' lover in a 'love simulation', so that she will have something to write about, but she is not convinced. Yukina then accidentally witnesses the supposedly 'nice guy' student, Shigure Kitami (Yūta Koseki), reject another girl's romantic advances. When Yukina finds Shigure's notebook, in which he has written details of all the girls he has rejected, she blackmails him into the eponymous 'missions of love', where he has to show her what is required in a romantic relationship. The first mission, she decides, is simply to hold hands. When Shigure hesitantly grasps her fingers, Yukina insists that they hold hands properly:

> Yukina: Not just your fingertips. Use your entire hand . . . until our body temperature becomes the same.

Shigure stares at her but does as she asks. Yukina does not look at him but begins describing the experience to herself, as if narrating a passage for her novel.

> Yukina [v/o]: I felt a warm touch from the palm of his hand.
> Shigure [pulling away]: That's good enough, right?
> Yukina: Do it until our body temperature becomes the same.
> Yukina [v/o]. When our fingers are entangled together our body temperature gradually merges together.

As gentle music plays, it seems that something romantic might be beginning, so Shigure roughly breaks away.

> Shigure: That's more than enough, right?

Yukina then replays the scene as a narrative for her novel (accompanied by non-diegetic writing on the screen), ending with '. . . And then infiltrates the depths of my heart'. The scene then cuts to Yukina's editor, who is commending her for adding the new romantic element to her writing. While Yukina's character is therefore shown as being innocent in romance, her strong will and determination to write from 'experience' (even if it is a confected experience) show that she feels she can keep an emotional distance from Shigure.

The gendering of the characters, with Yukina as the virginal innocent female and Shigure as the emotionally detached male who, at one point, boasts 'I won't fall in love with anyone,' follows the conventions of heteronormative cinematic representations in (most) Japanese high school films. As the film progresses, each 'mission' becomes more daring. Mission Four, for instance, sees Yukina summon Shigure to the school library to 'bite' her neck to help provide detail for a new vampire twist in her novel. She undoes the top buttons of her shirt, baring her neck. The scene suddenly takes on an erotic tone as he gently moves closer, caressing her neck and shoulder. As he leans in to 'bite' (kiss) her neck, she is overcome and slides to the floor in his arms. He apologises and leaves, while Yukina remains on the floor and begins another dreamy narrative:

> Yukina [v/o]: His eyes . . . his voice . . . even his fingertips. Everything about him made my heart race.

Shigure walks away, wondering how he has become smitten with Yukina, and her voiceover continues, 'To be continued . . . '

The gender role objectification in *Peach Girl* centres around Momo's behaviour, which leads to her being seen negatively as an 'easy girl', while the more promiscuous Okayasu is revered as a playboy. In one instance, Okayasu reveals to Toji (who has deep feelings for Momo) that he has sexual thoughts about her:

> Okayasu: I really wanna see what her tanned skin looks like behind that uniform of hers!

Toji slams the playboy into a tree:

> Toji: Don't ever get near her again!

A progressive view toward gender is displayed in *Ouran High School Host Club* when, midway through the film, Haruhii's father, Ryoji 'Ranka' Fujioka (Shigeyuki Totsugi), suddenly appears dressed as a woman. The only previous image of him was in a flashback, when Haruhii was small and together they witnessed her mother's collapse (and death) as they were leaving for a short trip. In the later scene, Haruhii is in a melancholy state as she wanders home after a difficult conversation with Princess Michelle. Haruhii's indeterminate gender (she is disguised as a male so that she can be accepted into the male-only Host Club), is played down for much of the film. As she walks home in the moonlight, an out-of-focus woman can be seen in the background, waving and calling her name. It is only when Haruhii turns and calls back 'Dad!' [*Otōsan*] that the audience realises that her father is now a transgender person. The previous success of *Ouran High School Host Club* as a manga (2002–10), TV anime (2006), live-action TBS TV series (2011) and mobile phone drama (2012) – the latter two shows also starring Haruna Kawaguchi as Haruhii – meant that Japanese audiences were attuned to the characters and the narrative deployment of gender issues and cross-dressing, without these being raised as controversial issues.

In *One Week Friends*, Yūki's unrequited love for Kaori is given further gendered significance through the motif of two pens, which Yūki buys for himself and Kaori to use when writing their 'exchange diary' to help prompt Kaori's memory. He buys a pink and a blue pen, and later hands the pink pen to Kaori. The pen is passed back each time they swap the diary. Towards the end of the film, Kaori has again forgotten their relationship, and as they are graduating from high school, Yūki asks her to sign his yearbook. In a poignant move, he hands her the pink pen, then pulls the blue pen from his pocket so that he can sign her yearbook. They finish signing and Kaori absent-mindedly slips the pink pen into her pocket and walks away. Meanwhile, Kaori's new boyfriend, Hajime Kujō (Shūhei Uesugi), has noticed and asks her how long she has been using that pen, but Kaori is unable to remember.

A more complex approach to physical intimacy is found in *Drowning Love*, in which Natsume's love interest, the white-haired Kō Hasegawa (Masaki Suda), is proactive in his pursuit of her, sneaking up on her, and intermittently running at her and away. His expressions of love are just as sporadic, and when Natsume spills a soft drink down her chin, Kō moves quickly to lick it sensually off her face before kissing her on the lips. In *Rainbow Days*, Tomoya Matsunaga (Taishi Nakagawa) and Mari Tsutsui (Yuri Tsunematsu) are eating down by the river, when Tomoya notices that Mari has some jelly (sauce) on her face. He cheekily leans over, as if he is going to lick it off her face. She pulls back and he reaches a finger out to wipe it off. The invasion of her personal space suggests a more romantic gesture than Mari is willing to concede. In a scene a short time later, Mari is at a food court with Anna and their friend Yukiko Asai (Mayu Hotta), who has been going steady with Tsuyoshi Naoe (Mahiro Takasugi) for nearly two years. Anna probes with some gentle questions before asking 'Well, have you two kissed and all?' Yukiko and Mari both choke on their drinks at the audacity of the question. Yukiko composes herself and responds: 'Of course we have! We are dating after all.' The conversation then turns to Mari and whether she has ever kissed a boy. While, in Western high school films, this discussion may seem a little too innocent for a group of seventeen-year-old girls, in Japanese high school films it is a moment of daring, seen as moving too quickly from one's private life to public disclosure. Mari is incensed at being asked and quickly gets up to leave.

Forbidden Love

When dealing with taboo relationships, *seishun eiga* draw on the famil-iar trope of a schoolgirl or schoolboy who has a crush on their teacher, such as in *My Teacher, My Love* or *Close Range Love*. Occasionally, this takes place as a romance beyond the school, such as in the manga-and anime-sourced *Policeman and Me/P to JK* (2017, dir. Ryūichi Hiroki), in which sixteen-year-old Kako (Tao Tsuchiya) lies about her age to enter a dating event and begins a relationship with Kōta (Kazuya Kamenashi), a twenty-four-year-old police officer. A reversal takes place in *The Liar and His Lover/Kanojo wa Uso o Aishisugiteiru* (2013, dir. Norihiro Koizumi), when Aki (Takeru Satō), a twenty-five-year-old rock musician, hides his identity to become involved in a relationship with sixteen-year-old Riko (Sakurako Ōhara). An even greater age dif-ference is found in *After the Rain*, in which seventeen-year-old Akira Tachibana (Nana Komatsu) falls for her divorced, slightly neurotic forty-five-year-old manager, Masami Kondo (Yō Ōizumi, fresh from his lead role success as an unwitting zombie killer in 2015's *I Am a Hero*), at the restaurant where she works part-time. After Akira expresses her love for the hapless Kondo, he tries to reason with her in a quiet conversation as he drives her home from work:

> Kondo: Tachibana-*san*. I'm already forty-five years old. What would others think?
> Akira: What others think has nothing to do with it.
> Kondo: Oh no, no, no! It does. I mean, I'm old enough to be your father.
> Akira: But you're not my father.
> Kondo: People would think it's compensated dating [*enjo kōsai*, or a paid escort].
> Akira: It's not compensated dating.

Akira suddenly turns to him, shouting 'I really love you!', catching Kondo off guard so that he nearly steers into an oncoming truck. They pull up, and once he catches his breath, they continue their conversation:

> Kondo: Just what is it you see in me?
> Akira: Do you need a reason to fall in love with someone?
> Kondo: It's true that you don't need a reason to like someone from the same gener-ation . . . but I think you need a reason if it's between us. [pause] Tachibana, I think it's better if you rethink this.

While it seems that the age difference is Kondo's main concern, he then stares straight ahead before stating his nihilistic view of his life:

> Kondo [sadly]: I'm already forty-five years old. I don't have dreams or aspirations anymore. I'm already an empty middle-aged dude.

Akira is silent, so he turns to her, only to see her smiling broadly, with tears in her eyes. He is taken aback:

> Akira: You called yourself 'dude'! You usually talk so formally, but you just talked like a kid.

Kondo is exasperated, telling her that she just does not understand the predicament she is placing them in, and suggests that maybe she should go on a date with him to see how gross he really is. She leaps across the seat toward him, catching him off guard again, her eyes wide open in anticipation:

> Akira: You just said that I should try going out on a date with you, right?

Unsure of himself, Kondo agrees that this is what he said and the scene cuts away, leaving the moment unresolved.

Depending on the type of film, such relationships can end either with the resolution of the student waiting to finish school before resuming the relationship as an adult (*Close Range Love*) or, more commonly, with the older protagonist ending the romance (*After the Rain*) and the student falling for a more age-appropriate classmate. Thus, issues of morality are dealt with in a way that transforms the narrative into a less controversial tale. In the *ecchi* film *The Hole of a Woman/Onna no Ana* (2014, dir. Kota Yoshida), based on a short-lived manga series, female student Sachiko Suzuki (Naoho Ichihashi) becomes convinced that she is an alien put on earth to procreate. She begins a romantic relationship with one young man, Mamoru Toride (Toshiyuki Fuse), but then has casual sex with her much older teacher, Murata-*sensei* (Toshiya Sakai). The issue of morality is largely set aside for comic/erotic purposes, as Sachiko wreaks havoc among the males in her 'orbit', both as an object of intense desire and as the kind of female character viewed as 'a threatening sexual Other' (Wada–Marciano 2008: 109). Resolution is left to the passive boyfriend, Mamoru, as he is the only one that seems to yearn for the 'decency' of a monogamous relationship.

A more offensive tone is prevalent in the 2012 short feature (with a run-time of 62 minutes), *Let's Make the Teacher Have a Miscarriage Club/ Sensei o Ryuzan saseru Ka* (by first-time director Eisuke Naito, who has gone on to make other high school horror-based films such as 2016's *Dorome: Girls' Side/Dorome: Joshihen*). As the title suggests, *Let's Make the Teacher . . .* is an unsettling film about a group of schoolgirls who wish to punish their pregnant teacher because she has committed the sin of having sex. The morality of the students, led by the sadistic Mizuki (Kaori

Kobayashi), suggests a loss of respect for their teacher, in a sense implying that their devotion to her authority has been destroyed by her personal behaviours. The use of a 'club' to organise Mizuki's followers reiterates the need for structure within the school, despite the club's horrific aim.

In *Close Range Love*, top-scoring student, eighteen-year-old Yuni, is struggling with just one subject, English, when her handsome teacher, Sakurai, begins to take an interest in why her grades in his course are so low. Outwardly, Yuni appears emotionless but Sakurai can sense her inner anxieties. When Yuni is injured after being bullied by a group of girls keen to spend more time with Sakurai-*sensei*, he comes to her rescue and carries her to the medical room. While being carried, Yuni finally seems to notice him (and his often remarked-upon cologne) and bends her head to him in a romantic gesture. In the medical room he gently applies a bandage to her sprained ankle before looking her directly in the eye and telling her:

> Sakurai: Kururugi, be more upfront about your emotions.

He stands and reaches out his hand as if to caress her face, but rather than make any move that might be misconstrued as romantic, he places his hand on her head, a kindly but patronising pat that suggests she will be alright. Yuni appears smitten, though, and gazes up at him. She begins to speak, addressing him formally:

> Yuni: *Sensei* . . . ? [Teacher . . . ?]

Before they can go any further, other teachers rush in to see if Yuni is alright and the moment is broken. When the two next meet in their one-to-one after-class tutorial, Yuni offers a small gift but Mr Sakurai refuses it:

> Sakurai: I can't take a present from a student. It'd be bad for me if people misunderstood.
> Yuni: I am not misunderstanding anything. It's just a thank you. [getting angry] There is no deep meaning!
> Sakurai: Why are you getting so serious? Did you actually fall for me? Have you lost it? Seriously? So dull. It was nice when you had no interest in me. I was being nice to you because it's my job.

Yuni slaps him.

> Yuni: I was just . . . trying . . . to thank you.

She begins to cry and he suddenly looks apologetic. He reaches out to touch her cheek but she pulls away, grabbing her schoolbag and running. This scene is the first to show how much emotional change has affected

Yuni, and that perhaps Mr Sakurai is feeling emotions beyond a teacher's expected pastoral care duties.

Of course, the sexual relationship between a minor and an adult carries with it legal ramifications, especially for the adult. When Yuni's guardian, also a teacher at the school, notices that Yuni seems emotionally affected by her tuition with Mr Sakurai, he arranges for the tuition to be cancelled – and while the school principal explains to Sakurai that there has not been any suggestion of a personal or sexual relationship between Yuni and Sakurai, there is no doubt a sentiment that one could develop. When Sakurai finally gives in to his emotions, he is seen kissing Yuni by another teacher (as noted in Chapter 1), his former girlfriend, Mirei, who accuses him:

Mirei: You really can't do this, Haruka. Love between a teacher and a student . . . If you were found out, you wouldn't be able to teach anymore. If it goes badly you could be sued!
Sakurai: [dismissive] I know that without you telling me.

Sakurai-*sensei* tries to keep his distance from Yuni, but eventually he confesses to her that he loves her and is willing to wait for her graduation, so that they can then marry each other. Sakurai soon reconsiders, though, as he begins to realise that this will cost him his career, and he reneges on the arrangement. When Yuni confides to her friend Nanami (Mizuki Yamamoto) that she still loves Sakurai, it is Nanami who begins to cry. Puzzled, Yuni looks at her friend:

Yuni: Why are you crying?
Nanami: Because you won't. So I'm doing it for you.

Nanami gazes at her friend and, slowly, Yuni begins to sob gently.

Setoka's various crushes in the romantic comedy *My Brother Loves Me Too Much* include her much older teacher, Yataka-*sensei* (Yūsuke Inoue), but perhaps more controversially, as per the title, her brother, Haruka. Early in the film, Haruka pins Setoka down on a table in their garden and leans ever closer to kiss her. The scene creates a brief moment of sexual tension with a sudden sound dropout, the instant silence hinting at the seriousness of a possible incestuous encounter, far more dramatic than the tone of the film has suggested up until this point. Luckily for Setoka, they are interrupted by another of her suitors, a young doctor named Takane Serikawa (Yūdai Chiba), who is passing by on his way to work. It is soon revealed (to the audience) that the two siblings are not blood relatives because Setoka was adopted when she was aged one and Haruka was two, a narrative that aims to remove some of the anxieties around incest. This revelation still makes the possibility of romance an awkward proposition, especially because Setoka believes that Haruka is her biological brother. This adds to tensions later in the film in an intimate scene when a near-naked Haruka (just out of a bath, which Setoka slipped and fell into) clutches her as she dries herself. Haruka nuzzles affectionately into her neck, and given that Setoka still believes they are biologically linked, she is confused at the feelings she has for him, and whether she can continue to suppress them.

Yataka-*sensei*, Setoka's English teacher who displays predatory behaviour, appears intermittently throughout the film. He inappropriately propositions Setoka in front of the other students but she struggles to understand his English. When his teaching contract finishes, he approaches her and explains that, because they are no longer teacher and student, that they can now openly start a relationship. Setoka smiles and bows, thanking him, and when she moves toward him his expectation rises; instead, she runs past him and out of the school, leaving him confused.

Setoka's destination is a meeting with the young doctor, Takane, but both know that their relationship seems unlikely to develop any further. Takane has also invited Haruka to their tryst (romantically, in a church), and gracefully steps aside to let Setoka, who now knows that she is not biologically related to Haruka, announce her feelings. Finally, they embrace, and although she continues to call him *onii-san* (brother), he gazes into her eyes and confesses his love for her, and they kiss. The film raises interesting ethical (and legal) issues around the relationships between adoptive siblings, and surprisingly comes out in favour of their coupling, and while their father is shocked, their mother gives their relationship her blessing. The final words uttered in the film reiterate the odd nature of the theme when Setoka says, 'Brother, you're cute,' then leans in to kiss him.

In *My Little Monster*, while the central focus is on the romance between Haru Yoshida (Masaki Suda) and Shizuku Mizutani (Tao Tsuchiya), the film's B-story is a developing relationship between Shizuku's friend, Asako Nazume (Elaiza Ikeda), and Haru's older cousin, the thirty-something Mitsuyoshi, or 'Mitchan' (played by Mokomichi Hayami). This relationship seems to be headed for scandal until Asako brings out into the open her affection for the older man as she sits at a table in his amusement parlour. She is dressed in casual clothes, with bare shoulders, trying to attract his attention with the exposed flesh. He acts indifferently, though, and offers an almost cryptic response:

Mitchan: The reason I'm kind to you is not because I want to face you eye to eye.

He stands several metres away from her, with his arms crossed and making no attempt to come close to her physically. Asako stands:

> Asako: I'm serious, I really like you.

Undeterred, she steps closer (Figure 7.1) and responds:

> Asako [cont.]: Is it because of our age gap? If that's the case, I'll be an adult in several years.

Mitchan puts a stop to this, coldly interrupting her:

> Mitchan: You have no place within me.

Asako looks at him, not convinced, but he continues:

> Mitchan [cont.]: To have more than what we have, I guess it would be a little more troublesome.

Shattered, Asako silently breaks eye contact with him, on the verge of tears, realising that she has over-estimated his affection for her.

In *The Dark Maidens*, the relationship between Itsumi and Mr Hōjō develops into a sexual one, and there is a scene of them in bed together (a very rare sight in Japan's high school films). As noted earlier, the scene takes place while they are on a school excursion to Bulgaria. As they lie in

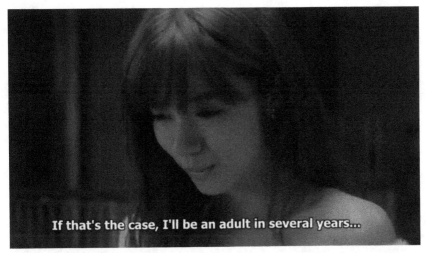

If that's the case, I'll be an adult in several years...

Figure 7.1 Out of school uniform, a forlorn Asako in *My Little Monster* (Toho, 2018).

bed together (Figure 7.2), Itsumi suggests that they should leave before the other students become suspicious. Her teacher/lover replies:

> Hōjō: I don't want to.
> Itsumi: Duh! You're like a little boy, Hōjō-*sensei*.

Hōjō moves across on top of Itsumi, looking down at her in a profile shot, and adopts a serious tone, warning her:

> Hōjō: Don't call me 'Mr'! [*sensei*]

Itsumi laughs, and they begin to kiss as the scene drops into a voiceover of Itsumi's story being read aloud.

> Itsumi [v/o]: The affection we spilled in Bulgaria was a moment's pleasure.

The scene cuts back to the high school in Japan, where Itsumi and her friend are climbing a set of stairs as the voiceover continues.

> Itsumi: As we returned to Japan, we became student and teacher again. Relationships are forbidden.

At this moment, Itsumi passes Mr Hōjō on a landing; they briefly exchange a glance and politely, formally, nod to each other, giving no indication to the surrounding students of the intimate scenes that have preceded this encounter.

Figure 7.2 Hōjō-*sensei* in bed with Itsumi in *The Dark Maidens* (Hakuhodo, 2017).

While it seems that this is the end of their relationship, the story takes on a more tragic tone when it is discovered that Itsumi is pregnant. She arranges a termination of the pregnancy, and under the instruction of Itsumi's father (the school's wealthy director), Mr Hōjō is banished to another, undisclosed location to live. However, Sayuri is able to locate Mr Hōjō and passes his contact details on to Itsumi. From that moment, Itsumi pieces together how the other girls in the literature club were involved in informing her father about the pregnancy. She then sets out to claim her revenge by staging her suicide, jumping from the school roof in front of them. The link between the institution of the school as a place of moral guidance and the personal, sexual relationship challenges the hierarchical system of the teacher/student association, providing a commentary on the fragile nature of the institution and its power over individuals.

Itsumi's carefully planned leap from the roof sees her land in a soft flowerbed, the same bed that she carefully cultivated earlier in the film. As Sayuri reads from Itsumi's diary:

Sayuri [v/o]: In order to stay with Mr Hōjō, I ran away from the hospital, and my embarrassed father declared that this was a tragedy. Or, rather, masked the real truth. Thus, at school, news stating that Itsumi Shiraishi is dead was spread. The rumours about my death will become a reality. In girl's schools, this dramatic imagination can always beat reality.

The forbidden nature of Itsumi's relationship with Hōjō is therefore covered up, saving face for Itsumi's family, and providing a supposedly tragic tale for the rest of the school's students.

As can be seen, many instances of what could be seen as age-inappropriate relationships are found in Japan's high school films. One final example is found in *Kiss Me at the Stroke of Midnight*, when acting superstar Kaede, in his twenties, becomes attracted to Hinana, who is acting as an extra in his high school-based film. Kaede invites the schoolgirl back to his apartment, and after eating a meal and watching a movie on TV, Kaede makes his move to kiss her. While Hinana shows no outward signs of being frightened, earlier scenes have shown that Kaede has a *hentai* fetish, looking at girls' bottoms. He pins the subservient Hinana down on the couch and is about to kiss her, when they are interrupted by Shigeo Takahashi (Kenichi Endo), Kaede's manager and 'adult' figure who provides pastoral care for the young actor. Shigeo has seen their passionate embrace and confronts Hinana, asking who she is and telling them to get away from each other:

Shigeo: How old are you?
Hinana: Sixteen years old . . .

In shock, Shigeo drops the shopping he is holding. The scene cuts to Kaede returning to Shigeo after showing Hinana out of the door.

> Shigeo: What the hell are you thinking? She's in high school! A sixteen-year-old high school girl! That's unbelievable man! [pause] This is a scandal! For crying out loud! How were you going to take responsibility for this? You'll be finished and lose your popularity alongside everything else!

Kaede wanders around his flat, seemingly not listening to the older man.

> Shigeo [cont.]: This is the most crucial time for your dramas, and movies too . . .

Kaede finally responds, but dispassionately:

> Kaede: I understand.
> Shigeo: If you understand then why are you doing this?
> Kaede [dreamily]: She's like an air purifier.
> Shigeo: What?
> Kaede: Don't interfere, okay?

He turns and heads up the stairs in his flat, ending the conversation. While Ryōta Katayose, the actor playing Kaede, is just over four years older than Kanna Hashimoto (Hinana), the inference in the film is that the age difference is much greater. Rather than deter Kaede, Shigeo's outburst does nothing to temper Kaede's affection for Hinana, and he soon hands her a key to his flat, further heightening the possibility of scandal.

Kaede and Hinana's relationship develops slowly, seemingly as a celibate relationship until Hinana nears her eighteenth birthday and her friend gently teases her about becoming an adult, the inference being that she is soon to lose her virginity. Before Hinana can celebrate her birthday, a breaking news story erupts when the press discover that the actor is dating a high school girl. Later, Hinana reconsiders whether her relationship with Kaede is suitable.

The idea of forbidden (heterosexual) love is therefore a relatively common theme in Japanese high school films. Some films, however, take a more progressive approach to issues of gender and sexuality, dealing with them either overtly or as side issues adjacent to the central narrative.

Same-sex Love

The muted way in which most *seishun-eiga* deal with female same-sex love (*dōseiai*), framed not in reductive homosexual or lesbian tropes but as implicitly close 'friendships', recreates familiar Japanese cultural narratives, as found in early fiction that 'features girls and women who are strongly attached to each other, valuing above all else their love and sisterhood' (Suzuki 2006: 575). Films such as *The Dark Maidens* toy with the premise of same-sex relations within the boarding school setting, sites long seen as 'breeding grounds for moral corruption' (Czarnecki 2005: 59). The film also features a sexual relationship between a student and teacher, resulting in a pregnancy that is then forcibly terminated by the student's powerful father, who owns both the school and a nearby hospital. Interestingly, an important theme found in many US high school films is homophobia, 'a widely accepted form of abuse for high school students' (Harrison 2017: 12), but notable for its absence (mostly) in Japanese films. Forms of physical weakness or shyness seem to be permissible themes to explore within the confines of bullying in Japanese high school films, but the topic of homosexuality in a generally conservative Japan, still seemingly coming to terms with how to deal with youth gender and sexuality issues, appears to be too divisive to include in work aimed at the wider commercial market.

Elements of homosexuality are sometimes presented as innocent crushes between students, or more suggestively: in *Girls' Encounter* and *Schoolgirl Complex/Sukūrugāru Konpurekkusu: Hōsōbu-hen* (2013, dir. Yūichi Onuma), for instance, there are languid, voyeuristic scenes of girls watching each other that seem to be heading toward possible sexual encounters. In an early scene in *Sayounara*, Yuki Kishimoto (Haruka Imō) receives an unexpected but not unwanted kiss from her friend Seto (Kirara Inori), a gently sensuous brushing of lips that leaves Yuki stunned (Figure 7.3). But tragedy strikes, and Yuki is left to ponder (in a school rooftop scene, untypically in the rain) whether there was more to their friendship than she had suspected. By the end of the film, things seem to be headed back to a heteronormative state, with the final scene showing Yuki being consoled in an embrace by longtime friend, Kieta (Amon Hirai), a boy who has been trying to win her heart. In avoiding a narrative based on a clear-cut LGBTQI story, the manga-based *Sayounara* offers 'a sophisticated look at teenage uncertainty' (Dimagmaliw 2019).

In *Please Don't Go Anywhere*, Akino Hayashi's (Natsumi Ikeda) crush on Okada (Yūsuke Kasai) takes a bizarre turn when Akino starts imagining that she shares her life with his girlfriend, Nacchan (Yūko Sugamoto). Akino's active imagination develops a strong relationship with her own concept of Nacchan (who she has not yet met at this point), and before long, she has fallen in love with her. As Nacchan sleeps on Akino's bed, Akino leans over in an intimate moment to kiss her (Figure 7.4).

Figure 7.3 Seto kisses Yuki in *Sayounara* (Spotted Productions, 2018).

Later, Akino asks Okada if they can go steady. Okada agrees, but says he must first break off his relationship with Nacchan. In the following days, Okada and Akino become closer, until Okada asks if he can kiss Akino. She closes her eyes in anticipation, but as he draws nearer, a sudden image of the sleeping Nacchan with pouting lips flashes across the screen (less than 1 second, perhaps only twenty frames) and Akino's eyes open quickly,

Figure 7.4 Akino moves to kiss Nacchan in *Please Don't Go Anywhere* (VAP, 2017).

causing Okada to pull back. The promise of a relationship with Nacchan is therefore quickly reinforced as underlying her reasons for going out with Okada.

Please Don't Go Anywhere soon shifts to Tokyo, where Akino is now in her late twenties and managing her friends' rock band and some other performance artists. She lives with Okada and they are soon to be married. While accompanying one of her acts to a TV appearance, she runs into Nacchan, now selling erotic pictures of herself on the internet. They spark up a platonic relationship based on nostalgia for their hometown and Akino's imagined memories of them being together, even though Nacchan has no recollection of ever meeting Akino. Any sexual chemistry that may have been present in the early parts of the film is absent, and it seems that this must have also been imagined until Akino suddenly attacks Nacchan in an unprovoked and violent way, pleading, 'I hate the way you make your living. You were always so sweet, why throw that away? Why can't you be the girl that I used to adore?' A wounded Nacchan lies on the ground, seemingly confused by what has happened, but suddenly sits up and embraces Akino, apologising for how her life has turned out. In this narrative shift, the film skirts the earlier emphasis on the possibility of a same-sex relationship and maintains a more 'innocent' dream-like facade that mirrors conservative attitudes toward on-screen representations of gender and sexuality.

The 2014 fantasy sex comedy, *What's Going on with My Sister?*, is based on both a popular manga and an anime series. Centred around a plot where it seems that a sexual relationship will take place between Mitsuki and her new step-brother, Yuya Kanzaki (Yukichi Kobayashi), Mitsuki dreams up a possibly imaginary 'mentor', another young woman named Hiyori (an actor known simply as Mayu). The mysterious Hiyori is mischievous and daring, as she seduces not only Yuya, but also Mitsuki.

Even in a film that seems structured to 'pair off' characters into heterosexual couples, *Rainbow Days* offers a moment of possible sexual ambiguity between Mari and Anna. Mari has been interfering in her role as a 'go-between' each time Natsuki wants to ask Anna on a date. In a confessional moment, as the two friends sit on a rainbow-coloured bench, Mari gazes at Anna before admitting:

Mari: Hey Anna? In this cultural festival . . . ?
Anna: Yes.
Mari: Hashiba said that he wanted to be with you.
Anna: Huh?
Mari: But I . . . told him no. I ignored your feelings.

Anna sits silently, stunned. Mari smiles at her.

> Mari: Sorry. But you know what? It's no good. Really.

Mari continues to smile but the strain is showing. Anna looks on, horrified, as Mari stands.

> Mari [cont.]: It's really no good.
> Anna: No good?
> Mari: I like you . . . You aren't just a friend. You're more special than that. I have special feelings for you.

Mari grows serious and nervously pulls at the buttons on her cardigan.

> Mari [cont., voice breaking]: I like you on another level. [fighting back tears] That's why I didn't want anyone to steal you from me. Sorry. I didn't really want to tell you this. But I thought I should tell you after all.

Anna stands, facing Mari, who is too upset to look her in the eye. The ambiguity in this scene, in which Mari is confessing her 'real' love for Anna, coupled with the film's rainbow theme look to be pointing it in the direction of girl love. Their conversation continues, underscored by low, melancholy music, rather than dramatic strains:

> Anna: I like you too Mari-chan!
> Mari: Will you continue to be my friend?

Anna rushes over to embrace Mari.

> Anna: I will always be [your friend].

They turn to face each other, holding hands, and again this looks more like a romantic gesture than one of platonic friendship. As they hold hands and gaze into each other's eyes, Mari urges Anna to go to the cultural festival with Hashiba, and Anna nods her agreement. On the surface, this reflects a return to the heteronormative world, but the ambiguity remains. Anna's long pause before agreeing to Mari's suggestion could also be read as her considering her own involvement with Mari.

The idea of same-sex intimacy is also used as a comedic trope, perhaps highlighting a homophobic streak in everyday media texts. In *Real Girl*, for instance, when Iroha admits to the school bully, Mitsuya Takanashi (Hiroya Shimizu), one lunchtime that she and Tsutsui are dating, he insults them. Tsutsui has convinced himself that he must follow the rules of dating and protect his girl. He begins to fight with Takanashi, but inadvertently, because he is not used to fighting, ends up in a series of holds that are designated romantic clutches narrated live by the other students in the cafeteria. Romantic music plays as their horrified classmates look on, calling out, firstly, 'a backhug!' as a moment of soft focus and a convenient lens flare provide a rainbow hue across the screen. Then, as Tsutsui slams Takanashi into a wall, he leans forward to balance himself with one hand on the wall, giving the appearance that he is preparing for a kiss. The students cry out, 'A *kabedon*! [wall pounding kiss that pins a girl to a wall]. Takanashi realises that the situation could be construed as a moment for gay lovers and roughly pushes Tsutsui away. Tsutsui bows deeply and apologetically but stands too quickly, catching Takanashi on the chin with the back of his head. A nearly concussed Takanashi slides toward the floor (still against the wall), so Tsutsui attempts to stop him by lifting his chin as the crowd yells, 'a chin lift!', which again has the appearance of preparing for a kiss. Finally, Takanashi manages to push Tsutsui off, but it is all too much of a spectacle for Iroha, who slides off her chair in a faint.

That the preceding scene from *Real Girl* is played as a comic moment reflects the schoolboy humour of possible homosexual relations (reinforced by each hold being accompanied by the rainbow lens flare). It reiterates how easily the concept of the geek is tied up with notions of a lack of masculine attributes. Iroha's fainting saves the situation, however, as Tsutsui is then forced to take on the decidedly masculine role of saving her, physically carrying her to the nearby medical unit. A similar event occurs in *Rainbow Days* when Mari is accidentally knocked out after another male student crashes into her, and Tomoya heroically lifts her and rushes her to the medical unit.

Later in *Real Girl*, the theme of same-sex love returns in a more serious vein when Tsutsui's best (male) friend, Itō, confronts Tsutsui in front of their friends. Tsutsui's girlfriend, Iroha, has run off into the woods, and Tsutsui is about to chase after her. Itō calls after him, wanting to talk, in what seems to be an opportunity for him to speak up for the shy Sumie Ayado (Moka Kamishiraishi), who is standing behind him. Ayado has an intense crush on Tsutsui, and it seems that Itō will disclose this to him. However:

Itō: Tsutsui. I like you.

The others gasp in shock.

Tsutsui: This is pretty important, right?
Itō: It is.
Tsutsui: Are you talking about, as a friend?
Itō: No. [pause] It is feelings of love.

The friends look on, their eyes wide in exaggerated disbelief as the scene plays out in a sombre tone.

> Itō [cont.]: You're nice to everyone. You think about your friends. You're awkward but you don't discriminate against anyone. You are the person I love the most in the world.

Ayado begins to cry, as Tsutsui answers:

> Tsutsui: I have accepted your feelings. But . . . I have her [Iroha]. That's why. Sorry. And from here on out . . . this may be selfish, but, will you still be my friend?
> Itō: That was my intention, anyway. Hurry up and go [to find Iroha]!

The scene breaks away from the otherwise heteronormative tone (apart from the earlier comic fight in the cafeteria), and hints that the film could suddenly break genre and become a *yaoi*, the popular 'boys' love'/*bōizu rabu* (or BL) category derived from manga, novels, games and anime; this presents homoerotic storylines, but is generally aimed at female or mainstream audiences rather being addressed to a distinct gay or lesbian niche audience. *Yaoi* films therefore present relationships in the same melodramatic, overly romanticised way as Japanese teen films. Tsutsui's quiet acceptance of Itō's admission of love reflects contemporary and mostly popular attitudes toward same-sex relationships among young Japanese people; however, it also points to Japan's legislative environment, in which same-sex marriage is yet to become enshrined in law.

The *bōizu rabu* concept features heavily in *Kiss Him, Not Me*, right from its opening scene of two teenage boys about to kiss, which snaps back to a close-up of a round-faced, bespectacled female student, Kae Serinuma (Miu Tomita), daydreaming on the school bus. In a voiceover introduction, as Kae enters the school gates, intensely watching two young men jokingly wrestling with each other, Kae admits that she is a *fujoshi*, or a boys' love *otaku* (obsessive fan). The plot moves into an even more progressive mode when Kae begins dancing for a new school production, and a new partner, Nishina (Satsuki Nakayama), dressed in a boy's tie and blazer, cuts in to dance with her. Nishina is soon seen to be wearing a skirt and is identified as being the daughter of one of the school's prestigious alumni. The gender 'confusion' is perhaps compounded by the fact that Nakayama (playing Nishina) is one of Japan's most well-established, genderless models.

Elements of homophobia are also found in *The Werewolf Game: Mad Land* when Ayana Sato (Arisa Matsunaga) confronts the arrogant and sadistic Sosuke Shoji (Hiroki Sana), on the rooftop of the abandoned school where they are imprisoned. The other students silently watch the exchange unfold. For their survival, Sato suggests the students split into two groups along gender lines, but Shoji ridicules the idea. Sato lashes out in a verbal spray:

> Sato: You're homosexual aren't you? Then it's a harem for you! You have one extra person anyway . . .
> Shoji: Hey!
> Sato: What? Do you have a complaint?
> Shoji: You said it!
> Sato: I called you a homosexual, dammit!
> Shoji [shouting]: Don't call me homosexual!
> Sato: You were bullied, weren't you?
> Shoji: Stop it, you bitch!
> Sato: You have no friends, do you?

Although brief, the argument suddenly puts Shoji into a position of perceived weakness, the homophobic slur intending to damage his credibility as a leader among the other students. The scene cuts to the four remaining female students who are meeting together, a visual sign that Sato 'won' the argument and enacted her plan. Soon after, Shoji is violently beaten by Taiki Shu (Shutaro Kadoshita), who yells 'You faggot! You fucking faggot!' as he punches his classmate.

In *You Are the Apple of My Eye*, Kazuki 'Ikii' Sugimura (Ryōsuke Yusa), one of Kōsuke's friends, who is already an outlier from mainstream codes by being overweight and subject to instant nosebleeds when under pressure, admits to Kōsuke that he 'likes' the athletic Kento Machida (Naoki Kunishima). This confession starts another nosebleed but Ikii feels he can trust his friend with the secret. Ikii's desire for Kento remains unexplored, though, with Kento seemingly unaware of his admirer and Ikii forced to watch sadly as Kento heads to Tokyo for a career as a professional sportsman. While it seems this is a convenient way of avoiding the non-traditional theme of male homosexuality, later in the film (post-school), Ikii is noted as having a boyfriend from India and there is a short scene showing them standing together, with Ikii proudly referring to him as 'my partner'.

The opening shots of *Ouran High School Host Club* feature a fantasy scene where the students are shown as pirates on a ship. Two male characters, Hikaru and Kaoru Hitachiin (played by twin brothers Shinpei and Manpei Takagi), stand on an upper level of the pirate ship, looking down on a group of girls assembled below. Brandishing an old-style pistol, Hikaru is in the middle of a brave speech to the girls below:

> Hikaru: . . . I feel I can't lose, no matter the foe!
> Kaoru: Hikaru!
> Hikaru: What is it Kaoru? [pause] Scaredy-cats should stay quiet.
> Kaoru [timidly]: But . . . I was worried you might get hurt because of your reckless actions.
> Hikaru: You're wrong, Kaoru.

Suddenly, Hikauru reaches out and grabs the other youth by the chin, turning the timid Kaoru to face him, mere inches away.

> Hikaru [cont.]: I'm doing this to keep you out of harm's way.
> Kaoru: Hikaru!

They draw closer, as if about to kiss. From below, the girls swoon, and call out 'Forbidden brotherly love!' as CGI stars emanate from them, flying toward the boys. That this happens in the first minute of the film indicates the way that heavily romanticised 'boys' love' can be seen as an accepted part of popular culture.

Kissing

In Japanese culture, it is commonly felt that any 'public displays of emotion, other than the ubiquitous smile, is still frowned upon, including touching another person' (Sandrisser 2018: 7). In this way, Japan's high school films accentuate the danger, the frisson of the physical touch between a boy and a girl, or as seen earlier, a teacher and a student. Historically, Sandrisser notes letters of outrage written to a major national newspaper on the issue of public kissing, 'by those who perceived the kiss as a special, private, human interchange, combining sensuousness, sexuality, and aesthetic sensibility' (8).

As in many cultures throughout Asia and the Middle East, Japanese custom dictates that the sight of an uncovered mouth may be considered vulgar, leading to men (at times), but especially women, 'covering their mouths with their hands, a fan, or the sleeve of their kimonos [. . .] a common sight in visual images dating back hundreds of years' (Sandrisser 2018: 10). As written in the seventeenth century, courtesans employed for companionship or sexual acts were judged not just on their appearance and conduct, '[b]ut for her to open her mouth and bare her teeth or to laugh in a loud voice is to deprive her instantly of all elegance and make her seem crude' (Sandrisser 2018: 11). Thus, despite the passing of time since this overview of courtesans was current, in comedies such as *My Teacher, My Love* the confident, outgoing nature of a female character like Ayuna can be easily rendered as uncouth because of her predilection for laughing out loud and not covering her mouth.

In Sandrisser's discussions with Japanese students, she found that they referred to their first kiss as their 'lemon kiss' because it tasted 'clean, fresh, like a lemon drop' (2018: 12). Sandrisser also notes the 'indirect kiss', where adolescents would indicate their liking of another in a coded way by 'starting to drink a soft drink from the same can and then sharing the can with that "special" person' (12). In *Say I Love You*, rather than the first time that Yamato kisses Mei being a desired 'lemon kiss', it catches her by surprise, and she is angry and storms off. He chases her, and after a short but heated exchange he kisses her again. Mei angrily tries to explain to him:

> Mei: A kiss without love! I'm not happy at all. Idiot!

She stops speaking, seemingly relieved to have told him what she thinks. He gently clutches her arm, then kisses her again:

> Yamato: That was my greeting kiss.

Mei does not resist, so he lifts her chin and gives her another short kiss.

> Yamato [cont.]: That was my 'I think that person is cute' kiss.

Mei closes her eyes as they kiss.

> Yamato [cont.]: That is the kiss I give to someone I want to develop a relationship with.

Mei leans into the kiss, extending the time their lips touch.

> Yamato [cont.]: That was a kiss for the person I like in front of me. There's still a lot of types. Now do you know the difference?

Toward the film's conclusion, after their relationship seems to have been torn apart, Mei is on her lonely walk home to the bus stop when she realises that she has been too timid in her approach to Yamato. She turns back and runs to the school, searching the rooms and corridors for him. Finally, they see each other amongst the cloisters, and she runs to him. He utters her name and she reaches out to grab his school tie, dragging him closer and landing a plump, full kiss on his lips. After several seconds, she pulls away, still clutching his tie, and breathlessly asks:

> Mei: The day we seriously kissed for the first time, you asked me if I like you, right? [pause] I couldn't answer you then. But right now, I'm certain of the answer. I like [love] you!

Mei's final phrase is the 'I love you' [*sukitte ii nayo*] of the film's title.

Sandrisser notes the storyline of Kōbō Abe's 1964 novel, *The Face of Another* (Abe wrote, among other things, *Woman of the Dunes/Sunna no Onna*, later made into a successful film): after a night of incestuous, erotic passion with her brother, a young woman takes her own life because her 'first kiss was so meaningful, amd so powerful that it could never be repeated' (2018: 13). In *Close Range Love*, the passionate kiss under the desk at the front of the classroom takes on such a power (although with less tragic consequences).

In a somewhat strange cultural intervention, American Occupation forces in post-World War II Japan 'wanted Japanese directors to include kissing scenes' and ordered one filmmaker to include them because the Americans felt that 'Japanese tend to do things sneakily [. . .] [t]hey should do things openly' (Sandrisser 2018: 14). In Japan, as in many nations, kissing is just one 'communicative act' that takes place between young people, yet 'there is evidence that adolescents especially yearn for building close relationships and having a strong anxiety toward failure in communication'; the rise of internet and mobile telephone communications can relieve (or momentarily transfer) some of that anxiety (Igarashi et al. 2008: 2314).

Communications

Communication between high school students is increasingly part of the digital age, and the intimacy of close physical interactions and communications can be 'replaced' with instant communication via SMS and direct messaging apps. The representation of these forms of communication is used to various degrees in Japanese high school films, but overall seems perhaps to be less prevalent than it might be in a real high school situation. A distinction emerges, though, in the relationship between the type of communication and the outcome of the communication, with Hirayama noting that '[a]ll junior high school, high school, and university students who were heavy users of mobile phone or e-mails had a higher rate of dating, kissing and sex than those who were heavy users of PCs' (2019: 101).

This pattern would seem to fit with stereotypes of the computer nerd, or geek, and their lack of social skills, especially with the opposite sex. In *Rainbow Days*, for instance, Natsuki needs prompting by his friends to try to obtain Anna's 'LINE' ID (Japan's most popular social media messaging app). When Anna is suffering with an allergy, he finally sees his chance and says that if she swaps 'LINE' IDs with him, he can send her his sister's allergy remedies.

While the swapping of contact details bodes well for the relationship between Natsuki and Anna, Anna's friend, Mari Tsutsui (Yuri Tsunematsu), becomes jealous. She is seemingly over-protective of Anna and angrily berates Natsuki's friend, Tsuyoshi Naoe (Mahiro Takasugi):

Mari: I need to get rid of his LINE.
Tsuyoshi: Why?
Mari: He's a bug after all! He's buzzing all around me!
Tsuyoshi: Don't call a stranger's friend a bug. Why are you being so bloodthirsty? Natsuki isn't a bad guy. And he's a friend of Kobayakawa [Anna], right?
Mari: What are you going on about? Shut up!

Mari's use of the word 'bug' is a play on the idea of a computer bug, an irritant in the technology that is interrupting her relationship with Anna.

The use of mobile phone technologies is used in *Closest Love to Heaven* to push the narrative forward. They are used for the delivery of heartbreaking news – either between individuals (the end of a relationship), or as a group communication with the students all being sent the same message, or in scenes where a group huddles around an individual as he/she receives important information on their mobile device. In *Closest Love to Heaven*, Ninon and Kira must communicate by text while Kira undergoes hospital treatment. When Ninon texts Kira to ask what he would like for Valentine's Day besides chocolate (he is on a strict diet because of his medical condition), he simply texts back 'Nino' (his nickname for her). The exchange therefore operates in a simple way that provides a further emotional conduit between the two lovers, but as Igarashi et al. (2008: 2321) note, the prosaic form of the text message can create 'an ambiguity in the meanings', whereby the receivers 'misunderstand the intention of senders'. Thus, a miscommunication arises when Ninon interprets Kira's response as an intimate sexual request.

In *You, I Love*, a remorseful Rin feels bad for calling Yū 'trash' and for saying 'I didn't expect you to be a bitch' when he saw her with another boy. Sitting at home, he anxiously cradles his phone (in a 'masculine' black and blue case) before finally dialling her number. When she answers, he freezes, eventually blurting out that he 'messed up' by calling the wrong number.

He hangs up but is frustrated at his inability to communicate with the girl he likes. Yū holds her ('feminine' pink) phone, staring at the screen of the now disconnected call, before slowly placing it on her desk but continuing to stare at it – the device quickly offering hope and then dashing it. Later, Rin arranges to meet another girl at the back of the school, and then immediately calls Yū, who nervously clutches the phone with both hands. While this part of the narrative helps to establish the characters' reliance on their phones, it also reflects wider cultural behaviours where young people 'may be obsessive about receiving and sending text-messages to avoid rejection, implying that text-message dependency is related to a compulsion for gaining approval from intimate friends' (Igarashi et al. 2008: 2313). Rin asks her to meet him in the same place behind the school, setting a trap for her to see him with the other girl and become jealous.

In the final scenes of *Rainbow Days*, the friends gather on the school rooftop after noticing a rainbow has appeared. Tomoya quickly pulls out his mobile phone and they hurriedly gather together for a 'selfie'. Once the photo is taken, the friends swarm around him to look at it, highlighting the social aspect.

The use of on-screen representations of text/SMS messages has proliferated in recent years due to the ability to produce digitally animated writing easily on the screen. In films such as *Peach Girl*, the audience is constantly shown the text messages as they are written, and in a tension-building feature that is now commonly used, highlights confessional texts that are are deleted or when there is a pause before hitting the send button. In the past, this would have been shown as the hesitation before dropping a love letter into a postbox. The close-up images of mobile devices also operate as a form of product placement that can be part of the industrial complex behind film funding: for instance, the close-up of Momo's phone in *Peach Girl* clearly shows that it is an iPhone, and as she erases the text message she was about to send to Toji, the camera lingers on her homepage and the apps (including the popular LINE social media app) that are installed. Later in the film, perhaps not surprisingly, LINE becomes the dominant means of phone communication for various characters.

Peach Girl's end credits are presented in a split screen mode with an image of an opened school notebook, Momo's pink iPhone lying across one page. Cast and crew credits and a story postscript are shown on the left 'page' of the screen, including still photos and video, while on the right the phone similarly presents credit information, still images, emojis, text messages and further postscript videos (a two–years–later 'After Story: 01', and then '02' and '03', as Momo and Kairi revisit their school).

Conclusion

Japan's cinematic approaches to romance and sexuality range from the contentious and controversial to the more subdued and coy, as found in its contemporary high school films. The on-screen ideal of romance is captured mostly as a part of a heteronormative society, and in films such as *Love and Lies* and *My Teacher, My Love*, the ultimate end appears to be to find a loving partner and arrive at some form of (formally) wedded bliss. Yet high school films also have the capacity for more progressive themes to emerge. While some of the works examined in this chapter objectify female characters, many of the narratives soon turn the tables, with male characters suffering retribution through some kind of punitive action for their behaviour. Some films toy with overly romanticised notions of *bōizu-rabu* or *gāruzu-rabu/yuri* that may push conservative moral boundaries, but these often fail to resolve relationships between their characters fully.

In more serious depictions of same-sex relations (often glossed over in those high school films that seem designed purely for box-office success or 'mainstream' attention) there are few depictions of physical or sexual interactions beyond that of the all-important 'first kiss'. One way of representing hesitancy in initiating physical contact between shy adolescents is through the use of mobile and internet technologies, whereby the intended romantic couple awkwardly thrust and parry their way through oblique or ambiguous text messages before arranging their first date. Japanese high school films therefore use a variety of ways to present romance and sexuality within accepted moral boundaries.

Conclusion

Early in this book I posed the question of whether there was an over-representation of high school films in the Japanese film industry. The sheer volume of these films in contemporary Japan indicates considerable enthusiasm for such a genre/subgenre among filmmakers, studios and audiences. Japanese high school films stake out a cinematic field that takes seemingly formulaic plotlines and stereotypical imagery to produce highly nuanced, richly sentimental texts that are a product of a nation that values the institutional role of the school system. In these films we find the 'repetitions of genre and of performers, and the recurring styles of costume and architecture' (Russell 2011: 9) that Russell identifies as key features of Japan's 'classical cinema' but which are now refigured for a contemporary audience.

This book is one small attempt to redress the dearth of Western academic literature on popular live-action cinema in Japan and to move beyond reductive assumptions that limit much analysis to studies of *auteur* cinema and anime. This omission, from Western scholarship particularly, is further proof of Steinberg and Zahlten's (2017: 2) claim that 'Japan, with one of the largest and most complex media industries on the planet and a rich and sophisticated history of theorisation of modern media, is nearly a complete blank spot on the Euro-American media-theoretical map.' This book therefore presents a select cohort of films as convergent texts that cross multiple forms of media as part of a much larger cultural and economic project in Japan. Furthermore, where many late twentieth- and early twenty-first-century studies centred on the concept of 'Cool Japan' as a form of soft power emanating outward, in this cohort of films we see a renewed focus inward. While the films are exportable products, at their heart they remain distinctly Japanese rather than being essentialised for global consumption.

As shown, the steady production of texts across many different mediums has been crucial to the rise of high school films, from the static drawings of manga to the audio-visual world of animated and live-action TV and feature films. Wada-Marciano notes the critical importance of just one of the links in this mix, where:

> [t]he television medium has indirectly supported the cinema's affinity with popular culture by assuming the role of launching new talent and nurturing existing old-time movie stars. This has led to a symbiotic relation between cinema and television . . . (2012: 17)

Beyond viewing this as the maintenance of an industry providing ongoing employment for Japan's actors, understanding the deeper cultural links between cinema and other popular forms of media in Japan gives us insights into an important element of contemporary Japanese culture.

Importantly, Japan's high school films capture the complexity of the 'social ecology' of the school and reflect this back to the audience through a generally accurate portrayal of how high schools 'are organized around multiple groups with meaningful identities that define the prevailing norms and values to which adolescents entering the school are exposed' (Crosnoe et al. 2018: 317). However, these popular texts can often be seen to break from realism in their 'over-emphasis on the negative aspects', with the focus on a portrayal where this social ecology is 'enforced by intimidation and bullying, demands conformity and chokes independence, and leaves psychic scars long after graduation' (317). This somewhat fatalistic approach may be applicable to Japanese high school films such as *The Blue Bird*, for example, where the teacher repeatedly suggests to his students that they are collectively responsible for their classmate's suicide, suggesting that 'the traumatic identity can also be developed by people not related to bullying personally' (Kiejziewicz 2018: 84). Yet such themes can be simultaneously viewed as part of the rules and conventions of creating narrative texts that push the novelist, screenwriter or filmmaker toward character confrontations in which tensions and conflict make for exciting viewing. While this emphasis on negative outcomes drives plotlines, in many of Japan's high school-based *seishun eiga* there is a decidedly more positive tone. Even those films that feature the death or impairment of a key character are framed in a way that emphasises the beauty of the individual character and their contribution to life and love within their school community.

In this book I have explored the physical (cinematic) setting of the school and its various disciplinary spaces to show how institutionalisation shapes the daily lives of high school students. But the cinematic space has more to offer than the built environment, so Japan's high school films make prominent use of locations external to the learning environment.

It is in these scenes beyond the classroom that much of the character development takes place and foreign audiences are given a closer insight into everyday Japanese life. For Japanese audiences, the background scenes and establishing shots may seem unexceptional or mundane, yet they reflect the 'real' streetscapes, homes and commuter experiences that have shaped their own identities.

The presentation of adolescent 'problems' around prescient issues of sexuality and violence in high school *seishun eiga* reflects the mostly conservative approach found in broader expectations of the school as a nurturing environment. The school is an institution created as 'an organizational mechanism of *human capital* development defined by *formal processes*' (Crosnoe et al. 2018: 318), and it is the emphasis on these formal, linear and teleological processes that create the framework for high school films. As noted, however, Western filmmakers tend to use high school-based films as sites for controversial adolescent behaviour that transcends or interrupts these formal processes. Japan's fictionalised high school characters, on the other hand, (mostly) represent young people that 'are happy to live under a ruling class' (Harrison 2017: 26) and the restraints of a functioning system of institutionalisation. Following Foucault's thoughts on the hierarchical 'training' role of institutions, this is because 'the subject class believe that one day they will become popular and rule alongside those who ruled over them' (26). Again, in Japan's high school films the students (characters) are mostly accepting of the linear processes of institutionalisation that dictate their orderly flow of life through Japanese society.

One way in which this acceptance is shown is through the assignment of the traditional gender roles manifest in Japan's institutions and clearly reflected in its high school films: from the normalising of uniforms along male/female divides, through to flippant comments, such as in *The Senior and the Girl* when Rika quickly guzzles some wine in order to get drunk to try to ease her pain at not being able to form a romantic relationship with Minohara. Minohara is told to take her home, and as he piggybacks her, he tells her, 'Tsuzuki, a drunken woman [pause] is unsightly.' The line is delivered in a matter-of-fact way, with Rika only commenting on the fact that her nemesis (Aoi) does not drink and is therefore not unsightly. That these films objectify female characters and tend toward the heteronormative and romantic may be a response to what Yoda (2017: 176) refers to as a part of the 'girlscape' that emerged in Japan in the 1960s and 1970s. This:

> refers not so much to the actual sites of shopping, recreation, and leisure designed for young female consumers. Rather, it is a mediatic milieu, disseminated via a variety of media channels, linking feminine bodies, affects, objects, and environment.

It was promoted as the setting of female pleasure and self-fashioning, autonomous of institutions of production and social reproduction, such as the family, the workplace, and school.

So, while the mediated girlscape linked young women with new consumerist images and means of identity construction, as shown in this book, complete autonomy still seems to be some way off. As an 'institution of production', the school remains capable of disciplining its students by way of demanding gender conformity, most visible in the compulsory wearing of the school uniform. More broadly, the uniform operates as an effective indicator of age, gender, ethnicity and even socio-economic status in Japanese society and is therefore an important visual indicator in high school films. It plays a pivotal role in creating links between the on-screen characters, the assumed teenage cinema audience watching them, and older audiences by evoking feelings of nostalgia.

The steady number of high school-based *seishun eiga* produced and released over the past decade may be a sign of a temporal 'fad', part of the cyclical trends in cinema that favour particular styles at certain times. Conversely, this means that the form could eventually fall from favour if audiences begin to reject the settings and narratives in search of other forms of storytelling. This is unlikely to occur, though, as the immense popularity of manga, anime and TV *dorama* continues to feed the cinema industry and shows no signs of slowing. Meanwhile, other regional cinemas reflect the influence of Japanese cinema with films and TV dramas set in high schools. In neighbouring South Korea, while films such as *Fashion King*/*Paesyeonwang* (2014, dir. Oh Ki-hwan) deal with high school narratives, they tend to be overshadowed by the decidedly more popular K-drama TV series such as *True Beauty* (2020), *The Liar and His Lover* (2017, based on a 2009 Japanese manga and 2013 feature film) or *Sassy Go Go* (2015), which draw the intense devotion of fans. Across China, Taiwan and Hong Kong, films such as *Fall in Love at First Kiss*/*Yī Wěn Dìng Qíng* (2019, dir. Frankie Chen), based on a Japanese manga, have found favour (with a $US29 million box-office gross); others such as *Take Me to the Moon*/*Dài Wǒ Qù Yuè Qiú* (2017, dir. Hsieh Chun-yi) (box office $0.7 million) have not been so successful.

The mixed success of locally made high school films in the region raises a number of pertinent questions about the influence and impact of Japanese high school films beyond Japan's borders. For instance, what significance do the Japanese films examined in this book have across the region? Is their success another case of cultural texts adding to Japan's 'soft power'? Is this a case of a Japanese homeland challenge to the decades-long Korean

Wave of popular youth-based media culture? If so, does this mean that the appeal of these films will remain almost exclusively within Japan? While these questions are beyond the scope of this book, I would encourage any further studies into the direct links between the wide variety of high school-based media texts in Japan and their distribution and popularity regionally or globally.

As we have seen, except for a minority of films with dark themes and ultra-violent or hypersexualised narratives, Japan's high school films are almost always on an upward trajectory in some form. Even in films where a central character looks like being 'written out' with an incurable disease (*Let Me Eat Your Pancreas* or *Closest Love to Heaven*), narratives are embedded with signs of hope or some kind of epiphany (usually moral) that emphasises 'goodness' in the world. The upbeat tone reflects a feeling of optimism about Japan and its people in a nation constantly challenged by concerns around its ageing population and sluggish economic growth. As a form of 'youth film' (to return to the original translation of *seishun eiga*), Japan's contemporary high school films provide a 'safe' nostalgia for their audience, with the iconographic and disciplined environment of the school clearly framing each narrative.

Films Cited

Note: abbreviations denote original or other forms of this text: [aff]= feature film anime, [atv]=television anime, [m]=manga, [n]=novel, [tv]= live action TV. Non-Japanese films are noted by their country of origin.

A Silent Voice/Koe no Katachi. 2016. Dir. Naoko Yamada.

After My Death/Joe Man-eun So-nyeo. 2018. Dir. Kim Ui-seok. South Korea.

After the Rain/Koi wa Ameagari no Yō ni. 2018. Dir. Akira Nagai. [m]

All About Lily Chou-Chou/Ririi Shushu no Subete. 2001. Dir. Shunji Iwai.

American Pie. 1999. Dir. Paul Weitz and Chris Weitz. USA.

Ano Ko No, Toriko/Girl Envy. 2018. Dir. Ryō Miyawaki. [m]

Assassination Classroom/Ansatsu Kyōshitsu. 2015. Dir. Eiichirō Hasumi. [atv][m]

Battle Royale/Batoru Rowaiaru. 2000. Dir. Kinji Fukusaku. [n]

Battle Royale II: Requiem/Batoru Rowaiaru: Chinkonka. 2003. Dir. Kenta Fukusaku and Kinji Fukusaku.

Blackboard Jungle. 1955. Dir. Richard Brooks. USA.

Blue, Painful and Brittle/Aokute Itakute Mori. 2020. Dir. Shunsuke Kariyama. [n]

Blue Spring Ride/Aoharaido. 2014. Dir. Takahiro Miki. [m]

Boys Love: The Movie/Bōizu Rabu. 2007. Dir. Kōtarō Terauchi.

Cheerfully/Chiafurii. 2011. Dir. Shō Tsuchikawa.

Chihayafuru Part 3/Chihayafuru Musubi. 2018. Dir. Norihiro Koizumi. [atv][m]

Close Range Love/Kinkyori Ren'ai. 2014. Dir. Naoto Kumazawa. [m]

Closest Love to Heaven/Kyō no Kira-kun [lit. *Today's Kira-kun*]. 2017. Dir. Yasuhiro Kawamura. [m]

Crazed Fruit/Kurutta Kajitsu. 1956. Dir. Kō Nakahira.

Cruel Story of Youth/Seishun Zankoku Monogatari. 1960. Dir. Nagisa Ōshima.

Daily Lives of High School Boys/Danshi Kōkōsei no Nichijō. 2013. Dir. Daigo Matsui.

Daytime Shooting Star/Hiranaka no Ryūsei. 2017. Dir. Takehiko Shinjō. [m]

Deep-Sea Fishes/Shinkai Gyogun. 1957. Dir. Nagisa Ōshima.

Dorome: Girls' Side/Dorome: Joshihen. 2016. Dir. Eisuke Naito.

Drowning Love/Oboreru Naifu. 2016. Dir. Yūki Yamato.

Easy A. 2010. Dir. Will Gluck. USA.

Eighth Grade. 2018. Dir. Bo Burnham. USA.

Election. 1999. Dir. Alexander Payne. USA.

Fall in Love at First Kiss/Yī Wěn Dìng Qíng. 2019. Dir. Frankie Chen. HK/China.

Fashion King/Paesyeonwang. 2014. Dir. Oh Ki-hwan. South Korea.

Fast Times at Ridgemont High. 1982. Dir. Amy Heckerling. USA.

Ferris Bueller's Day Off. 1986. Dir. John Hughes. USA.

Five Feet Apart. 2019. Dir. Justin Baldoni. USA.

Flashdance. 1983. Dir. Adrian Lyne. USA.

Flying Colours/Biri Gyaru. 2015. Dir. Nobuhiro Doi. [n]

Forget Me Not/Wasurenai to Chikatta Boku ga Ita. 2015. Dir. Kei Horie. [n]

From Today It's My Turn!!/Kyo kara Ore wa!!: Gekijoban. 2020. Dir. Yūichi Fukuda. [m][tv]

Girl Asleep. 2015. Dir. Rosemary Myers. Australia.

Girls' Encounter/Shōjo Kaikō. 2017. Dir. Yūka Eda.

Girls Step/Gāruzu Suteppu. 2015. Dir. Yasuhiro Kawamura.

Harry Potter and the Half-Blood Prince. 2009. Dir. David Yates. UK. [n]

Have a Song on Your Lips/Kuchibiru ni Uta wo. 2015. Dir. Takahiro Miki. [m]

Head On. 1998. Dir. Ana Kokkinos. Australia.

Heathers. 1988. Dir. Michael Lehmann. USA.

Hentai Kamen/Pervert Mask [aka *HK: Forbidden Super Hero*]. 2013. Dir. Yūichi Fukada. [m][n]

Heroine Disqualified/Hiroin Shikkaka. 2015. Dir. Hanabusa Tsutomu. [m]

HIGH School. 2010. Dir. Adrien Brody. USA.

Himizu/Mole. 2011. Dir. Sion Sono. [m]

Honey/Hanii. 2018. Dir. Kōji Shintoku. [m]

Hot Gimmick: Boy Meets Girl/Hotto Gimikku: Gāru Miitsu Bōi. 2019. Dir. Yūki Yamato. [m]

House of Hummingbird/Beol-sae. 2018. Dir. Kim Bora. South Korea.

Hyouka: Forbidden Secrets/Hyōka. 2017. Dir. Mari Asato. [m]

I Am a Hero / Ai Amu A Hīrō. 2015. Dir. Shinsuke Satō. [m]

Ichi the Killer / Koroshiya Ichi. 2001. Dir. Takashi Miike. [m]

I Give My First Love to You / Boku no Hatsukoi o Kimi ni Sasagu. 2009. Dir. Takehiko Shinjō. [m]

If You Count to Five, It's Your Dream / Itsutsu Kazoereba Kimi no Yume. 2014. Dir. Yūki Yamato.

Infinite Foundation / Mugen Fandēshon. 2018. Dir. Akira Ōsaki.

In the Realm of the Senses / Ai no Koriida. 1976. Dir. Nagisa Ōshima.

I Wish / Kiseki. 2011. Dir. Hirokazu Koreeda.

Kamen Teacher: The Movie / Gekijōban Kamen Tiichā. 2014. Dir. Kentarō Moriya. [m][tv]

Kids on the Slope / Sakamichi no Apollon. 2018. Dir. Takahiro Miki. [m][n]

Kill Bill Volume 1 and *Kill Bill Volume 2*. 2003 and 2004. Dir. Quentin Tarantino. USA.

Kiss Him, Not Me / Watashi ga Motete Dosunda. 2020. Dir. Norihisa Hiranuma. [atv][m]

Kiss Me at the Stroke of Midnight / Gozen O ji, Kiss Shi ni Kite yo. 2019. Dir. Takehiko Shinjo. [m]

Kotodama: Spiritual Curse / Gakkō no Kaidan Noroi no Kotodama. 2014. Dir. Masayuki Ochiai.

Ladybird. 2017. Dir. Greta Gerwig. USA.

Lean on Me. 1989. Dir. John G. Avildsen. USA.

Let Me Eat Your Pancreas / Kimi no Suizō o Tabetai. 2017. Dir. Shō Tsukikawa. [aff][m][n]

Let's Go, Jets! From Small Town Girls to U.S. Champions?! / Chiadan: Joshi Kōsei ga Chiadansu de Zenbei Seiha Shichatta Honto no Hanashi. 2017. Dir. Hayao Kawai.

Let's Make the Teacher Have a Miscarriage Club / Sensei o Ryuzan saseru Ka. 2012. Dir. Eisuke Naito.

Lights in the Dusk / Laitakaupungin valot. 2006. Dir. Aki Kaurismäki. Finland / Germany / Italy / Sweden.

Looking for Alibrandi. 2000. Dir. Kate Woods. Australia.

Love and Lies / Koi to Uso. 2017. Dir. Takeshi Furosawa. [m]

Love Exposure / Ai no Mukidashi. 2008. Dir. Sion Sono.

Love, Simon. 2018. Dir. Greg Berlanti. USA.

Make a Bow and a Kiss / Ichirei Shite, Kisu. 2017. Dir. Takeshi Furusawa. [m]

Marmalade Boy / Mamarēdo Bōi. 2018. Dir. Ryūichi Hiroki. [m][n]

Me and Earl and the Dying Girl. 2015. Dir. Alfonso Gomez-Rejon. USA.

Missions of Love / Watashi ni XX Shinasai. 2018. Dir. Tōru Yamamoto. [m]

My Brother Loves Me Too Much/Ani ni Ai Saresugite Komattemasu. 2017. Dir. Hayato Kawai. [m]

My Little Monster/Tonari no Kaibutsu-kun. 2018. Dir. Shō Tsukikawa. [m][n]

My Neighbour Totoro/Tonari no Totoro. 1988. Dir. Hayao Miyazaki.

My Pretend Girlfriend/Momose, Kotchi o Muite. 2016. Dir. Saiji Yakumo. [n]

My Teacher, My Love/Sensei Kunshu. 2018. Dir. Shō Tsukikawa. [m]

Napoleon Dynamite. 2004. Dir. Jared Hess. USA.

Night and Fog in Japan/Nihon no Yoru to Kiri. 1960. Dir. Nagisa Ōshima.

Nisekoi: False Love/Nisekoi. 2018. Dir. Hayato Kawai. [m]

Norwegian Wood/Noruwei no Mori. 2010. Dir. Anh Hung Tran. Japan and France. [n]

Now is Good. 2012. Dir. Ol Parker. UK.

One Cut of the Dead/Kamera o Tomeru na! (lit. 'Don't Stop the Camera!'). 2017. Dir. Shin'ichirō Ueda.

One Week Friends/Isshūkan Furenzu. 2017. Dir. Shōsuke Murakami. [m]

Orange/Orenji Mirai. 2016. Dir. Kōjirō Hashimoto. [aff][atv][m][n]

Our Meal For Tomorrow/Bokura no Gohan wa Ashita de Matteru. 2017. Dir. Masahide Ichii. [n]

Ouran High School Host Club/Gekijōban Ōran Kōkō Hosutobu. 2012. Dir. Satoshi Kan. [atv][m][n][tv]

Peach Girl/Pichi Garu. 2017. Dir. Koji Shintoku. [atv][m]

Please Don't Go Anywhere/Nacchan wa Mada Shinjuku. 2017. Dir. Rin Shutō.

Policeman and Me/P to JK. 2017. Dir. Ryūichi Hiroki. [m]

Prince of Legend. 2019. Dirs Hayato Kawai and Kentarō Moriya. [tv]

Principal! Am I a Heroine in Love?/Purinshiparu: Koi Suru Watashi wa Hiroin Desu ka? 2018. Dir. Tetsuo Shinohara. [m]

Psycho. 1960. Dir. Alfred Hitchcock. USA.

Rainbow Days/Nijiiro Deizu. 2018. Dir. Ken Iizuka. [atv][m]

Rashomon/Rashōmon. 1950. Dir. Akira Kurosawa. [short story]

Real Girl/3D Kanojo Riaru Gāru. 2018. Dir. Tsutomu Hanabusa. [m]

ReLIFE/Riraifu. 2017. Dir. Takeshi Furusawa. [atv][m]

Run! T High School Basketball Club/Hashire! T Ko Basuketto Bu. 2018. Dir. Takeshi Furusawa. [n]

Sailor Suit and Machine Gun/Sērāfuku to Kikanjū. 1981. Dir. Shinji Sōmai.

Saki Achiga-hen: Episode of Side-A. 2018. Dir. Yūichi Onuma. [m][tv]

Sakura. 2020. Dir. Hiroshi Yazaki. [n]

Sayounara/If That's True. 2018. Dir. Yūho Ishibashi.

Schoolgirl Complex/Sukūrugāru Konpurekkusu: Hōsōbu-hen. 2013. Dir. Yūichi Onuma. [photobook]

Season of the Sun/Taiyō no Kisetsu. 1956. Dir. Takumi Furukawa.

Second Life/Sunhee-wa Seul-gi. 2018. Dir. Park Young-ju. South Korea.

Second Summer, Never See You Again/Nidome no Natsu, Nidoto Aenai Kimi. 2017. Dir. Kenji Nakanishi. [m][n]

Seven Days: Monday–Thursday/Sebundeizu MONDAY→THURSDAY. 2015; and *Seven Days: Friday–Sunday/Sebundeizu FRIDAY→SUNDAY.* 2015. Dir. Kenji Yokoi. [m]

Shino Can't Say Her Own Name/Shino-chan wa Jibun no Namae ga Ienai. 2018. Dir. Hiroaki Yuasa. [m]

Sierra Burgess is a Loser. 2018. Dir. Ian Samuels. USA.

Spiral/Uzumaki. 2000. Dir. Higuchinsky [Akihiro Iguchi]. [m]

Spring Has Come/Supuringu Hazu Kamu. 2017, but made c.2015. Dir. Ryūhei Yoshino. [tv]

Stand and Deliver. 1988. Dir. Ramón Menéndez. USA.

Stand By Me. 1986. Dir. Rob Reiner. USA.

Street Without End/Kagirinaki Hodo. 1934. Dir. Mikio Naruse.

Strobe Edge/Sutorobo Ejji. 2015. Dir. Ryuichi Hiroki. [m]

Suicide Club/Jisatsu Sākuru [lit. *Suicide Circle*]. 2001. Dir. Sion Sono.

Sundome. 2007; and *Sundome 2* and *Sundome 3.* 2008. Dir. Daigo Udagawa. [m]

Sundome New. 2017; and *Sundome New 2.* 2017. Dir. Kazuhiro Yokoyama. [m]

Tag/Riaru Onigokko. 2015. Dir. Sion Sono.

Take Me to the Moon/Dài Wǒ Qù Yuè Qiú. 2017. Dir. Hsieh Chun-yi. Taiwan.

Tetsuo: The Iron Man/Tetsuo. 1989. Dir. Shin'ya Tsukamoto.

The Anthem of the Heart/Kokoro ga Sakebitagatterunda. 2017. Dir. Naoto Kumazawa. [aff]

The Ashes of My Flesh and Blood is the Vast Flowing Galaxy/Kudakechiru Tokoro o Misete Ageru [aka *My Blood and Bones in a Flowing Galaxy*]. 2021. Dir. SABU. [n]

The Black Devil and the White Prince/Kurosaki-kun no Iinari ni Nante Naranai. 2016. Dir. Shō Tsukikawa. [aTV][m]

The Blue Bird/Aoi Tori. 2008. Dir. Kenji Nakanishi. [n]

The Breakfast Club. 1985. Dir. John Hughes. USA.

The Dark Maidens/Ankoku Joshi. 2017. Dir. Saiji Yakumo. [n]

The Family Game/Kazoku Gēmu. 1983. Dir. Yoshimitsu Morita.

The Fault in Our Stars. 2014. Dir. Josh Boone. USA.

The 400 Blows/Les Quatre Cents Coups. 1959. Dir. François Truffaut.

The Hole of a Woman/Onna no Ana. 2014. Dir. Kota Yoshida. [m]

The Kirishima Thing/Kirishima, Bukatsu Yamerutteyo. 2012. Dir. Daihachi Yoshida. [n]

The Liar and His Lover/Kanojo wa Uso o Aishisugiteiru. 2013. Dir. Norihiro Koizumi. [m][tv]

The Senior and the Girl/Senpai to Kanojo [aka *Senior and Her*]. 2015. Dir Chihiro Ikeda. [m]

The Werewolf Game: Mad Land/Jinroh Gemu Maddo Rando. 2017. Dir. Shinya Ayabe. [n]

To Sir, with Love. 1967. Dir. James Clavell. UK.

Wander Life/Kakuga, Mama. 2018. Dir. Naho Kamimura.

What's Going on with My Sister?/Saikin, Imōto no Yōsu ga Chotto Okashiinda ga? 2014. Dirs. Yūki Aoyama and Iggy Coen. [atv][m][n]

Wolf Girl and Black Prince/Ōkami Shōjo to Kuro Ōji. 2016. Dir. Ryūichi Hiroki. [atv][m]

Yarukkya Knight/Yarukkya Naito. 2015. Dir. Katsutoshi Hirabayashi. [m]

Yell for the Blue Sky/Aozora Ēru. 2017. Dir. Takahiro Miki. [m]

You Are Brilliant Like a Spica/Shigatsu no Kimi, Supika. 2019. Dir. Kentarō Ōtani. [m]

You Are the Apple of My Eye/Ano Koro, Kimi o Oikaketa [aka *Those Years, We Went After You*]. 2018. Dir. Yasuo Hasegawa. [n]

You, I Love [aka *We Love*]/*Ui Rabu.* 2018. Dir. Yūichi Satō. [m]

Your Lie in April/Shigatsu wa Kimi no Uso. 2016. Dir. Takehiko Shinjō. [atv][m]

Your Name/Kimi no Na wa. (anime). 2016. Dir. Makoto Shinkai. [n]

References

Allison, Anne. 2019, c. 1996. *Permitted and Prohibited Desires: Mothers, Comics, and Censorship in Japan*. New York: Routledge.

Altman, Rick. 1984. A Semantic/Syntactic Approach to Film Genre. *Cinema Journal* 23 (3): 6–18.

Arai, Andrea G. 2003. Killing Kids: Recession and Survival in Twenty-First Century Japan. *Postcolonial Studies* 6 (3): 367–79.

Bamkin, Sam. 2018. Reforms to Strengthen Moral Education in Japan: A Preliminary Analysis of Implementation in Schools. *Contemporary Japan* 30 (1): 78–96.

Bazin, André. 1982 (c. 1975). *The Cinema of Cruelty: From Buñuel to Hitchcock*, translated by Sabine d'Estrée. New York: Seaver.

Blackwood, Thomas and Douglas C. Friedman. 2015. Join the Club: Effects of Club Membership on Japanese High School Students' Self-concept. *Japan Forum* 27 (2): 257–75.

Bomford, Jennifer. 2016. Blocking the School Play: US, Japanese and UK Televisual High Schools, Spatiality, and the Construction of Teen Identity. Master's thesis: University of Northern British Columbia.

Bordwell, David. 1995. Visual Style in Japanese Cinema, 1925–1945. *Film History* 7 (1): 5–31.

Corrigan, Peter. 2008. *The Dressed Society: Clothing, the Body and Some Meanings of the World*. London: Sage.

Craik, Jennifer. 2005. *Uniforms Exposed: From Conformity to Transgression*. Oxford and New York: Berg.

Crosnoe, Robert, Lilla Pivnick and Aprile D. Benner. 2018. The Social Contexts of High Schools. In *Handbook of the Sociology of Education in the 21st Century*, edited by B. Schneider. Cham, Switzerland: Springer International, 317–35.

Czarnecki, Melanie. 2005. Bad Girls from Good Families: The Degenerate Meiji Schoolgirl. In *Bad Girls of Japan*, edited by Laura Miller and Jan Bardsley. New York: Palgrave Macmillan, 49–64.

Dimagmaliw, Ben. 2019. Indie Forum 2019: Osaka Asian Film Festival. *Indievisual*, 6 May 2019. Available at: <read.indie-visual.net> (last accessed 21 April 2021).

Driscoll, Catherine. 2011. *Teen Film: A Critical Introduction*. New York: Bloomsbury.

Eiren (Motion Picture Producers Association of Japan). 2021. Available at: <www.eiren.org> (last accessed 21 April 2021).

Federov, Alexander, Anastasia Levitskaya, Irina Chelysheva, Olga Gorbatkova, Galina Mikhaleva and Ludmila Seliverstova. 2019. *School and University in the Mirror of American, British, French, German and Russian Movies*. Moscow: ICO Information for All.

Foucault, Michel. 1977 (c. 1975). *Discipline and Punishment: The Birth of the Prison*, translated by Alan Sheridan. London: Penguin.

Furukawa, Hiroko and Rayna Denison. 2015. Disaster and Relief: The 3.11 Tohoku and Fukushima Disasters and Japan's Media Industries. *International Journal of Cultural Studies* 18 (2): 225–41.

Galloway, Patrick. 2006. *Asia Shock: Horror and Dark Cinema from Japan, Korea, Hong Kong, and Thailand*. Berkeley, CA: Stone Bridge Press.

Goffman, Erving. 1961. *Asylums: Essays on the Social Situation of Mental Patients and Other Inmates*. New York: Anchor Books.

Greene, Barbara. 2018. High School of the Dead and the Profitable Use of Japanese Nationalistic Imagery. *Electronic Journal of Contemporary Japanese Studies* 18 (3): article 9.

Greene, Doyle. 2012. *Teens, TV and Tunes: The Manufacturing of American Adolescent Culture*. Jefferson, NC: McFarland.

Grenfell, Michael James. 2007. *Pierre Bourdieu: Education and Training*. London and New York: Continuum International.

Gwynne, Joel. 2013. Japan, Postfeminism and the Consumption of Sexual(ised) Schoolgirls in Male-authored Contemporary Manga. *Feminist Theory* 14 (3): 325–43.

Harrison, Mark. 2017. How Female Students Are Portrayed in Relation to Established Hierarchies Featured in the High School Movie: An Analysis of the Sub-genre in Contemporary American Cinema (1985–2015). Unpublished essay: University of Salford, Manchester.

Hebdige, Dick. 2003 (c. 1979). *Subculture: The Meaning of Style*. New York and London: Routledge.

Hirayama, Maki. 2019. Developments in Information Technology and the Sexual Depression of Japanese Youth since 2000. *International Journal of the Sociology of Leisure* 2: 95–119.

Igarashi, Tasaku, Tadahiro Motoyoshi, Jiro Takai and Toshikazu Yoshida. 2008. No Mobile, No Life: Self-perception and Text-message Dependency among Japanese High School Students. *Computers in Human Behavior* 24: 2311–24.

Jasper, Cynthia R. and Mary Ellen Roach-Higgins. 1995. Role Conflict and Conformity in Dress. In *Dress and Identity*, edited by Mary Ellen Roach-Higgins, Joanne B. Eicher and Kim K. P. Johnson. New York: Fairchild, 139–46.

Jones, Richard. 1990. Educational Practices and Scientific Knowledge: A Genealogical Reinterpretation of the Emergence of Physiology in

Post-Revolutionary France. In *Foucault and Education: Disciplines and Knowledge*, edited by Stephen J. Ball. London and New York: Routledge, 57–77.

Joseph, Nathan. 1995. Uniforms. In *Dress and Identity*, edited by Mary Ellen Roach-Higgins, Joanne B. Eicher and Kim K. P. Johnson. New York: Fairchild, 182–6.

Kawamura, Yuniya. 2012. *Fashioning Japanese Subcultures*. London and New York: Berg.

Kiejziewicz, Agnieszka. 2018. Bullying, Death and Traumatic Identity: The Taboo of School Violence in New Japanese Cinema. *MASKA: Performing Arts Journal* 39: 75–89.

Kinsella, Sharon. 2002. What's Behind the Fetishism of Japanese School Uniforms? *Fashion Theory* 6 (2): 215–38.

KOFIC (Korean Film Council) 2019. *Korean Cinema 2018*, vol. 20. Busan: Korean Film Council.

Kondo, Dorinne. 1995. The Aesthetics and Politics of Japanese Identity in the Fashion Industry. In *Dress and Identity*, edited by Mary Ellen Roach-Higgins, Joanne B. Eicher and Kim K. P. Johnson. New York: Fairchild, 475–9.

McDonald, Keiko I. 2006. *Reading a Japanese Film: Cinema in Context*. Honolulu: University of Hawai'i Press.

McVeigh, Brian J. 2000. *Wearing Ideology: State, Schooling and Self-Presentation in Japan*. Oxford and New York: Berg.

Martin, Daniel. 2015. *Extreme Asia: The Rise of Cult Cinema from the Far East*. Edinburgh: Edinburgh University Press.

Miller, Toby, Nitin Govil, John McMurria and Richard Maxwell. 2001. *Global Hollywood*. London: BFI.

Mizuno, Koh, Kazue Okamoto-Mizuno and Kazuki Iwata. 2019. Napping Behaviors and Extracurricular Club Activities in Japanese High School Students: Associations with Daytime Sleep Problems. *Clocks and Sleep* 1: 367–84.

Morrison, David. 2012. Framing Loneliness in Painting and Film. In *Framing Film: Cinema and the Visual Arts*, edited by Steven Allen and Laura Hubner. Bristol and Chicago: Intellect, 203–19.

Okano, Kaori and Motonori Tsuchiya. 1999. *Education in Contemporary Japan: Inequality and Diversity*. Cambridge: Cambridge University Press.

Osanami Törngren, Sayaka and Yuna Sato. 2019. Beyond Being Either-or: Identification of Multiracial or Multiethnic Japanese. *Journal of Ethnic and Migration Studies* 47 (4): 802–20.

Pagel, Caren. 2011. Fearing the Youth: Economic Turmoil, Adult Anxiety and the Japanese *Battle Royale* Controversy. Unpublished thesis: Florida Atlantic University.

Paule, Michele. 2016. *Girlhood, Schools and Media: Popular Discourses of the Achieving Girl*. New York and London: Routledge.

Pickering, W. S. F. (ed.). 1979. *Durkheim: Essays on Morals and Education*. London: Routledge and Kegan Paul.

Phillips, Alastair and Julian Stringer (eds). 2007. *Japanese Cinema: Texts and Contexts*. London and New York: Routledge.

Richie, Donald. 1972. *Japanese Cinema: Film Style and National Character*. London: Secker and Warburg.

Rubinstein, Ruth P. 2001. *Dress Codes: Meanings and Messages in American Culture*, 2nd edn. Boulder, CO: Westview Press.

Russell, Catherine. 2011. *Classical Japanese Cinema Revisited*. New York: Continuum.

Sandrisser, Barbara. 2018. The Kiss in Japan. In *Sensorial Trajectories*, edited by John Murungi and Linda Ardito. Newcastle upon Tyne: Cambridge Scholars, 7–17.

Schilling, Mark. 2018. Japan Debates the Ethics of Making Films on the Cheap. *Variety* (30 May).

Steinberg, Marc. 2012. *Anime's Media Mix: Franchising Toys and Characters in Japan*. Minneapolis: University of Minnesota Press.

Steinberg, Marc and Alexander Zahlten. 2017. Introduction. In *Media Theory in Japan*, edited by Marc Steinberg and Alexander Zahlten. Durham, NC: Duke University Press, 1–29.

Suzuki, Michiko. 2006. Writing Same-Sex Love: Sexology and Literary Representation in Yoshiya Nobuko's Early Fiction. *The Journal of Asian Studies* 65 (3): 575–99.

Suzuki, Michiko. 2017. Reading and Writing Material: Kōda Aya's *Kimono* and Its Afterlife. *The Journal of Asian Studies* 76 (2): 333–61.

Takakura Minoru, Wake Norie, and Kobayashi Minoru. 2010. The Contextual Effect of School Satisfaction on Health-risk Behaviors in Japanese High School Students. *Journal of School Health* 80 (11): 544–51.

Tamura, Yurika. 2017. Lacerated Girls' Uniforms and What the Cuts May Engender. *Feminist Formations* 29 (3): 25–48.

Tanioka, Ichiro and Daniel Glaser. 1991. School Uniforms, Routine Activities, and the Social Control of Delinquency in Japan. *Youth and Society* 23 (1): 50–75.

Vick, Tom. 2007. *Asian Cinema: A Field Guide*. New York: HarperCollins.

Wada-Marciano, Mitsuyo. 2008. *Nippon Modern: Japanese Cinema of the 1920s and 1930s*. Honolulu: University of Hawaii Press.

Wada-Marciano, Mitsuyo. 2012. *Japanese Cinema in the Digital Age*. Honolulu: University of Hawaii Press.

Yoda, Tomiko. 2017. Girlscape: The Marketing of Mediatic Ambience in Japan. In *Media Theory in Japan*, edited by Marc Steinberg and Alexander Zahlten. Durham, NC: Duke University Press, 173–99.

Yoneyama, Shoko. 1999. *The Japanese High School: Silence and Resistance*. London: Routledge.

Yoshimoto, Mitsuhiro. 2007. Questions of the New: Ōshima Nagisa's Cruel Story of Youth (1960). In *Japanese Cinema: Texts and Contexts*, edited by Alastair Phillips and Julian Stringer. London and New York: Routledge, 168–79.

Zahlten, Alexander. 2019. 'The Prerogative of Confusion: Pink Film and the Eroticisation of Pain, Flux and Disorientation'. *Screen* 60: 1, pp. 25–45.

Index

Durkheim, Emile, 1, 6–7, 11, 137–8, 140, 152–3
dyed hair, 78–9

E-Girls, 121
Easy A (Gluck, 2010), 4, 16, 38, 121
ecchi (erotic) films, 128–30, 161
education reforms (*kyōiku kaikaku*), 6, 83, 140
Eighth Grade (Burnham, 2018), 4
Election (Payne, 1999), 35, 121, 122
elite schools, 9–10, 59, 96
entrances, 16, 17
eroticism, 128–30
establishing shots, 10, 16–18, 23, 35, 52, 68, 184
ethnicity, 75–9
examinations, 9, 11, 124
EXILE, 120
extra-curricular diversions, 84–8

'face', loss of, 124
Face of Another, The (Abe), 178
Fall in Love at First Kiss/Yī Wěn Dìng Qíng (Chen, 2019), 185
family, 13–14, 89–95, 145
Family Game, The/Kazoku Gēmu (Morita, 1983), 124
fashion, 60, 66
Fashion King/Paesyeonwang (Ki-hwan, 2014), 185
Fast Times at Ridgemont High (Heckerling, 1982), 16, 121
fathers, 92–3, 94–5
Fault in Our Stars, The (Boone, 2014), 118
female characters *see* girls
Ferris Bueller's Day Off (Hughes, 1986), 4, 16, 83, 121–2
festivals, 106–7
fetishes, 154
Five Feet Apart (Baldoni, 2019), 118
flashbacks, 51–2, 91, 97
Flashdance (Lyne, 1983), 66
Flying Colours/Biri Gyaru (Doi, 2015), 53, 69, 88, 92, 125–7
forbidden love, 14, 160–8
Forget Me Not/Wasurenai to Chikatta Boku ga Ita (Horie, 2015), 23, 27–8, 117
Foucault, Michel, 1, 10, 11, 16, 19, 20, 27, 184
Discipline and Punishment, 8
and judgements, 18
and time, 23

framing, 24, 26–7, 28, 31, 33, *34*, 35
France, 11, 24, 103
'Freaks and Geeks' (TV series), 131
friendship, 25
From Today It's My Turn!!/Kyo kara Ore wa!!: Gekijoban (Fukuda, 2020), 100

gakkyu hōkai (classroom chaos), 8
gakuen-mono (school thing), 2, 3
Galloway, Patrick, 137
ganguro girls, 110
gāruzu-rabu/yuri (romanticised notions), 34, 181
gates, 16
gender, 46–7, 54, 59, 184–5
and cultural identity, 75
and sexuality, 157–9
and tradition, 80–3
and uniforms, 69–70
see also boys; girls; same-sex relationships
GENERATIONS from EXILE TRIBE, 120
geography, 59, 70
Girl Asleep (Myers, 2015), 6
girls, 7–8, 184–5
and bedrooms, 56–7
and 'boss' gangs (*sukeban*), 61
and cycling, 51
and delinquency, 73
and empowerment, 81, *82*
and 'popular', 1, 83
and sexuality, 128–9, 153–4
and toilets, 37–41
and uniforms, 60, 62, 66, 67
Girls' Encounter/Shōjo Kaikō (Eda, 2017), 106, 144, 146, 169
girls high schools, 11
Glaser, Daniel, 7, 63, 71–2
Glee (TV series), 22, 131
Goffman, Erving, 58–9
'golden ratio' (*ōgonhi*), 74
graduation, 9
Great Kanto Earthquake, 60
Greene, Doyle, 4, 101, 109
Grenfell, Michael James, 103
gymnasiums, 13, 35–6, 37, 41

haafu (*hāfu*) (mixed-race), 76–9
hair *see* dyed hair
hallways, 13, 20–5
Hamabe, Minami, 65, 107
Harrison, Mark, 4, 7–8, 9, 58
Harry Potter films, 16, 37

Printed in the USA
CPSIA information can be obtained
at www.ICGtesting.com
JSHW011454150823
46583JS00003B/234